The ANSI/SPARC DBMS Model

The ANSI/SPARC DBMS Model

Proceedings of the Second SHARE Working Conference on
Data Base Management Systems
Montreal, Canada, April 26-30, 1976

edited by

Donald A. Jardine

Department of Computing & Information Science
Queen's University
Kingston, Ontario, Canada

1977

NORTH-HOLLAND PUBLISHING COMPANY
AMSTERDAM • NEW YORK • OXFORD

North-Holland ISBN: 0 7204 0719 2

QA
76.9
.D3
S5
1976

PUBLISHERS:
NORTH-HOLLAND PUBLISHING COMPANY
AMSTERDAM • NEW YORK • OXFORD

SOLE DISTRIBUTORS FOR THE U.S.A. AND CANADA:
AMERICAN ELSEVIER PUBLISHING COMPANY, INC.
52 VANDERBILT AVENUE, NEW YORK, N.Y. 10017

PRINTED IN THE NETHERLANDS

INTRODUCTION

In the three years since the first SHARE Working Conference on Data Base Management Systems (July 1973) major advances have been made in the clarification of structure and definition of interfaces in data base management systems. In 1975 the ANSI/SPARC DBMS Study Group produced an interim report describing a model for a data base management system, including identification and description of interfaces. The purpose of this report was to provide a framework for further discussion and refinement of those interfaces which could be considered for more formal standardization efforts.

The second SHARE Working Conference held in Montreal April 25-30, 1976 took as its theme the ANSI/SPARC Study Group report. An expository paper on the report itself and several papers on various aspects of the report were presented and generated extensive discussion. These discussions, which clarified many of the concepts contained in the Study Group report, are included in edited form.

In addition, papers on other aspects of current data base technology were presented at the conference. Important survey papers on end-user interfaces, data security, data base administration, and status of the CODASYL Data Description Language, together with discussion, are contained in the proceedings.

The papers are printed in order of presentation, and it is possible from the discussions to see a developing concensus on the strong (and weak) points of the ANSI Study Group Report. Panel- and open-discussion sessions clarified many points.

The editor would like to express his appreciation to Sandra Pryal, who was responsible for text entry. The text itself was prepared on a locally developed cursor-driven screen-oriented text editor running under the Bell Laboratories UNIX time-sharing system on a PDP-11/45, and was formatted using the UNIX text formatter. Typographical errors are the responsibility of the editor.

D.A. Jardine
Queen's University
Kingston, Ontario
December, 1976

CONTENTS

THE ANSI/X3/SPARC/SGDBMS ARCHITECTURE

Beatrice Yormark
The Rand Corporation
Santa Monica, California

INTRODUCTION

In late 1972, the Standards Planning and Requirements Committee (SPARC) of the American National Standards Committee on Computers and Information Processing (ANSI/X3) established an ad hoc Study Group on Data Base Management Systems. This Study Group was charged with investigating the subject of data base management systems with the objective of determining which, if any, aspects of such systems are, at present, suitable candidates for the development of American National Standards. As part of their scope of work, the Study Group was charged with defining an overall structure for an information system in order to identify those portions which are within the scope of Data Base Systems.

In February 1975, the ANSI/X3/SPARC Study Group on Data Base Management Systems completed and published an Interim Report [1], which explained in detail, the gross architecture they had developed for information systems. This paper will review the most salient features of this architecture and, in so doing, describe the flow of definitional information through the architecture. The paper begins with an overview of the data base management system architecture, followed by discussion of the components of the architecture and ending with a discussion of data independence.

In order to provide a context for the ensuing discussion of the architecture, it is necessary to understand the working definition of data base management as employed by the Study Group. Quoting directly from the Interim Report, the discipline of data base management is viewed as" . . . records, fields, files, sets, and the descriptions for all of these, and all the indices, mapping techniques, access methods, file organizations and end-user languages . . ."

DATA BASE MANAGEMENT SYSTEMS ARCHITECTURE OVERVIEW

The gross architecture being described is displayed in Figure 1. The architecture is partly based on the concept of "nested machines" (sometimes referred to as as "onion"). The outermost "machine" is the most closely aligned to the functionality and support of the data base; as we descend inwards through successive layers of machines, we pass from the highest level of the "real world" view, through the various logical views of the data base and on to its physical attributes, until ultimately we arrive at the actual secondary storage device.

The information and data flow through the multiple layers of the architecture is accomplished by describing the kind of information and data which passes across interfaces, at both the same level of machine and through various levels. The Study Group recognized early in its work that unambiguous characterization of different interfaces and the information flowing across them is ultimately where standardization of the data base management function will occur, if at all. The gross architecture depicted recognizes the need for data manipulation interfaces for multiple classes of users as well as multiple data declaration interfaces for effecting data independence.

1

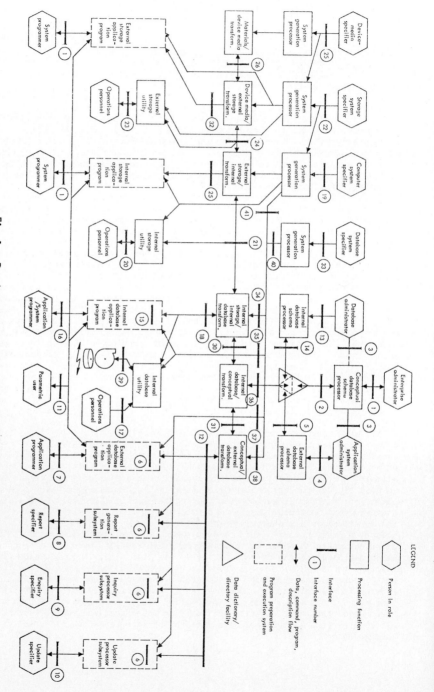

Fig. 1 — Database system prototypical architecture

Three Schema Approach

At the outermost layer of the onion we have what is perhaps one of the most essential components of the architecture--the concept of the Conceptual Schema. This fact has also been noted by Nijssen [2]. The conceptual schema embodies the "real world" view of the enterprise being modelled in the data base. It represents the current "best model" or "way of doing business" for the enterprise [3]. It provides an unconstrained, long-term view of the enterprise. In addition, the conceptual schema provides the basis for integrity and security declarations imposed by the enterprise onto the various data base users, as well as providing a data description basis for restructuring. The conceptual schema also acts as the common denominator between optimized storage descriptions and multiple-user views. This latter function will be discussed in greater detail elsewhere in this paper.

The various users of the data base management system operate on subsets of the total enterprise model which are relevant to their particular needs. These subsets of the model, as seen by the users, are depicted in the gross architecture as the external schemas.

The "machine view" of the data is described by the internal schema. This schema describes the stored representation of the enterprise's information. The architecture imposes no restriction on the actual storage strategy employed. Any "theology" may be accommodated (e.g. tree, hierarchy, network, flat-files, etc.). In addition, the internal schema contains the description of "how" the data are stored, i.e. record implementation techniques, field implementation techniques, syntax of data values, etc.

Figure 2 contains a simplified view of the gross architecture depicting the interrelationships between the conceptual, external and internal schemas.

Administrator Roles

The following three administrator roles have been identified for providing to the data management system a particular view of the necessary data.

Enterprise Administrator
Application Administrator(s)
Data Base Administrator

Each of these roles has the responsibility for describing and maintaining the currency of the schema relevant to their specific view of the data.

The enterprise administrator is responsible for providing a definition of the conceptual schema. In this role, the enterprise administrator is responsible for defining the entities of the enterprise and their associated properties, relationships and constraints to be applied on access, values and relationships. It is worth reiterating that the conceptual schema is a "real and tangible item made most explicit in machine readable form, couched in some well-defined and potentially standardizable language." [1]

An application administrator provides an external schema defining a particular application's (or application class) view of the data base. The external schema specific to an application is the sole source through which an application programmer (hence an application program) obtains the data descriptions germane to the application. All external schemas must be consistent with, and mappable from, the conceptuaml schema, and, as such cannot contain data descriptions for entities which are not defined in the conceptual schema.

The data base administrator has the responsibility for defining the internal schema and maintaining the internal data base. The data base administrator chooses implementation techniques consistent with, and mappable from, definitions in the conceptual schema. It is the data base administrator who determines how the data is to be stored.

Referring to Figure 2, it is across interface 3 that both the application administrator and data base administrator roles are provided with information from the conceptual schema necessary for defining their respective schemas (i.e. external and internal).

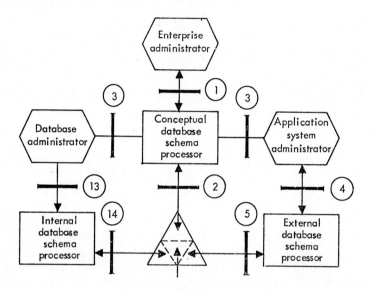

Fig. 2—Administrator roles

COMPONENTS OF THE ARCHITECTURE

The preceding sections of this paper have provided an overview of the prototypical architecture and introduced the notion of the conceptual schema as the real world model of an enterprise. Additionally, three key roles associated with the architecture were characterized. This section of the paper will describe, in greater detail, the information and data flow through the architecture and across the various interfaces.

In Figure 1, all of the interfaces below, to the left of, and including interface 21 are beyond the scope of this discussion. These interfaces and their associated processes can be classified under the headings of either "storage" or "resource" management and hence do not intersect with the definition of data base management previously given. Thus, the remaining sections of this paper will exclude these interfaces and processes from discussion. Figure 3 is a simplified schematic of the prototypical architecture with the storage management function removed.

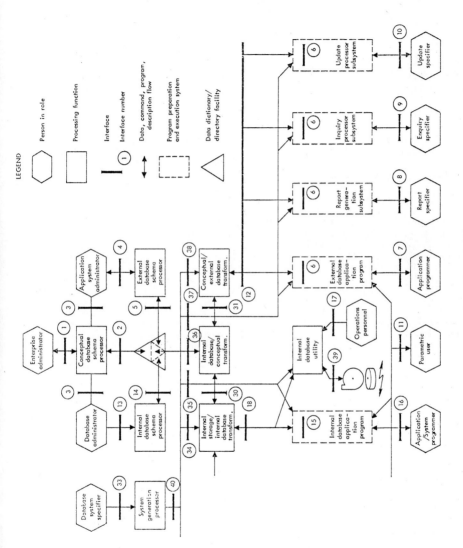

Fig. 3—Simplified system architecture

Defining the Conceptual Schema

The enterprise administrator defines the conceptual data and entities describing the model of the enterprise. The objects used for describing the entities of the conceptual schema consist of:

                attributes (conceptual fields)
                conceptual groups
                conceptual records
                conceptual plexes
                conceptual record set
                conceptual data base

Interface 1 - the source format of the conceptual data description is the interface by which the enterprise administrator makes known to the data base management system declarations concerning the nature of the enterprise. The enterprise is described in terms of the entities with which the enterprise is concerned, the attributes by which they are described and the relatinships existing between them. See Steel [4] for a proposal for formalizing the conceptual schema. The conceptual data base schema processor accepts this information model from the enterprise administrator, checks it for syntax and internal consistency, and encodes it into a machine readable form, passing the edited and encoded model to the rest of the data base management system across interface 2, to be stored in the data dictionary/directory. It is the machine readable format of the conceptual schema that is utilized by both the external data base schema processor and internal data base schema processor for validating the external and internal schemas, respectively, against the conceptual schema.

The application administrator(s) and data base administrator have the conceptual data description displayed to them across interface 3. They use this information to prepare external and internal schemas consistent with the specifications in the conceptual schema.

It is across interfaces 1, 2 and 3 that the comprehensive enterprise model is made known to the rest of the data base management system. The entities of interest, and the relationships among them are passed on, as well as any and all constraints to be applied to implementation and usage of the entities. This includes addressing matters of security, integrity, recovery, permissible operations upon objects and other rules/ restrictions as may be necessary to accurately model the enterprise.

Defining the External Schema

The application administrator provides a description of an external model (i.e. an external schema) for a specific class of application programs, consistent with the view of the data base necessary for that application class. The objects defined in an external schema are:

                External fields
                External Group
                External Record
                External plex
                External record-set

These objects are visible to and manipulated by the class of application programs utilizing the specific external schema.

Interface 4 - The source format of the data description is the interface across which an application administrator makes known to the data base management system his declaration of an external schema. The external schema contains the names and characteristics of the objects visible to a family of applications, as well as the associations and structures in which they are related and the operations permitted upon these objects. The external data base schema processor accepts this external schema from the application administrator and validates it, checking for internal

consistency, correct syntax and consistency (i.e. derivable from) with the
conceptual schema. This latter edit is effected through mapping functions
from the external schema to the conceptual schema defined across interface
5. The edited external schema is transmitted to the rest of the data base
management system across interface 5, the object format of the external
data description interface. The edited external schema may be stored in
the data dictionary/directory.

Defining the Internal Schema
The data base administrator prepares an internal schema which contains
the descriptions of the objects that are components of the internal model
in the data base. The requirements analysis which determines the exact
nature of the objects in the internal model are determined by the
enterprise administrator when the conceptual schema is defined. It is the
role of the data base administrator to define the "steady state" operation
of the data base. The objects defined in the internal schema are the
internal data storage organizational components of internal data. These
include:

> Internal Model Space
> Internal field (data element)
> Internal field aggregates
> Internal record (stored record)
> Internal record aggregate
> Space extent
> Form extent
> Internal record-set (data set)
> Internal data base
> Data bank

By defining the data in terms of the above objects, the data base
administrator provides a precise definition of how the internal data is
represented, how it is organized, stored and accessed.
The source format of the internal data description interface (interface
13) is the interface across which the data base administrator makes known
to the data base management system his declaration of the internal data
base schema. The internal data base schema processor accepts this
declaration, edits it for syntax, internal consistency and external
consistency (i.e. consistent with the specifications in the conceptual
schema). The mapping structures relating the internal data base to the
conceptual data base are made known through interface 14. The edited
internal schema is transmitted to the rest of the data base management
system across interface 14, the object format of the internal data
description.
Figure 4 displays that portion of the architecture relevant to the schema
preparation function.

Mapping Functions
As was indicated above in the sections on schema preparation, the data
base administrator and application administrator(s) must prepare their
respective schemas to be consistent with, and derivable from the entities
declared by the enterprise administrator as being in the conceptual schema.
The mechanism for accomplishing this is to define mappings between the
conceptual schema and the various external schemas as well as from the
internal schema to the conceptual schema. Figure 5a is a representation of
the DBTG mapping mechanism, whereby introduction of a new schema (i.e. a
new internal schema) in DBTG causes new mappings to be defined between the
new schema and the existing subschemas (i.e. external schemas), resulting
in previous mappings becoming obsolete. Figure 5b depicts how the same

situation (i.e. new internal schema, existing external schemas), is handled
via the ANSI/SPARC proposed architecture. Using the SPARC architecture,
only the mapping from the internal schema to the conceptual schema needs to
be redefined. Since all external schemas are, by definition derivable from
the conceptual schema, the mappings from the conceptual schema to the
external schemas stay fixed.

In order to accommodate changes to any one of the three schemas it is
necessary to establish the relationships between the schemas to understand
the ramifications of any change. Within the framework of the SPARC
architecture, this is accomplished by specifying mappings between the
schemas and processing these mappings by explicit transformation processing
functions. Figure 6 displays that portion of the architecture relevant to
defining and transmitting the mapping structures between the schemas to the
rest of the data base system.

The mappings relating external data base objects to conceptual data base
objects are stored in the data dictionary/directory by the external data
base schema processor across interface 5. Similarly, the mapping structure
representing the relationships between internal data base and conceptual
data base objects are stored in the data/dictionary directory by the
internal data base schema processor via interface 14. The relevant mapping
structures, along with the conceptual data base schema object descriptions
stored in the data dictionary/directory via interface 2, are transmitted
from the dictionary across interface 36 to the internal data base to
conceptual data base transformation module, and interface 38 to the
conceptual data base to external data base transformation module to
establish the correspondence of models necesary to maintain consistency
across schemas. Thus, changes to schema definitions will result in
redefining the relationships between the new schema definition and the
existing schemas; that is, changing the mapping structures.

The above discussion has focused on mappings which define the
relationships between the internal and external schemas with the conceptual
schema and the transformation functions which bind an application to its
data. Another class of mappings represented in Figure 6 are those mapping
structures which relate end-user programs to both the external and internal
data base object tyes. These mappings, coupled with the schema mappings,
insulate user programs from changes to either the external or internal
schemas. External data base to user program mapping structures are stored
via interface 37; internal data base to user program mapping structures are
stored via interface 35. Interfaces 30 and 31 are utilized during
execution time for transmitting access commands and data between the
internal storage, internal data base, conceptual data base and external
data base (i.e. through several layers of the onion-machine). These
commands and data are transformed into the object types known at each level
by the relevant transformation processing function.

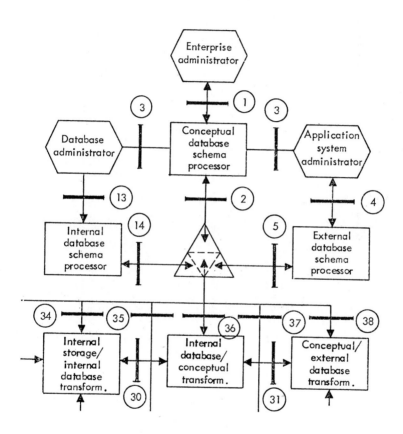

Fig. 4— Schema preparation

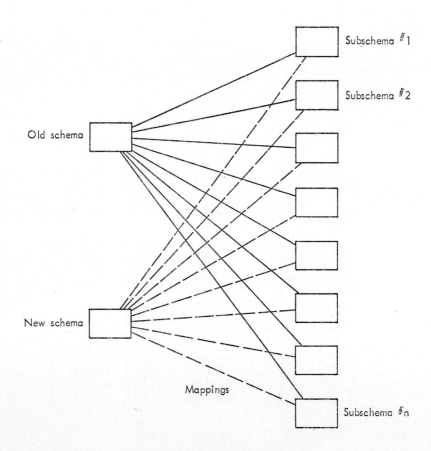

Fig. 5a — DBTG mapping mechanism

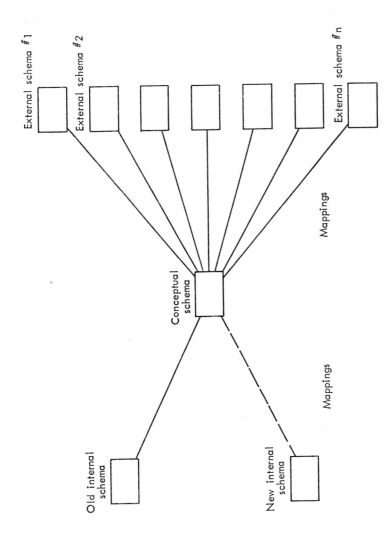

Fig. 5b—ANSI/SPARC mapping

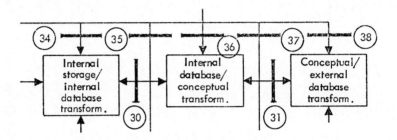

Fig. 6—Mapping Preparation

End User Interface

The major portion of the preceding discussion has centered around those data description and data manipulation interfaces necessary for each administrator (i.e. enterprise, application, data base) to successfully prepare his respective schema and define its relationships to the other schemas.

In order to complete the discussion of the components of the architecture, and hence describe the information flow through the total data base management system, it is necessary to describe the multiple data description and manipulation interfaces which exist for the many classes of end-users who access and manipulate the data of the enterprise. Referring to Figure 7, the SPARC architecture characterizes five types of end-users:

        Parametric User
        Application Programmer
        Report Specifier
        Enquiry Specifier
        Update Specifier

It should be noted that this is not an exhaustive list; it is meant to be representative of end-users having different degrees of sophistication and making different demands upon the data base management system. Other classes of end-users may be accommodated, each interacting with the data base management system through a unique language interface.

The application programmer as end-user communicates with the data base management system through an external data manipulation language interface (interface 7). The application programmer specifies, across interface 7, the selection and manipulation statements on the external data objects which are defined in the external schema for the specific application class. It should be noted that there is one such interface (i.e. interface 7a, 7b, 7c, etc.) for each host language (e.g. COBOL, PL/I, FORTRAN, etc.).

Interfaces 8, 9, 10, 11 are interfaces through which specialized end-users can communicate with the data base management system in a manner which is most convenient and specific to the type of user and application. For example, the Enquiry Specification Language interface (interface 9) is the interface across which the enquiry specifier, as end-user, describes a particular inquiry to be answered (i.e., a request for data from the external data base). Similarly, interfaces 8, 10 and 11 are the data manipulation language interfaces through which report specifiers, update specifiers, and parametric users (e.g. doctors, clerks, engineers) respectively, make requests for data known to the data base management system.

In order for the external data manipulation statements specified by the end-user across interfaces 7, 8, 9, 10, and 11 to be compiled/translated/interpreted against the external data descriptions specified in the external schema, it is necessary for the external data description to be made known to the host language compiler/translator/ interpreter. It is across interface 6 that the external schema is presented to the program development function in order that this compilation/translation/interpretation of the program can occur.

At execution time, all requests for data are passed across interface 12 to the data base management system which, in turn, provides the necessary transformation from external, to conceptual, to internal, to internal storage form.

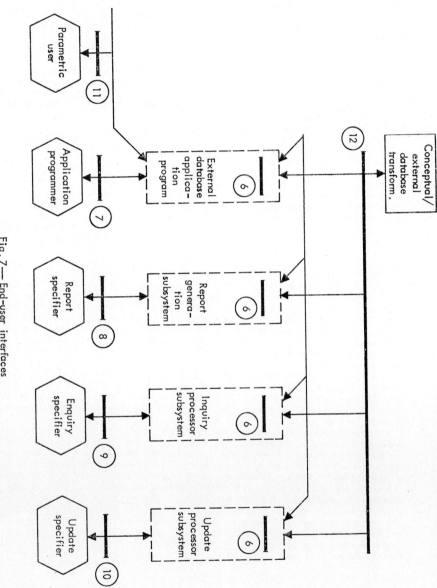

Fig. 7 — End-user interfaces

DATA INDEPENDENCE

Presentation of a prototypical architecture for data base management systems would be incomplete without a discussion of how the architecture meets the objectives of data independence. The working definition of data independence employed by the Study Group is:

> "Data independence is the capability of a data management system to permit references to stored data especially in programs and their data descriptions, to be insulated from changes and different usages in the data environment: the data as stored, as shared by other programs, and as reorganized to improve data base system performance."

Given this definition, the questions to be answered are:

How does the proposed architecture

. permit theinformation system to evolve easily?

. permit the optimum use of computer and human resources?

. preserve the enterprise's investment in existing programs, which are logically correct, in the face of data base restructuring?

In order to answer the first question, it is necessary to understand that the model of the information system is characterized by the entities of the conceptual data base. If an enterprise radically changes its way of doing business, then presumably, the concern is not to preserve prior investments, but to re-orient or re-adjust to the "new enterprise". However, given that in most cases an enterprise only augments its current mode of operation by adding new entities, the assumption is made that the new conceptual schema is not totally different from the old schema, and furthermore, that the transformation from the old schema to the new schema can be explicitly stated. The proposed architecture can accommodate these changes by introducing new mappings between the conceptual schema to the existing external schemas and internal schema such that the existing schemas can stay fixed. It may be necesssary, however, to prepare new external schemas incorporating the new functions of the enterprise. What is most important to note however, is that changes can be made to the conceptual schema, and that the changes affect only the mappings and transformation processors and need not interfere with existing applications.

The second and third questions are answered in a similar fashion. That is, any change in the internal schema affects only the mappings between the internal toconceptual schema; external applications are insulated from these changes. (refer again to Figure 5b). New external schemas may be added as new application areas are needed by defining new mappings from the conceptual schema to the new external schema, without affecting either existing application programs or the existing internal schema.

To summarize, the prototypical architecture responds to the objectives of data indepedence through the concept of the conceptual schema. By preparing external and internal schemas against the relatively stable conceptual schema, changes to the data base environment for economic reasons (e.g. restructuring of internal data base) or to add new application classes (e.g. new external schemas) can be absorbed with a minimum of impact to the surrounding environment.

Summary

This paper has presented a prototypical architecture for data base management systems developed by the ANSI/X3/SPARC Study Group on Data Base Management Systems. The most significant aspect of this architecture is the benefit to the enterprise gained from the three- level approach to data base modelling. By introducing the concept of a Conceptual Schema, the information model of the enterprise is formalized, thereby producing a

framework for systematic evolution of the information system.   The notion
of the conceptual schema also promotes data independence by providing a
relatively stable basis for data descriptions.

REFERENCES
[1] ANSI/X3/SPARC Study Group on Data Base Management Systems Interim
    Report
[2] Nijssen, G.M., "An Evaluation of the ANSI DBMS Architecture and
    Conceptual Schema as in the February 1975 Report," working paper
    prepared for IFIP WG 2.6, May 1975 meeting
[3] Sibley, E.H., "Data Management Systems - User Requirements," Data
    Base Management Systems, Donald A. Jardine (ed.), North Holland
    Publishing Company, 1973
[4] Steel, T.B. Jr., "Formalization of Conceptual Schemas," IFIP TC-2
    Working Conference on Modeling in Data Base Management Systems,
    January 1976 Meeting

DISCUSSION

PRATT: You made a statement that there may be no materialization or machine
description of the conceptual schema.   It seems to me that the entire
notion of data independence and mapping depends on a materialization of the
conceptual schema.

YORMARK: What I meant was the conceptual schema provides the real world
model.   Actual one-to-one mapping may not exist between the entities of
interest in the conceptual schema and the data that are actually stored.
There may be an entity in the conceptual schema which maps onto several
objects in an internal schema. We re talking about descriptors of those
objects rather than the actual objects.   They may be materialized in
several objects in the actual stored data representation.

TAYLOR: I have three questions.   First of all you said during your
presentation that the external schema was "equivalent" to a DBTG sub
schema. Could you expand on what you mean by equivalent.

YORMARK: The notion is equivalent. It's the users view of the data base,
some subset of the stored data.

TAYLOR: This does not mean that for every notion in a DBTG subschema
there's an equivalent notion in an external schema and conversely, which
would be the mathematical idea of equivalent.

YORMARK: Correct. They are not equivalent in a mathematical sense.

TAYLOR: How does a notion of a distributed data base get incorporated into
an internal schema?

COHN: There was some discussion of the distributed data base, but primarily
it is on the agenda for subsequent work.   There was an effort by Don
Jardine in a SHARE committee at one time, where we took the SPARC study
group model and attempted to distribute it. We physically distributed the
internal data base, and we discussed how it would be controlled through the

conceptual schema. We concluded (with a very primitive study) that it could work. There was nothing in what we had done in the study group that appeared to be unworkable in a distributed data base.

TAYLOR: A conceptual schema is supposed to model the enterprise, and I assume it will model the data entities and relationships and also the operational entities of that enterprise. You said further that interface 1 in particular (the interface between the enterprise administrator and the conceptual schema transformer) was one on which you were going to take positive action. When I think of something as being a candidate for standardization, I think of a language which has existed in the field for some period of time and has met the test of being under fire. I don't know of any language which incorporates notions like data abstraction that are in the field now.

STEEL: Positive action can mean more than one thing. We were not necessarily saying there is an existing candidate for standardization. We were trying to say that this is an area in which it seems like standardization is extremely desirable, and development efforts should be put under way in order to generate candidates for standardization. That is considered equally positive action.

NELSON: I'd like to convey the depth of my objection to the approach you described, at least as a way to describe information system architecture. I don't think you have an architecture that is suitable for use in a small systems environment. In doing a commendable job of analyzing all the possible ways in which you could decompose a system, you've overanalyzed. This results in a system which only a few very large installations could cope with, either conceptually or practically. Most of the people who could use a data base system couldn t handle a system of this level of complexity.

YORMARK: I don't understand what smallness or largeness has to do with the concept of defining an enterprise s data in terms of a real-world view, and providing mapping or definitions of that enterprise through to an external view and an internal view, passing across as many interfaces as you need to to map from the conceptual view to actual stored data.

NELSON: I m concerned about your information system architecture and its 40 odd interfaces, and the extent to which that implies a system complexity incommensurate with the information systems now in existence, for example, the System/3 shop with a single person who is the chief financial officer and the chief programmer and the data base administrator.

KIRSHENBAUM: The three functions we [the ANSI Study Group] talked about in data description are roles, not necessarily organizations or staffs. In a big company, each of those might be a staff of possibly several dozen people. As the company gets smaller, the number of people would decrease. The first roles to be combined would be the data base administrator and the enterprise administrator. The next thing would be that either all three would be combined, or the application systems administrator role would be performed by the programmer. At the next level of interfaces, some of the transformations on a smaller machine are null transformations. In the actual execution of the system there does not have to be a mapping from external to conceptual to internal. Those could be compiled, so that efficiencies could be achieved in a smaller machine. Some at the left hand side could be prespecified by the vendor. It's quite possible that the data

base description language would be either in hardware or specified by the
vendor.   The Study Group's interfaces must be the superset of all possible
interfaces. It doesn't mean that any one or any group of them will be
visible at any given implementation.

NELSON: I have a further objection. The architecture is described in terms
of 40-odd interfaces. If you are trying to convey something that complex,
it would be better to have a simpler version of it to begin with, one in
which the complexity can unfold as a matter of refinement. You have made a
system as complicated as it is because you are trying to make distinctions.
This is the role of the analyst. When block diagrams are that complex it s
time for a simplicist to try to find some way to organize it conceptually,
so it makes a more coherent picture.

STEEL: I'd like to comment on this last observation in particular. One of
the most dangerous things in the world is to oversimplify something that
really is fundamentally complicated.

YORMARK: If you are trying to define an architecture for a generalized data
base management system, you must define it for the most complex system and
have a smaller system utilize that portion of the model which is necessary.
The three level approach is not inherently complex, not even to a small
user. Most data bases being developed by large companies need the level of
abstraction represented by our architecture. I don't think we have closed
any roads for the smaller systems.

SENKO: First a remark on abstract data types, and then I'd like to come
back to the other question. Abstract data types have been talked about by
programming language people for a few years. For those in the data base
area, you can think of them as a relatively small portion of data
independence and consistency constraints. If you are familiar with those,
you find that they cover quite well what the programming language people
are trying to do with abstract data types. In fact, data independence is a
much more general concept.   Coming back to the question about small
systems, I think that the ANSI/SPARC people have done a neat job in the
three level concept.   You can build a small system without getting the
properties of the three levels. For instance, you could give up data
independence and functions of that nature. But there is another aspect of
it also. The three level concept (and additional levels within it), which
my group had looked at in DIAM, gives you a chance to build a simpler
system. The systems we have at the present time are all built up by
generalizing systems which were originally payrolls, and parts systems, and
so forth. They've excessively complex because we try to generalize them by
adding pieces. They've been incoherent and redundant. With a fresh look we
find that in many cases you get more power and more simplicity in the same
step.   With regard to the number of interfaces that the ANSI/SPARC people
have mentioned, I think they can simplify the number. It's a first pass,
and a little bit more looking will in fact allow them to cut down.

STEEL: While the number of interfaces actually runs to 41, there are about
18 of them that have disappeared under the covers of the machine. They
were things that were identified as essential, but after eyxamination it
was clear that they were inappropriate for even consideration for
standardization. Most of them will, in fact, be built into hardware.

JARDINE: Conceptual schemata are going to get extremely complex. The idea,
it seems to me, of having a single conceptual schema for the enterprise is

probably not practical. The result of this will be a number of separate and distinct conceptual schemata in a particular enterprise. And now we have created an absolutely horrendous problem which exists even if there were only one conceptual schema; that is, the problem of how does the conceptual schema processor check the conceptual schema for validity.

KIRSHENBAUM: I question the basic assumption, that because of complexity we may need more than one conceptual schema. I disagree with that completely. You must separate what is stored about the conceptual schema and what human beings see about the conceptual schema at any one point in time. Don Moerke of A.O. Smith has done a lot of work on a concept called data hiding. Presumably the enterprise administrator would only look at a small part of the total schema at any point in time. No one human being is ever going to try to grasp the whole thing. You start with a very small piece of it, keep adding to it, and only look at a part of it through a window, perhaps somewhat darkly. You can mask out the levels of detail that you re not interested in.

ROBERTSON: You have compared the external schema with the DBTG subschema and, presumably on purpose, avoided any such comparisons of the internal schema and conceptual schema. Could you try to make such a comparison with a corresponding DBTG concept?

YORMARK: I can't make a comparison with the conceptual schema. The DBTG schema is not mathematically equivalent to the ANSI/SPARC internal schema.

ROBERTSON: So you're saying that the internal schema is as close to the DBTG schema as the external schema is to the subschema.

YORMARK: I'd say yes, but Jon Turner is shaking his head no.

SENKO: Most things in the conceptual schema are relatively implicit in the record structure and to some extent in the set structure of DBTG That is, associations between fields or between names are really what the conceptual schema describes. DBTG also says a lot about how those associations are represented, which is really the internal schema.

ROBERTSON: Why have you not proposed that interface 13 (the data base administrator's interface to the internal schema) be a good candidate for standardization?

YORMARK: The proposal for positive action, negative action, and undecided, came about as a consensus opinion, and does not represent the views of all of the members of the study group. There were some of us who thought that we should go a step further.

STEEL: The ones we said were positive were ones that were overwhelmingly endorsed by the vote. The ones that we said were negative were overwhelmingly disposed of. The others including, I think, Number 13, fell into the category in between. I believe the majority was leaning in favour of having positive standardization. I think the logic of those who voted against it had to do with the fact that the particular model was tied to economics; that is, economic control of the data base is the responsibility of the data base administrator. If it were to be tied to hardware constraints or to taking advantage of hardware opportunities, then it should be free to take advantage of technology. On the other hand, some people said, from the users point of view, there ought to be ways of

specifying what you want as the economic objectives in that interface.   It
should be standardized in some way, and the vendors could figure out how to
satisfy it. The argument did not get sophisticated enough to resolve the
point.   There were people on both sides of it, so it was left for further
study.

YORMARK: With many of the interfaces that had to do with an unclear
boundary between hardware and software, the vote was not very clear cut.
If things could be really tied to the hardware, we had much more of a
problem reaching consensus than otherwise.

SWENSON: Have you considered a mechanism for building conceptual schemas,
and are you going to do that in your standardization effort? Also, I
wonder if you've properly distinguished between the simplicity   or
complexity of that mecchanism vs. the simplicity or complexity of the
resulting schema.

YORMARK: We have not had any prolonged discussion on what kind of
information or language is available to the enterprise administrator in
creating a conceptual schema and passing it across Interface 1 to the rest
of the data base management system.   The further study that we will
recommend will be to try to come up with a candidate. At that point in the
study, SPARC may or may not create a whole new group to study Interface 1.

ROBERTS: Your slide presentation states that both   the   data   base
administrator and the applications administrator have responsibility for
economics. Could you clarify that?

YORMARK: The problem was in the use of the term 'economics' in both cases.
The data base administrator is concerned with the economics of the data
base in terms of storage, redundancy, access techniques, and so on. When I
talk about the applications administrator, I refer to the economics
afforded by a definition of an external schema which contains only those
entities or data items of interest to a particular application class. It's
the economics of size of the objects that are available to work with, not
the economics of being able to control the internals of the data base for a
specific application. The economics I was referring to at the external
level were the economies afforded to an application by not having to view
irrelevant data.

TAYLOR: In this discussion about Interface 1 a couple of comments were made
that perhaps ANSI would appoint a group that could write some sort of
specifications of what sounded to me like functional requirements. How is
it that ANSI does things which tend to lead to development?

STEEL: The answer to your question is not an easy one.   It is something
that ANSI has not done generally in the past. In computers and information
processing there are several areas where, because the technology is
changing so rapidly , it has been appropriate to at least find a
development group. I give you the example of CODASYL in the COBOL work.
There is a specific agreement between ANSI X 3J4 (the COBOL standards
committee) and CODASYL that specifications will be developed by CODASYL and
delivered to X3J4 for processing as an American National Standard. It
seems not inconsistent that the same sort of thing happened in the area of
PL/I where a specific ANSI committee took an existing language, did a great
deal of development work on it, and then proposed a standard. It seems not
unreasonable that the same thing can happen in the area of data base,

particularly if the people who are studying the situation feel that there is a need for that kind of development work and don't see it going on anywhere else.

BRODIE: In your specification you've picked a few interfaces to recommend for standardizaation. Wouldn't it have been better to pick a minimum set of specifications that should be specified in order to come up with an operatable system. As it stands now the interfaces that you have picked won't allow anyone to come up with a complete system that will do anything.

YORMARK: It would have been too good to be true if we could have gone from interface 1 through some of the mappings and at least to interface 7, so that an application programmer could write a program against a data base management system. It's not that we couldn't reach consensus. We came to a consensus that standardization efforts at this point were premature. If a development effort does go on in terms of standardizing or coming up with a standard for interface 1, it may, in fact, clarify the mapping interfaces in between. You're right...we stand here open kimono. We have not been able to say that we can standardize on interfaces which would allow us to have a workable data base management system. I think a lot of it has to do with the ambiguity surrounding definition of a conceptual schema. I don't think we can start an effort on standardizing mappings until we know what a conceptual schema looks like, and how somebody might be able to utilize a conceptual schema in defining a data base or the entities of interest.

KIRSHENBAUM: What you're talking about would be the equivalent of having in, for example, a COBOL standard, everything from the COBOL source language itself to the object language that it's specified in. In fact, there is no such standard, and yet people do build 'standard' COBOL language compilers. What we've tried to do is specify the ones that were important to standardize, not the ones that had to exist to build a system. What we're saying is; given the standard set plus others that are not standard, someone can build a system. We said it wasn't important or useful to standardize for example, the transformation algorithms between the transformation boxes because that's technology dependent.

SENKO: I'd like to get some middle ground on the conceptual schema, whether it's one or multiple. From a standpoint of philosophy, we who are outsiders tend to attack the group, and try to put things in. On the other hand, the group, to avoid being pushed all over the place, puts their feet in concrete. It turns out that people whose feet are in concrete end up being drowned. I think it will be hard to prove you can only have one conceptual schema for an enterprise, because you have first of all to find what an enterprise is. An enterprise could very well be a division or several divisions of a company, so in one sense you have one conceptual schema and in another sense you have many. One thing to be said for the conceptual schema is that it will be simpler than we have now, so it will be at least easier to construct. It still may not be possible, but it will be easier.

PANEL DISCUSSION ON ANSI/X3 DBMS STUDY GROUP REPORT

PANEL MEMBERS

T.B. Steel,Jr.   L. Cohn
F. Kirshenbaum   H. Kunecke
C.E. Mairet   J.A. Turner
B. Yormark

STEEL: Every member of this panel has been intimately involved in developing the ANSI/SPARC report, and in deliberating on the current and future activities of the committee. Let me begin by making some comments on what the study group is supposed to do. There is an report called a SPARC document 90 which is an outline proposal for action on standardization. It has eleven sections to it; I won't go through all of them in detail, but essentially it asks any proponent of standardization action to first describe precisely what it is they propose to have standardized. Second and perhaps most important, to give a cost-benefit trade-off on the development of the standard and the economics of having such a standard. Third, to describe a program of work and schedule for developing such a standard. The formal end-product of the ANSI/SPARC Study Group on Data Base Management Systems is supposed to be a series of such reports recommending for or against standards actions. The study group concluded rather early on that the only things appropriate to consider for standardization are interfaces, and these interfaces we have idenfified and these are the ones we discuss. As Bea Yormark said earlier, there are some that we considered, more or less unanimously, inappropriate for standardization. Mostly they were internal interfaces, those that are technology dependent and that perhaps belong in hardware. There are some that we were undecided about and a handful that we considered were indeed significant and appropriate. After some discussion, the study group concluded that interface 7, the data manipulation language interface, was not, as a single interface, technically feasible to standardize. We've subdivided Interface 7 as a, b, c, d, etc. The sub-interfaces were carefully chosen in the order in which the programming languages were considered for standardization.

There is no other implication by the order of any significance with respect to the programming languages. Therefore, interface 7(a) is Fortran, Interface 7(b) is COBOL, Interface 7(c) is PL/I, and so on. We decided, further, because of the extensive efforts of CODASYL and because there are existing proposals, that the appropriate first step was to consider Interface 7(b) and look at the candidate or candidates for a data manipulation language for COBOL. We spent six rather excruciating months at it. The results of that were a report that we sent to our parent committee in October of last year. I'm going to ask Bea to comment on that.

YORMARK: Essentially what I'll do is read to you the content of the letter that we sent to SPARC in October:

"After publication of the interim report in February [1975] the Study Group undertook an investigation of Interface 7, the External Data Manipulation Language - Source Form, as it relates to COBOL. This

choice of task was made because of the consideration of the CODASYL Data
Base Facility by X3J4, making this investigation seem the most urgent.

After four meetings the Study Group has evaluated the Data Base
Facility specification as a candidate for meeting the intent of
Interface 7. It was agreed that certain changes in these specifications
are essential for acceptability of this candidate as a standard and
these are outlined in the attachment. However, the Study Group has
failed to reach agreement on how much change would be required, the
areas of disagreement being outlined in the attachment. As a result of
the impasse, these areas of disagreement must be considered as partial.

....

The Study Group recommends the following activities as appropriate for
future work.
   a) finish the interim report, especially the detailed interface
      definitions.
   b) evaluate existing data base management systems to determine their
      functional capabilities.
   c) on a selective interface basis, evaluate potential candidates and
      recommend actions; in particular interfaces 1, 3, 4 and 9."

I'd like to outline to you the areas of agreement that the study group
reached with respect to interface 7(b). Declarations which are present in
the schema should never be overridden by declarations in the subschema or
by programmer action and declarations present in the subschema should never
be overridden by programmer action. The current mechanism of privacy locks
violates the principle set forth above. The current mechanism for data
integrity, that is, the set occurrence selection, violates the above
principle also. The current mechanism for shared access control, i.e.
KEEP, FREE, and RE-MONITOR is considered to be incorrect and uncorrectable.
The current REALM concept seems to be a mixture of logical and physical
considerations. The study group feels there is a need for a file concept
at the subschema level which is entirely independent of storage
considerations. The current mechanism does not seem to adequately cover
recovery and restart requirements. A facility is needed to notify the
recovery and restart facilities and shared access facilities that the
programatic actions prior to the execution of the command are logically
independent from those that succeed it. It is necessary to introduce a
command which permits a programmer to request a concellation of data base
actions carried out during a sphere of control. Implied is the recovery of
other run units which have been affected by the actions of the run unit.
The run unit itself is not terminated. Errors exist in the specification
of how currency indicators are updated, and finally, facilities in the data
manipulation language should only be dependent upon declarations in the
subschema, and all vestiges of storage considerations should be removed
from the subschema.

These were areas of agreement. The areas of disagreement, those which
have hung us up for the past six months, are the following:

1. Whether the currentmechanism for defining the record occurrence to be
manipulated via the currency indicators should be replaced by an explicit
cursor mechanism.

2.Whether the data base key mechanism should be removed. [Ed. note: see
Manola's paper in this Proceedings concerning removal of data base key.]

3. (this is one of the most fought about) Whether the specification should provide manipulation capability for data model other than networks (data structure sets).

Those were our areas of disagsreement where we have as yet failed to reach consensus among the study group members.

STEEL: The letter referred to by Bea Yormark is a public letter. It is a letter to SPARC from the SPARC Data Base Management Study Group, on the study group status. It is available from CBEMA, which is the secretariat for ANSI/X3, Computers and Information Processing. It is dated 75/10/27.

KIRSHENBAUM: The letter was initially presented to the SPARC committee (which is our parent committee). At a meeting in November, the SPARC committee felt that the appropriate thing to do was to take the areas of agreement and the areas of disagreement and pass them to X3J4, the COBOL Standardization Committee within ANSI. It was also forwarded to both DDLC and PLC explaining what action had been taken. As I understand it, X3J4 is beginning to work on the areas of agreement and disagreement now.

KLAUS: DDLC has taken action and removed the data base keys from the DDLC description language. However, I think it should be clear that what we´re talking about is the ability of the applications programmer to reference data base keys as they existed in the DBTG report, rather than the basic mechanism of identifying record occurrences. What has been removed, must be partially replaced, but in such a way that it´s transparent to the user.

KIRSHENBAUM: The problem in the discussion of other data models was the problem of migration. When you talk about having only the network model, or only the relational model, or any one particular model, one must consider the substantial number of companies who are running data base systems other than what some people are proposing as a standard. They must have some migration path. Consider the following information from Datapro (August to December 1975):

TOTAL		750
System 2000		300
ADABAS		100
IDMS		66
DMS2		75
IDS		475
DMS1100	250 to	300
IMS		400
DOS DL/I		100

If you compare DBTG to non-DBTG, there are 1725 non-DBTG and 841 DBTG systems, which means that two-thirds of the data base management systems being used are not DBTG systems. Those installations systems represent a substantial investment in data base management systems and their migration path to any standard must obviously be considered.

STEEL: The next point for us to address is that it is not just a small group in ANSI that has considered this approach. There has been considerable international activity of various kinds. I am going to ask Larry Cohn to talk about that.

COHN: ISO is the international standards body. Within ISO, there is TC97,
which is the equivalent of ANSI X3 in Computers and Information Processing.
Within TC97, there is SC5, which is a committee on programming languages.
One of the member countries of TC97 is the Netherlands and, in late 1973,
they recommended to TC97 that the DBTG report be submitted to SC5 for
development of an ISO standard. TC97, following its procedure, sent the
Netherlands proposal around to the member countries of TC97 for comment.
As a result of the comments, TC97 asked SC5 to sponsor a study group to
investigate where things stood relative to   standardization   at   an
international level.   As the ANSI SPARC representatives, some of us have
been participating in the ISO meetings. I´d like to report to you on two
of those meetings. I feel that I´d better read it because every word that
is on here had to withstand the potential of World War II being fought
again,   and they went through six drafts and hours of commentary until the
specific wording was agreed upon. The member nations that participated in
the first meeting in June of 1975, were the United States, Germany, France
and Sweden. The conclusions were as follows:

1. The Study Group concludes in response to the Netherlands Proposal on
    Data Base Management, (ISO/TC 97/598), that any standardization
    action in the area of data base management systems based on existing
    proposals is premature in the absence of criteria against which to
    measure such proposals.
2. The Interim Report of the ANSI/X3/SPARC Study Group on Data Base
    Management Systems (ISO/TC 97/SC 5 (USA-75) N359) is accepted by the
    ISO/TC 97/SC 5 Study Group on Data Base Management Systems as an
    initial basis for discussion on a gross architecture of data base
    management systems.
3. The Study Group acknowledges the need to identify all types of data
    base management systems users and to specify their requirements.
4. The Study Group proposes to review and augment the terminology used
    in N359 and the concepts therein. As the initial effort, the Study
    Group will establish priorities in terms of interfaces identified in
    N359 for further investigation. These priorities will be chosen to
    optimize the benefits derived from standardization.
5. As a parallel activity to those identified above, the current
    CODASYL data base specifications will be evaluated. The Study Group
    notes at this time that preliminary studies by various national and
    international bodies have indicated that the CODASYL specifications
    are not suitable for standardization as they stand.
6. The Study Group will recommend development work for those interfaces
    appropriate to standardization for which no adequate candidate
    exists.

Seven months later, in Paris, there was a second meeting of that group.
The same four countries returned. Also attending the second meeting were
the U.K., Netherlands and an observer from Italy.   The conclusions that
resulted from that meeting were best described in this scope of work which
also went through lots of argument. They decided the ISO Study Group´s job
was to recommend:
(a) any actions appropriate to data base standardization;
(b) actions appropriate to technical development; and
(c) priorities with regard to the before two mentioned items.
As a means of accomplishing the objectives above, the following actions are
necessary:
1. Review current data base activities within the standardization

technical and commercial communities.

2. Identify or develop a framework for describing the components and interfaces for an architecture of a prototypical data base management system.

3. Identify users of data base management systems and establish their requirements for such systems.

4. Define criteria for judging existing and future approaches to data base management systems with respect to suitability for standardization.

5. Evaluate existing and proposed data base facilities and languages against this criteria.

6. Determine the advantages and disadvantages of standardization with regard to particular interfaces defined within the architecture earlier mentioned.

7. Review and develop terminology as necessary to support the above activities.

Final comment: The architecture to be developed will use as its principle basis the concepts of the interim report that the ANSI SPARC Study Group has issued.

We set ourselves a work program in 1976 of commenting on, revising, doing whatever we felt was necessary to two basic documents:

1. the Interim Report that the ANSI SPARC Study Group produced and
2. a statement of requirements that was produced by the French member body.

We expect to meet again in January, 1977 to see whether we are converging or whether we are diverging.

That's the activity of ISO. Another activity that should be mentioned in Europe is ECMA. They have chartered Technical Committee 22 whose task is to develop a standard in data base, COBOL flavoured.

STEEL: There have been some other activities in Europe. The International Federation for Information Processing has Technical Committee 2 on programming, which has a Working Group 2.6, on data base management systems. This committee has sponsored several working conferences on various aspects of data base management systems, and one of them was concerned to a considerable extent with the ANSI/SPARC architecture. It was held in Freudenstadt, Germany last January, and I would like to ask Frank Kirshenbaum to comment on his observations.

KIRSHENBAUM: The meeting concentrated basically on the conceptual schema, what would be in it and what would not be, and it led to some very lively and useful debate. It was not a bi-polar discussion between two opposing camps, as many of these have been in the United States.

JONES: It is now 11 years since standardization work started on PL/I and we don't have an accepted standard. Those who think it is time for a data base standard must consider that time frame, and the fact there was no existing accepted PL/I product when the standards activity began. There is now no existing data base product that everybody uses.

STEEL: I've taken a look at the length of time between the first proposal and ultimate stadardization in several complex areas, programming languages in particular. The mean time to standardization seems to be 12 years from the first publication of a proposal until the formal standard comes out. I submit that data base is probably somewhat more complex than a single

programming language, so it may take even longer, especially when there has
been so much early debate about what's right and what's wrong. We can
expect it will be 1980 or 1981 before reasonable data base standards will
appear.   There is a lot of preliminary work to be done, and a need for a
lot of interaction and feedback among the professional community in order
to determine what is reasonable.   I came up with 1981 on the basis of the
original publication of the CODASYL DBTG report in 1969.   There has been
sufficient controversy in the data base area that I suspect it's going to
take longer, so it may take 15 years.   1984 is eight years away, so that's
perhaps not unreasonable, since there seems to be the beginning of some
kind of consensus. The SPARC study group has attempted to devise a scheme
that permits all data models to be encompassed within a single system if
someone wants to implement it that way. That's been one of the objectives.

PEEBLES: Is this the UNCOL of data bases?

KIRSHENBAUM: The paper speaks not at all to the specific data models,
except in saying that we must allow them. This is an architecture that
will allow you to describe multiple data models. I would presume that most
vendors will not offer all the data models, in the same way that the U.S.
Federal Government has divided COBOL into several levels and modules.
There may be a particular vendor who chooses to offer only the hierarchical
model within the standard system. Others may offer only the network model
or the relational model.   Some may choose to implement two or three.
Within an installation or a company, they may choose to implement only one,
even if there were several in the delivered package.

KLAUS: I want to go back to the question of proliferation of programming
languages.   I don't believe that we're ever going to end up with one
programming language. However, I'm concerned about the absence of guidance
and/or standards specifications for communications between languages,
between languages and DBMS's and between languages and operating systems.
All these questions need to be resolved in terms of the DBMS architecture
and interface specifications.

STEEL: Data Base Management Systems is a big enough job for this study
group that we can't take on the problems of programming languages and
operating systems and operating system control languages. That's for our
parent committee to worry about. There are other study groups in these
areas.

KLAUS: I am concerned only with the interface. I'm not talking about the
features or the functions of a particular language, or operating systems
command language; I'm talking about the interface, for example, parameter
passing.

KIRSHENBAUM: Look at the diagram of the architecture. I'll pick one
example, interface 12, which is an attempt to do something like what you
are describing. At the point where a request is passed to the data base
management system there is one interface, not one for each language. While
there are 7 (a), 7(b), 7(c), etc. for languages, there is only one
interface 12. In that sense, we've answered your question.

COHN: The conclusion on interface 12 was that the generation of that single
interface from any language, through its interpreter or compiler, would
most likely be a hardware-architecture dependent interface, so it was voted
down as a standardization candidate.   It was not the objective of this

study group to develop the specifications for a standard. It was the
objective of this group to review existing candidates, to establish
criteria against which to measure these candidates, to propose positive
action if there were no candidates in an area where we thought that there
ought to be, and to tell SPARC which areas were ready for standardization,
based on the candidates that existed, and which were not. As part of the
methodology of developing the criteria to measure things against, we
developed an architecture and we described the roles and functions against
which a candidate had to be measured. It was not our job to take whatever
terminology or architecture we developed and to put a specification behind
that as a standard. However, if somebody comes to us with any part of
CODASYL DBTG or a relational system or any other product, and says that
ought to be a standard, we can ask ourselves in terms of the function of
the architecture and the roles and interfaces described, whether it meets
the requirements. One of the early conclusions of the study group in our
interaction with SPARC and the Netherlands proposal, was that major
objectives like dynamic data independence were apparently not satisfied by
any existing products, and we felt that we had to define an architecture
that would enable us to portray where and how that would have to be
accomplished so we could measure and evaluate candidates. We're not the
specifiers of the standards.

JARDINE: I am a little concerned about the activity that's going on in
various parts of the world in various groups looking at the possibility of
standards for DML's. It seems to me we're starting at the wrong end of the
horse. It's not clear to me how you go about designing a DML to manipulate
things that have not yet been defined and furthermore, for which the
defining mechanism has not been defined. Until we know what the objects of
interest are, as defined in the conceptual schema, it seems to me it is
entirely inappropriate to go around worrying about the mechanism by which
we manipulate these undefined quantities.

COHN: First point is that in any of the efforts that are underway regarding
a DML carry along their subschema with them. The second question you raise
is a more interesting one, and that's the problem of: do you have to have
a conceptual schema as a standard before you have a Fortran standard or a
COBOL standard? We came to a conclusion that you could consider Fortran or
COBOL disjointly from the conceptual schema, and that any conceptual schema
worth its salt would have to allow for any end-user view that could be made
consistent. Any decent conceptual schema should be able to map to any
decent self-contained and consistent user view, and in that sense, I think
you could in a disjoint fashion arrive at a COBOL standard before you have
a conceptual schema standard.

JARDINE: I don't necessarily agree that just because you have carried along
the subschema with the DML that you're out of the woods. On the other
hand, I agree that it is probably inappropriate to wait as long as it will
take to develop any kind of conceptual schema definition capability before
trying to get somethiing into the programming languages. If this problem
is to be solved by having a conceptual schema with sufficient horsepower to
generate any kind of reasonable end-user view, I'm concerned that the
conceptual-to-external schema interface is not sufficiently well defined.

YORMARK: I'm beginning to feel that we're losing sight of what this
committee is trying to do. In terms of setting a context for discussion of
standardization, we have defined an architecture which defines models in
which certain kinds of information are kept and are passed to other parts

of the data base management system. Although the form of the information
passing across interfaces is not known, what these things are is known, so
that we can indeed define data manipulation language interfaces to be
consistent with the architectural view of what belongs in a DML as opposed
to what belongs in the conceptual schema without a precise definition of
what is the form of interface 1. The exact implementation of interface 1
is not necessary for arriving at a standard for interface 7. However, the
objects of interest at interface 7 and the objects of interest at interface
1 have been clearly defined by the architecture.

TAYLOR: We've been talking mostly about interface 7. Could we spend some
time on the others, particularly No. 4, which Tom Steel said was also a
debated one.

STEEL: We chose interface 7(b) as the first thing to look at, largely
because we thought it would be the simplest. Well, we spent about eight
months on it, something like four meetings totalling 12 days arguing with
one another, and as you see did not reach consensus. The last meeting of
the Study Group was the end of October, 1975. The anticipated next step
would be interface 4. It is the hope of the group that one can come up
with a way of describing external schemas, not particular external schemas,
but ways of describing them that are language independent. Obviously
interface 1 is something we feel needs a lot of development work done.
Interface 39 is a tough one, something that we feel needs more discussion
in the study group before we can really talk about what has to be there,
although it seemed like an important one to do something about.

KIRSHENBAUM: To return to Don Jardine's point, the whole process of
interfacing programming languages with the data base management system is
not a process of adding. It seems to me that it's a process of taking
away.   As more and more of the function slides back into the data base
management system or the operating system, elements are ' removed from the
language, not added to it. That's what every data base system currently on
the market today is doing to a greater or lesser degree.   Even the data
manipulation verbs are going out. We had discussions in the Study Group
about whether the equivalent of read or write is necessary, and as a matter
of fact, some of us believe it may not be. If you say in a language like
COBOL, ADD A TO B GIVING C, the system at some level of technology may know
enough so that you don't have to define A, B, or C in the program, nor the
read and write operations involved in acquiring that data. The problem may
be psychological. In all of the committees dealing with programming
languages they tend to think in terms of a charter which states that they
are to expand the language.   It is inconsistent with that charter and
psychologically very difficult to say the time has come to take something
out.

NELSON: I think you have spotted a trend, and this is something that
ANSI/SPARC should be concerned about that is, how to reduce the content of
existing programming languages, particularly in a data base environment.
However, you're not getting rid of data description languages when you push
them back into a data dictionary interface.   What you're saying is, a
number of declarations which must be supplied in order to write a data
manipulation program, has been diminished. A need for describing data
hasn't gone away.

KIRSHENBAUM: I agree with you.   What I meant to say is that data
description is coming out of each individual programming language, and out

of each individual occurrence of a program. There is obviously still a need for more and more sophisticated data definition languages, but they are not programming languages in the way we tend to think about them today. Certainly they are not coded at the same logical point in time.

NELSON: The declaration of data has become the most important part of the process of describing information systems, and has a context that is much broader than the manipulation programs. I would like, on a second point, to get some comments from people here who might be representing DML or DDLC standardization efforts. I have heard comments from people who are working on standardizing a data manipulation language for COBOL, and their view is that they are taking the 1971 DBTG Report intact, and trying to describe the data manipulation portion in the meta-language of COBOL, and that they are not trying to improve, amplify, distort, or otherwise change the DBTG language specifications. On the other hand, we've talked to people who are working on describing data description languages withiCn CODASYL. These people have taken the 1971 report as a baseline from which they expect to do substantial development, modification change, correction, etc. On that basis I think Professor Jardine's comments were too quickly brushed aside. If that's in fact what is happening, then I think it doesn't make any sense at all for a data manipulation language to be standardized while the DDL is moving rapidly in another direction.

KIRSHENBAUM: The work that's gone on in PLC in the DML area has also carried a COBOL subschema along with it. Of the three part definition of the 1971 DBTG Report, subschema, schema, and data manipulation, two parts went to PLC (the data manipulation and the subschema), and the third part went to DDLC. DDLC is also looking at a host-independent subschema, because PLC picked up specifically the DML and subschema with a COBOL flavour. The COBOL Journal of Development has an approved extension (April, 1975), for a subschema and DML.

NELSON: PLC is developing and maintaining a language which exists, and therefore is also taking into consideration economic factors of actual installations, rather than things that might happen in the future. DDLC takes the point of view that it's developing a language that does not exist as a standard yet. So you have two different operations: one of which deals with a language which is a standard, and therefore is subject to a lot of pressures from the field, and one which deals with a language which is not a standard and feels that it's totally in the development stage. On the other hand they obviously do depend on each other. You can't arbitrarily develop a COBOL data base system completely independent from the DDL.

COHN: I just want to suggest to you that your use of the word 'standard' is inappropriate relative to the definition that Tom Steel gave. It is an accepted specification from CODASYL, which has been implemented in several place. It is not an ANSI standard.

JARDINE: I'd like to hear a little bit more, if it is appropriate, about the internal SPARC Study Group discussion concerning the addition of other data models.

MAIRET: It would be very difficult to relate the essence of all the conversation without getting into personalities, because this was one of the areas where we ran into a major impasse. There was considerable discussion about different views, hierarchical, network, and relational. The only conclusion we came to was that we couldn't reach agreement. There was considerable discussion about the possibility that in the framework of talking about a COBOL interface 7, there might be three standards; one for relational, one for network, and one for hierarchical, and maybe more. That didn't seem very probable for some people, but imposing one data model on other people who do not choose to use that data model, seemed to be an unfair imposition. My personal feelings are that I believe the industry is running headlong into what I consider to be a very serious problem, and that is premature standardization. I've spent several years working in the field of data base, the last three and a half in some very painful and agonizing arguments, debates and discussions in the Study Group. It has become obvious to me, and because of this conversation we've had here today, it may be obvious to some of you also, that we don't really know what is the job to be done. We don't have the disciplines in place on how to define the data of an enterprise. We don't understand well enough the whole problem of how to manage data as a resource. My own personal opinion is that we're quite premature. I think there are some very serious questions that have just come up about COBOL. Please understand these are personal remarks. My company has been a COBOL user ever since it was available, and is predominantly a COBOL shop right now, so we have a vested interest in COBOL. We're also very upset and concerned with the direction that it's taking, and it seems like every time a new version comes out, it's got more system concerns exposed to the business application programmer. My position is, we should be taking systems concerns out. There should be less and less dependenceupon the underlying system. I consider the communication facility a step backwards, and I consider the data base facility, if it were included in the standard, as a step backwards. These facilities put more and more technical systems problems in the hands of the business appplications programmer, and this does not solve the business problems of the enterprise. I believe we will have to make the programmer independent of how the user puts a transaction into the computer system, and independent of how the data resource is stored within a system. There is a serious question about the direction of high-level languages in terms of their objectives in the beginning. Until questions like that are answered, I don't see how we can proceed, because we may be proceeding in the wrong direction.

JARDINE: One of the things that concerns me, and I've seen more and more of it in the last fifteen or twenty minutes, is the problem of binding the programming language definition to a particular data model. We have been talking for several years about data independence and yet the first thing we do when we design subschemas and data manipulation constructs, is bind to a particular view of the world. As Chuck [Mairet] and several other members of the panel have said, having multiple data models available to the applications programmer doesn't seem to be a rational way around that. I'd like to ask the question: Why are we exposing the data model to the application program?

KIRSHENBAUM:
  There should be les and less need. I'm not sure if the answer is none, but less and less of the data model should be exposed to the application program. I, too, am concerned about this direction. The CODASYL data base facility proposal (and the numbers for the communication facility are quite similar) adds seven new verbs, fourteen new special registers, and over 50 reserved words to the COBOL language. I'm really concerned about thecomplexity that adds to the language. Commercial programmers should only be interested in solving the business problem they've been asked to solve. It can be very dangerous to give them this level of complexity to

to deal with.

COHN: BASIC started out as a very simple language and when they get
finished with it in another ten years, it is going to put COBOL to shame.
It will be a very detailed system-oriented language doing eveything that
you could conceivably think of. I think that when people get together and
they want to expand a language, they will sit down and do so. The concerns
on the part of Chuck[Mairet], Frank [Kirshenbaum], and Don[Moehrke], as
users, is that this is not accomplishing what they would like to accomplish
from a business point of view. I am not quite sure what the outlet for
that kind of sentiment is, until somebody at, for example, an ANSI/X3 level
votes down a proposed standard and says stop, I am choking to death on what
you are giving me. However, I have not seen any signs of that happining
despite the views expressed in this room. I think we should be realistic
about these expansions and,, as yet I have not seen any concerted movement
to stop it.

KENT: I'm a little puzzled about Professor Jardine's question about
exposing data models to the programmer, unless we have very different
notions of what the model itself means. I understand a model to be that
which defines the semantics of the data to the programmer. He must think
of it as a sequential file, or as a one level store with indexed or
associative retrieval, or as a configuration of named relationships, or as
a hierarchical model, but he must think of it in some way. He must have
some context in which his verbs have some semantic meaning. I just don't
understand the notion of not exposing models to the programmer at all.

JARDINE: There are specifications I can make that do not present any
particular data model. Remember what a data model is. A particular data
model as seen by a program is a representation of a model. I maintain that
we really want to make programs representation independent. The CODASYL
proposal chose a particular representation of the model described in some
conceptual schema (if they had it). They chose an owner-member coupled
representation. I know of no case whatsoever where an algorithm written in
English ever has to know about a sequential file or an indexed file or a
hierarchy, or anything else. A particular representation does, and I get
concerned about how far we've become dependent on the representation of the
models we talk about.

KENT: What we're dealing with is just differences in a definition of what
model means. In order to be able to write any algorithm, you're going to
have to write in some more or less fixed terminology. In my definition of
model, the fact that you're dealing in a universe of named entities and
relationships and you have certain prescribed ways of talking about which
relationships among which entities you want to deal with in that algorithm,
is in itself a model. It's on this difference of what the term 'model'
means that this whole discussion rides.

WINTER: I've learned to be a pessimist in my experience with development
efforts, and I would guess that it will be nine years before we see the
standard out of ANSI if this program is followed. My primary concern with
waiting nine years is that the rest of the world might not wait. If people
who have real problems to solve that hinge on standardization have to wait
nine years, maybe they'll turn to some other, non-ANSI, solution. By the
time the ANSI solution comes along, it will have little force. What can
you do or say to reassure people who might like to make an investment in
the ANSI approach, that when it comes, it will be effective, and that the

world can somehow be encouraged to wait for it.

KIRSHENBAUM: While you pointed out the dangers of not standardizing fast enough, there is an opposing side that says you can standardize too fast. At the time that the Study Group started, to the best of my knowledge the only available papers on the relational approach were two by Ted Codd. Since that time, there has been major contributions to the field; a significant new approach has appeared since the time the Study Group started. We haven't reached the knee of that curve - there's more yet to come. The danger of standardizing too quickly and having enough people move to it, is that you've excluded what may be major breakthroughs in technology and in thinking about the solutions to these problems. There's always the chance that you're going to be wrong, whichever way you do it. If you're wrong, it's going to cost a fortune.

KLAUS: I'd like to take issue with the idea of waiting too long to standardize. If we were to standardize syntax or specific implementations, I could agree. However, standardization of interface specifications is long overdue, and I believe some of the problems we have in conversion are due only to the fact that interface standards have not been defined in the past. If we wait too long, even if you come out with a good standard in the end, nobody will know how to get there, or nobody will be willing to pay the price.

MAIRET: One of the ways in which premature standardization would impact progress toward better solutions is that as soon as there is a standard, every vendor is going to feel compelled to allocate his resources to development of products to meet that standard, and there will be less money spent trying to solve some of the real problems that we're wrestling with right now.

DATA ADMINISTRATION: MANAGING AN IMPORTANT RESOURCE

Charles E. Mairet
John Deere and Company
Molines, Illinois

ABSTRACT

The requirements for a data administration function will be discussed. Important questions concerning how to manage data as a shared resource will be discussed. Then a description of data administration responsibilities will be presented using the three human roles of the ANSI/SPARC/DBSG architecture. The presentation will conclude with a presentation of John Deer's experiences in implementing the data administration function.

In the past few years, many enterprises have recognized data as one of their most valuable resources and have taken steps to implement data base concepts in an attempt to manage this important resource. The principal concept is that of managing data as a shared resource. The effective implementation of data base concepts requires coordination that usually does not take place spontaneously between and/or among organizational units. Data administration, the management of data, becomes an important function that is required to fully exploit the advantages of data base technology.

DATA ADMINISTRATION: MANAGING AN IMPORTANT RESOURCE

I. Importance of Data to an Enterprise.
   A. Information is the I/O of decision process.
   B. Data is the raw material of information.
   C. Data is a resource.
   D. Data is an investment.
   E. Data is needed to manage other resources.
   F. Data is an important resource about all other resources.
   G. Data should be managed like most shared resources.
      - Money
      - Manpower

II. How Do You Manage Data?
   A. What are the data of the enterprise?
   B. What are the relationships of data to processes?
   C. What are requirements for controls?
   D. How do you plan data base development?
   E. What tools are available?
   F. What new methodologies are needed?
   G. What staff is needed?

III. ANSI/SPARC/DBSG View of Data Administration
   A. Human roles.
   B. Importance of conceptual schema.
   C. Importance of three level data definition.
   D. Central role of DD/D.
   E. Enterprise Administrator responsibilities.

    F. Data Base Administrator responsibilities.
    G. Application Administrator responsibilities.

IV. Implementation of Data Administration.
    A. Probably must evolve.
    B. Evolution at John Deere.
        - Standard Dictionary - 1967
        - Data Base Administration - 1972
        - Data Systems Department - 1974
        - Data Systems expanded Charter - 1975
    C. Current organization.
    D. Current problems.
        - Tools inadequate
        - Acceptance of change
        - Understanding of mission
            - Techniques
            - Methods

V. Conclusion
    A. Importance of managing data.
    B. Future evolution of data administration.

In the past few years many enterprises have recognized data as one of their most valuable resources and have taken steps to implement data base concepts in an attempt to better manage this important resource. The principal concept is that of managing data as a shared resource. These concepts promise to provide many advantages over past practices. The effective implementation of these concepts requires coordination that usually does not take place spontaneously between and/or among organizational units. Data administrarion, or the management of data, becomes an important function that is required to fully exploit the advantages of emerging data base technology.

Data administration is important because of the importance of data to an enterprise. People in all functional areas of our enterprises - such as manufacturing, marketing, distribution, and personnel - use information every day in their day-to-day work. Information is used in nearly every decision made. Information is both the input and the output (I/O) of the decision making process. The output of one decision becomes input to other decisions and so on. A part of the information available to these people is the result of outputs from a data processing system. It is no great revelation that information is a valuable resource, but it is too often a point missed when we talk about data.

What is the relationship of information to data?

Before we explore this question, we should caution ourselves about one area of confusion. In our communications we jump from realm to realm without warning. The realms are: the realm of reality, the real world; the realm of information, the ideas about the real world existing in the minds of men; and the realm of data, the symbols stored on some medium representing these ideas.

We tend to use these three realms almost interchangeably, making it difficult to know whether we're referring to the data, the information, or the real entity in the real world. The term entity refers to a person, place, thing, concept, or event, real or abstract, of interest to the enterprise. Some examples of entities are employees, parts, jobs, products, sales, purchases, etc. These are the things of reality that we want information about. For example, consider the set of all persons employed by an enterprise. We refer to them as employees. One of those employee's name is John Jones, he works in department 90, he is a shear operator, he is 40 years of age, etc. Another example would be a part that is a gear, it is Part Number E23561, it is 5 inches in diameter, it has 40 teeth, it fits on a one-half inch shaft, etc. This is information about the specific part identified and described by this information. Data are stored symbols representing information in the form of data, and information is what we need to make decisions involving the entities of concern to us. If we are concerned with the assignment of employees to jobs or the parts required to make a particular product, we are expecting this kind of information from systems intended to meet our information needs. Realizing that information is an extremely valuable resource that is needed to manage all other resources, leads us to the realization that since data is a stored representation of information, then data is a valuable resource.

Data is a valuable investment.
Our enterprises spend a great deal of money collecting, converting, storing and maintaining data so that we can provide information services to functional people so that they can make informed decisions. Bad data presents them with bad information which may result in a wrong decision. Then bad data can adversely affect the productivity of our enterprises. The fundamental motivation for pursuing data base concepts is to treat data as a resource and to provide better control of our investment. We have little difficulty realizing that people are an important resource, that facilities are an important resource, that money is an important resource. These are but a few of the recognized resources of our enterprises. We have management systems and resource control systems for all these resources, to guarantee their availability, their integrity, and their proper utilization. These systems collect a great deal of information, convert it to data, maintain it, process it, and convert it back to information. If each of these systems could work independently of each other, each would control its own resource of data. This is not the case. Real world relationships require that these sytems work together and thus they have common data requirements. Effective control of this shared resource requires a management system and resource control system separate from each of the others.
Data is a valuable resource and investment that needs control like all other resources.
- Information is the I/O of the decision making process.
- Data is the raw material of information.
- Data is a resource.
- Data is an investment.
- Data is needed to manage other resources.
- Data is an important resource about all other resources.
- Data should be managed as are other shared resources.

How do we manage data?
In general, data administration amounts to applying the basic notions of resource management to the resource of data. In detail, it becomes quite involved due to the lack of definition and understanding of the characteristics of the data resource that makes it different from other resources. It is the "how" and not the "what" that differs. This is because of the lack of fundamental approaches, long accepted practices, and well conceived tools with which to do the job. All of these will come but with time. Meanwhile, let's briefly look at the job to be done. I'll do this by making some brief observations in answer to some basic resource control questions.

What are the data of the enterprise?

One of the first steps is to "take inventory". This involves defining what are the data of the enterprise. This may differ from some notions of inventory in that it does not involve counting how many we have of predefined items. Rather, it involves defining the items (i.e., the meaning of every field of data). This definition must include (1) the entity about which the data represents information, (2) the property of the entity being represented, (3) the role, and (4) the domain. The definition must be specific and complete so that there is no ambiguity concerning the meaning of the data. This definition step is absolutely necesary and one should not underestimate the complexity or size of the task. The establishment of a data dictionary of standard terminology and data definition is an effective way to get started. One cannot hope to manage an undefined or ill defined resource.

What are the relationships of data to processes?

One needs to know the relationships of data to processes since this analysis will provide you with the source of each field as well as a directory to all its uses. It is difficult to administer controls for integrity and security of the data resource if its source and its uses are not known.

What controls are required?

To determine just what controls are required is a very difficult but important aspect of managing data. This is difficult because current controls are usually poorly documented and are imbedded implicitly in the logic of programs. In some cases, in our rush to apply the computer to an application, we have ignored adequate controls. The definition and exercising of controls is important because we can never claim to manage a resource and yet ignore controls for its integrity and security. In addition, management and society will soon demand it.

What data bases are needed and when are they needed?

The planning of data base development is completely dependent upon planning for the development of application systems. If application systems planning is done at the field level then data base planning becomes a factoring out of data requirements. If application systems planning is done at a very gross level, then data base planning must rely very much on conjecture. What is needed is a planning methodology that plans both application systems and data base development in concert with eachother. IBM's Business Systems Planning methodology is an example.

What tools are available?

Compared to the practices of managing other resources, the management of data is extremely new. Because of this situation there is an extreme shortage of adequate tools. The two most important tools needed are a Data Base Management System (DBMS) and a Data Dictionary/Directory (DD/D). There are several of each of these to choose from, all of varying degrees of inadequacy.

What new methodologies are needed?

The establishment of a data administration function requires the extraction of responsibilities (functions) from existing data processing organizational units. This has an impact on how they do their work. A new organization also increases the communication interfaces required. These two changes require new methods for developing data processing systems and for project control.

What staff is needed?

You will need a combination of business and management oriented analysts and technically proficient analysts. The number of people and the mix depends upon the amount of your data processing activities and the manner in which you organize for the data administration function.

ANSI/SPARC/DBSG VIEW

Let us now review the ANSI/SPARC/DBSG view of the data administration function. The human roles identified as being involved in the management of data are: the enterprise administrator, the data base administrator, and the application administrator. Notice that these are roles as opposed to individuals. The same individual may function in different roles and one role may involve several individuals simultaneously. It is critical, however, that there is only one enterprise administrator and one data base administrator, while there may be many application administrators.

Each administrator is responsible for providing to the system a particular view of the necessary data, the relevant relationships among that data, and the rules and controls pertinent to its use. Presently some data base management systems provide for two views of the data. These roughly equate to (1) the programmers view, and (2) the systems view of how the data is stored. In the ANSI/SPARC/DBSG architecture these views are expressed by the application administrator and data base administrator respectively. The study group also recognized the necessity of a third view; the enterprise's view of its data and its structure that it is attempting to model in the data base. This central view of data is to be expressed by the enterprise administrator. This is the view informally (normally because it's undocumented) invoked when there is a dispute between the user and the programmer over exactly what was meant by program specifications. In a shared data environment this view must be made explicit and, in fact, made known to the DBMS. The mechanism for doing this is the conceptual schema. An application administrator expresses his view through an external schema and the data base administrator expresses his view through the internal schema. These latter two views must necessarily be consistent with the view expressed by the conceptual schema.

. Particular emphasis must be given to the conceptual schema. It is a real and tangible item expressed most explicitly in machine readable form, available to the system, and in fact, is a central control mechanism over the system. The conceptual schema is a formal model of the enterprise, even though it may be logically incomplete when the real world situation is most complex. It contains the definitions of entities and their properties. This definition is the "inventory" of the enterprises' data. No entities or properties can be referenced in the data base unless they are defined in the conceptual schema. The relationships amongst these entities will also be defined as well as the constraints on the values (of properties) and relationships and their usage.

The conceptual schema is one of central importance in that it is the definition of what are the data of the enterprise and it is where security and integrity provisions are defined. This conceptual model is a model of the data in its own right and not how it is manipulated by the system or used by applications. The model is to be in terms of the entities of the real world and to be independent of both how data representing information about these entities is stored or used.

The construction of such a model will lead to a better understanding of an enterprises' data requirements, but its primary benefits are (1) assisting in managing the change in data requirements and technology and (2) providing administrative control over the DBMS and the enterprises data

resource. It accomplishes this by providing a model which, when placed
between the internal and external schema, provides for program and data
independence and for controls.

We can assume that our enterprises will continue to experience
environmental changes affecting their information systems. We can assume
that information management technologies will continue to change. Our
enterprises must be able to continue to make progress in the use of
information systems to imrpove their productivity. In order to do this,
they must be able to effectively manage their data resource in this "sea of
change". An extremely high degree of program and data independence must be
available in its DBMS. Also the DBMS must be administratively controlled.
The three levels of data definition, including as the central one the
conceptualmodel, provide an architecture that can support this needed
independence and administrative control.

The data dictionary/directory (DD/D) is an important tool for
administrators involved in managing data. It is appropriate then that the
DD/D play a very central role in the ANSI/SPARC/DBSG architecture. The
DD/D is a data base about data. The DD/D facility is an information system
(or resource control system) for administrators responsible for managing
data. The DD/D is referenced by administrators and through the appropriate
schema processors is maintained by them. The DD/D is of central importance
to the hardware/software components of the system. Thus the DD/D is
central to both the human and system roles required in managing the data
resource.

Administrative responsibilities
A brief outline of the enterprise administrator's responsibilities:
1. Defines conceptual data.
2. Defines conceptual data relationships.
3. Protection of data.
   a. Security/privacy
   b. Integrity
4. Data retention.

A brief outline of the data base administrator's responsibilities:
1. Defines and organizes internal data base(s).
   a. Data representation.
   b. Storage strategies.
   c. Data base performance tuning.
2. Protection of internal data base(s).
   a. Recovery/restart.
   b. Physical data security/integrity.
3. Define mapping to conceptual schema (consistent with same).
4. Monitor actual usage.

A brief outline of the application administrator's repsonsibilities:
1. Define external data (application view).
2. Define mapping to conceptual schema (consistent with same).

A more detailed discussion of these administrative roles is available in
the ANSI/SPARC/DBSG report. Let's now turn our attention to the
implementation of the data administration function.

IMPLEMENTATION OF DATA ADMINISTRATION
The data administration function probably must evolve. This is because
it will take time to gain management understanding and approval, to gain
acceptance of change, and to develop needed tools and experienced staff.
Data administration should evolve because it will take time and experience

to determine what should be done and how it can best be accomplished in a
particular organization. Data administration has evolved and continues to
evolve at John Deere.

In the mid 60's some data base related studies were made in John Deere.
The first outcome of these was in 1967 and was the formation of a Corporate
staff responsible for establishing the John Deere Dictionary of standard
data element terminology. A Corporate procedure was established that
required system development projects to use or define data elements in the
dictionary. Thus the dictionary has evolved and grown in applicability and
size. It is currently approaching 10,000 data element definitions.

The second major step was the design, development, and implementation of
a Data Base Management System. This took place in the 1969-70 time frame.
This effort provided a needed tool and also developed additional staff with
data base experience and expertise. Many of the personnel involved in that
project are now involved with data administration. That DBMS is still in
production but we are migrating applications to IBM's IMS.

In 1972 John Deere appointed a Data Base Administrator within the
Planning Division. With this change data base design was centralized for
Corporate systems development efforts. This included systems for the
general company and marketing units but not systems developed by the
decentralized manufacturing system development units. However, the DBA was
responsible for coordinating all unit data base design activities.

In 1974 John Deere formed the Data Systems Department. This change
involved a significant increase in charter and staff. However, the charter
still pertained only to Corporate system development efforts. Then in 1975
the Data Systems charter became companywide and was broadened to include
important functions for data integrity and security.

DATA SYSTEMS AT JOHN DEERE

Data Systems' major concern is with the management of the Company's data
resource. To meet this responsibility the department is organized into
three divisions. They are Data Structure, Data Maintenance, and Data
Management Systems. Data Structure is concerned with the identification,
definition, storage, and documentation of data. Data Maintenance is
concerned with the protection of data including back-up, recovery,
integrity, and security. Data Management Systems is concerned with the
effective use of DB/DC technology in systems development. Specific
responsibilities of these divisions are as follows:

Responsibilities of Data Structure

- Design all Data Structures. This includes the design of both physical
  and logical IMS data bases companywide and also conventional files for
  Corporate systems development efforts.
- Data Base Documentation. All data base documentation is produced
  automatically by the DD/D system. This includes automated preparation
  of all IMS control blocks as well as printed documentation required for
  system development personnel. Thus, the same source of data
  description is used for both the system and human roles. This same
  information is available on-line through CRT's. The dictionary portion
  is printed on microfiche as back-up and for use by those without CRT
  access.

- Provide a Data Dictionary/Directory Deere & Company uses the UCC-TEN
  Data Dictionary/Directory system of the University Computing Company.
  This on-line system is the data processing system of the data

administration function. The IMS data bases of this DD/D are the data
bases about data, its structures, and uses. This system and these data
bases are important tools in the management of the data resource, as
important to data administration as the personnel system is to the
personnel manager or the accounting system to the accountant.

- Performance Monitoring.   This is a function shared with the IMS
  software personnel in computer operations.   The data analyst is
  involved primarily to evaluate the effectiveness of data structures and
  their use by application systems.

- Maintain a Data Dictionary/Directory System. This is one of the few
  software support functions in Data Systems. It is placed here mainly
  because of the amount of enhancement work tht is needed at this point
  in time and the fact that data analysts are the principle users and,
  therefore, generating nearly all requests for enhancements. This is a
  significant effort.
     At Deere & Company the above responsibilities currently require a
  staff of twelve data analysts and one manager. This information is
  intended only to help yu understand the scope of effort involved in
  these responsibilities. The effort will of course vary from company to
  company.

Responsibilities of Data Maintenance

- Develop and Maintain Test Data Bases. In a shared data environment the
  testing of applications becomes more critical since the adverse impact
  of one incorrect application is much broader.   Also one application
  development team may not know the data requirements of all other
  sharing applications. For these reasons the development of test data
  bases is provided by data analysts. This service is required for
  Corporate system development efforts and optional for decentralized
  efforts fo the Company units. However, policy requires that all units
  maintain current test data bases.

- Establish Back-up and Recovery Procedures.   The sharing of data
  requires that the back-up and recovery functions be separated from
  applications, since the unilateral actions of one user may be quite
  detrimental to other users. Also the IMS log tape is a system-wide or
  shared resource in that it is used to log the actions of all
  applications.   This log tape is critical for data recovery. The
  unilateral recovery actions of one user may adversely impact the log
  tape such that it would impair other recoveries. Therefore, this
  function was centralized.

- Implement Data Security Procedures. This is a very difficult area, but
  one in which we feel compelled to work. Our responsibilities are
  concerned with the unauthorized logical access of data through the
  computer system.   One data analyst is assigned full-time to our
  efforts. There are other people in the organization concerned with
  overall security program coordination and phsyical security of computer
  systems and data. Our approach to data security involves three phases.
  The first phase involved identifying and documenting all exposures.
  That study is complete.   The resulting report is a blueprint to
  disaster and therefore has had very limited distribution. We are

currently involved in phase two, which is to provide quick near-term fixes for the more serious exposures. Security reviews have also been incorporated into the system development review points of our System Integrity Review Procedure.

- Audit Computer System Test Results. This responsibility is placed in Data Maintenance to provide a review of testing outside the program development organization and to test for data integrity. The latter is required since the sharing of data exposes data not in the purview of the application to accidental invalidation. This requires testing to insure that a program is not doing more than specified as well as validating what was specified.

    We use the Test IMS Utility and have found it to be a real productive aid in testing. The data analyst works with system development personnel in the beginning of a project to develop a test plan for that project. One other effort related to testing is what we call our Quality Auditing Program. This involves a data analyst interviewing systems analysts and users to determine all known validity audits for all data of a data base. He then constructs a program that exercises those audits for that data base or a statistical sample of the data base records. The program reports all exceptions to the audits which include consistency checks between data elements and relationship audits to other data bases. These programs are used periodically on production data bases to review user maintenance of data. This is a consequence of shared data. This approach has also proved valuable in testing as it points out errors in maintenance logic and missed audits.

- Loading and Reorganization of Production Data Bases. As new applications and changing data requirements occur new and restructured data bases must be loaded. This responsibility has been separated from applications because of sharing by multiple applications. However, the application areas are involved since they are responsible for gathering and providing input data for the loads. Reorganization of data bases for processing efficiency is also the responsibility of this group.

    At Deere and Company the above responsibilities currently require a staff of six data analysts and a manager. Again, the scope of this effort will vary for each company.

Responsibilites of Data Management

- Coordination of DB/DC Project Activities. The development and implementation of application systems exploiting DB/DC concepts and technologies is, at least for now, more complex. This is due in part to the newness of concepts and the newness (inadequacy) of tools, but also due to the increased specialization and attendant organization changes. There are a number of actions that must be done with fairly precise timing and coordination in order to implement a DB/DC system without impacting development schedules. This is further complicated by the number of organizational units involved (software, operations, users, three development groups, and three Data Systems groups). The Data Management group is chartered to provide this coordination on a Companywide basis for all DB/DC projects in the Company.

    One of the tools they have developed to accomplish this is an "IMS Development Checklist". This is a checklist of every action that must be completed in order to successfully implement an IMS application.

Use of this checklist has been incorporated into our Systems Integrity Review Procedure. A tailored checklist with dates and individual responsibilities is produced for each project.

Another tool developed by this group is an "IMS Handbook". This contains IMS policies, standards, guidelines, procedures, aids, and 'do's' and

- Coordinate Implementation of Data Management Systems. This involves working with software personnel in coordinating the implementation of software such as IBM's IMS and Informatics' MARK IV with application development needs. They distribute manuals to users of these products and also provide assistance in their use. In-house education is a form of that assistance.

- Development of Data Base Load Programs. Essentially this is in this group because of the need to separate it from application development team efforts (data sharing) and also the need to maintain a programming skill in this group.

Currently at Deere & Company these responsibilities require a staff of four data analysts and one manager. Again, this will vary from company to company.

CURRENT PROBLEMS

Too often presentations on approaches to solving problems and/or organizations tend to make them sound like they work better than they do in practice. While we have had some success in implementing data administration at John Deere, we are not without some current problems. Also many problems were encountered in the past. I consider there to be four classes of current problems; (1) acceptance of change, (2) the management of change, (3) inadequate tools, and (4) inadequate methods.

One cannot implement new concepts that affect organization and methods of performing work without expecting some resistance to change. Acceptance of this type of change takes time. This is especially true and justified when the concept, the needed technological tools, and methods are all new and developing. However, if we wait for their development they won t develop since a base of experience is needed for proper development.

In most cases data administrationis implemented in an environment where a considerable investment in data and programs already exists. In thise cases an evolutionary approach must be taken. The implication of this is change. It means change to data bases as they grow in scope. Without a DBMS that provides a significant level of data independence, this means frequent changes to prior applications to accommodate change caused by new applications. When data is shared across multiple applications it does not take long to reach a situation where you have multiple concurrent application system development projects involving multiple versions of several data bases. Managing projects and data in this situation is extremely difficult.

Both the above problems are in part created by two other problems. Our tools for data administration are inadequate and the required methods and practices are not yet developed. Let's look at these problems in more detail.

Inadequate Tools

The most serious area of inadequacy is the lack of program and data independence. In order to develop and manage data as a resource independent of applications our DBMS must provide a considerable degree of program and data independence. In a shared data environment one soon reaches a point of little progress because each change to the data prompted by a new application requires multiple changes to multiple applications. The tools needed are documented by my earlier comments on this subject and in the ANSI/SPARCC/DBSG document.

The naming, definition, and description of data, its structure, and its usages is difficult enought to do for other human roles let alone for computer systems (DBMS). Most DBMS's have very inadequate Data Descriptive Languages (DDL).

In fact, you may question if some even have a DDL. This language when teamed with a capable data dictionary directory (DD/D) had DBMS becomes the data processing system of the data administrator. They are the principal tools used by him to maintain needed information about the resource for which he is responsible.

One of the characteristics required in a DD/D is a flexible way to handle multiple concurrent designs of data bases and applications. Most DD/D's assume a rather fixed design, which requires that the analyst know future as well as all current data requirements. Obviously this is an impossible situation. What is needed is an approach similar to that used by product engineering personnel in the design and subsequent modification of both current and future product designs. This approach allows for the concurrent statement of the removal of certain aspects of a product and the insertion of other aspects by stating an 'effective' or 'as of' date for each change. Thus by giving a date you can extract a product specification 'effective' or 'as of' that date. This same flexibility is required in the design and subsequent modification of data bases.

Another area of growing inadequacy is security, privacy, and auditability. This inadequacy is growing becuase there is very little progress in improving the tools, but considerable improvement in the statement and imposition of the requirements. The access protection provided by most DBMS's is easily circumvented because they are built on top of the operating system (rather than an integral part of its design), and thus provide no better protection than the operating system itself, which is inadequate. Another example of inadequacies in this area is that there exists no adequate facility for automatically producing an audit trail of activities related to a data base for a critical or controlled company resource. Most 'logging' or 'journaling' facilities of current DBMS's are for back-up, recovery, and restart purposes and not suitable for auditing.

I referred earlier to the 'data processing system of the data administrator'. The data processing industry must apply systematic and computerized methods to their own work. We have been busy systematizing and computerizing the work of all our users, yet we have ignored the manner and tools with which we do this work. The work of the data administrator must be integrated with the work of application development ersonnel and operations personnel, therefore, his system must be integrated with any systematic tools they use. What is needed is an integrated data processing system for data processing personnel.

Inadequate Methods

Often the miscommunications between users and those constructing systems and between the different personnel involved in construction of systems is due to different perceptions of data requirements. These miscommunications cost us in personnel time. My experience has been that they are caused by ambiguous or missing data definitions. Missing definitions is a management problem. What is needed to solve the ambiguous definition problem is a more structured and disciplined method of naming, classifying, and defining data. Critical to such a method is a rigorous way of insuring that all the qualifiers have been stated that are required to remove all ambiguity. Given such an approach, it could and should be integrated into the total system development methodology so that it is of benefit to the system analyst as well as the data analyst.

An integrated set of data bases that adequately address data requirements with appropriate timeliness cannot be developed without a development plan. Such a plan must exist within an overall plan including applicatiion system development. What is needed is a methodology for jointly planning the development of applications and data bases in concert with the information system needs of the business. As mentioned earlier, IBM's Business Systems Planning (BSP) and follow-on Information Systems Planning (ISP) methodologies are an example.

The design of data bases involves far too much art and not enough science. The development and use of design and simulation aids is essential. Our method today requires building the data base and trying it in order to test our design. Wouldn't we laugh at architects who built buildings to test their designs? We must become more scientific and professional in our methods and practices.

FUTURE EVOLUTION OF DATA ADMINISTRATION

The motivation for implementing the data administration is to manage data as an important shared resource and to provide better control of our investment in data. This occurs when data is recognized as a shared resource. As data becomes increasingly more important to higher levels of management and the ability (tools and methods) to manage data as a shared resource improves, the data administration function will grow in importance to an enterprise. I am confident that in time these situations will improve and data administration will grow in importance to an enterprise. Management and staff levels will probably increase accordingly. I am also sure that today most senior management would find these expectations optimistic. The business-like and professional manner in which we approach the development of the data administration function will determine its future evolution and our involvement in it.

DISCUSSION

RYLAND: At John Deere, how do you handle data not currently in the data management environment? Does your data systems group deal with data in both environments?

MAIRET: We do not have all the data documented in our data dictionary-directory needed to fully control the data base management system. At the time we started there were two schools of thought: either document everything and then start on a data base management system, or, get started, and as you construct, define. We've taken the latter approach. As we construct a data base, however, we do a preliminary design trying to use the concepts of the relational data model to identify the entities so that we can start without preconceived notions of embedding data at lower levels, when in fact, it's going to migrate to the top later. We also gather from users data they have of interest to them about that entity before we build that data base. Considering the amount of change we have to data bases, I would have to say we're not doing a very good job of that.

STEEL: Would you comment on where you ultimately see the collection of data managers reporting in terms of level in the company, particularly in view of the decentralized nature of the organization.

MAIRET: We are presently encouraging and helping in the implementation of a data administration function in our decentralized units. We see that as a necessary function. In most companies all the data administration function will probably not be in one place and be one huge organization, reporting at one level. I think we're going to find it dispersed. You find this with other resources, such as the financial resource. We have a controller in every one of our decentralized units; department managers have some financial responsibilities and budget constraints. We have a corporate controller, we have internal auditors, all involved to some extent in financial resource management. I think we're going to find the same thing in managing the data resource. We're broadening ourselves in that we're thinking more in terms of the business as we approach this program, and less in terms of the technical problems of running a DMS on a computer, although we have to face those problems because we have to do our job. Our vice president of corporate planning made an observation at one of our planning sessions to the effect that nowhere in the entire enterprise can you find anyone who has the opportunity to know the total business, and to look across the total business, than the data processing area and the business systems department do.

TAYLOR: How do you manage and co-ordinate necessary changes to application programs when a data base is logically restructured.

MAIRET: The division manager responsible for the areas of application and change and my management team work it out together. It's very difficult because of the sharing of data, and as we get more and more sharing, the problem gets more acute.

COLLINS: You mentioned the need for new methodologies. Can you give us any more hints on that?

MAIRET: Our current efforts in the methodology area starts with the business problem statement. The next step is a set of functional specifications to which the user agrees before we do any systems construction. We are still in the mood of those two big steps. We must get out of that mode. The industry must move in the direction of developing more discrete and smaller pieces. We must build systems driven by events, and not build big application systems. To do that, you have to have a coordinated information systems and data plan driven by the business plan. We don't have that at John Deere.

JEANNIN: How do you manage to get the user in your decentralized environment involved in the definition process?

MAIRET: We do involve the user in the development of the data definition. The application analyst who is responsible for that particular project is required to get the user to agree to the statement of definition. In some cases, the user has done the job completely; in other cases we've had to do it and ask him for his review. We have gone to the users for review and

acceptance of the definitions that we wrote down, and in many cases have
had a few misconceptions straightened out. To enforce the data definition,
all our COBOL 01 levels are generated automatically from the data
dictionary-directory system. If the data element is not in the dictionary,
then they cannot generate their own levels and can't construct their
system. There is a human audit to make sure they haven't picked up some
names that are in there and used them for something else. The data analyst
does that audit, and he has to understand it because he's constructing the
data base.

JEANNIN: Is the contents of your dictionary available for the whole
company, or only to those data suppliers that are involved.

MAIRET: The data dictionary directory is a corporate-wide system that
everybody uses. Those who do not have on-line terminals receive microfiche.
We provided all them with microfiche readers, at our cost, because we could
do that cheaper than we could print it.

JEANNIN: Do you use the dictionary system on-line, or do you make the
information available constantly in another form?

MAIRET: We maintain the data dictionary-directory system in an on-line
environment. Our twelve data analysts are using it as a design tool day in
and day out. That's the way they do their job. The data definitions are
entered that way as they are established. We do have a small problem in
that the people involved want to batch it. They tend to want to work on
all the definitions and get everything all straightened out before they put
it in. We're encouraging them to use the data dictionary-directory on line
more as they learn; to use it as a documentation or as an information-
gathering tool.

GUILLORY: You made the statement that not all data was defined to the data
dictionary. I assume you have some old systems that have not yet been
upgraded into a data base management environment. What criteria did you
use to exclude this old information? Did you go back and get any of the
critical files? What determined the criticality of that information?

MAIRET: We are going back to systems constructed in the past to define that
data that system requires, even though there isn't any project approved to
reconstruct that system in a DBMS environment. When we set priorities with
the development management, we use the data base construction plan for the
next eighteen months to determine which ones to define. In that way we get
the data defined before data base construction.

RASMUSSEN: As the scope of data administration broadens, I see the
dictionary becoming more and more of a tool to not only describe the data
resource, but also to describe how it's used, where it's used, and in what
processes. You're starting to run into a head-on collision with what's now
known as records management and what they view as their responsibility.
Records management is a particular job title that is established in many
governmental and university institutions right now. They have
responsibility for forms design, for archival information, for the actual
documentation of the data resource, where it is, how it's used, and how it
flows from one part of the organization to another. They have professional
societies in the United States today, and meetings similar to this one, and
we're going in the same direction.

MAIRET: I think that's good. The problem is that most enterprises, outside of the ones you mentioned, don't have that type of function with that broad a definition. We have a records and retention department at John Deere, but what that amounts to is running a warehouse with paper in it that people can't get rid of for legal reasons.

RASMUSSEN: Many organizations we're involved with have already developed a data administration function and I do see a collision at some point.

MAIRET: In other words, you see the data processing function within those same organizations as developing a data administration function also. I can see that as a problem. Maybe one of those is going to be the enterprise administrator, and the other one is going to be the data base administrator.

COLLINS: I'd like to emphasize this last point. There is a body of professionals who meet at national conferences, who talk about data administration, data element standardization, data dictionary, and so on, and they don't mean by these terms exactly what we mean. They get a hearing also, and consider themselves professional, which they certainly are. They're represented on ANSI X3, but I'm aware of precious little interaction between the attendees of their conferences and those who attend the data base management system conferences. This could bode ill in the future. For example, there are legal steps being taken in certain states to require a data dictionary for health-related information for all institutions in that state which collect and retain such information. What's going to happen at a high managment level when it's discovered that the data dictionaries on which we've spent a fortune are in no way oriented toward that particular use of a data dictionary, the data description aspect of it. As you know, many of the data dictionaries we use don't provide us with any real usable formalism for describing the data semantics. The Bureau of Standards is a reference point. There have been two national conferences in this area, the proceedings of the first of which have been published.
   The particular question I wanted to raise was on the SPARC report. It specifies a title, Enterprise Administrator, which sounds almost like the President of the Company...Surely the SPARC Study Group couldn't have been unaware of the public relations problems in that sort of title. I'm wondering what is wrong with Data Administrator? The Enterprise Administrator doesn't define the information of the enterprise; he defines the data of the enterprise.

MAIRET: I don't think the authors of the document intended to say that they were describing the role of the president, or chairman, or chief executive officer of a company. I think what motivated the choice of such a name, was to drive home the point tha we must broaden our perspective and think beyond just the technical problem of data bases. Maybe there should have been another qualifier, such as Enterprise Data Administrator.

KLAUS: Could you give me a little more idea of the scope of the problem that you ran into in terms of the size of the data dictionary. What I really want to get at is the number of elements you started with, and the number of elements you you ended up with due to the elimination of redundancies, etc.

MAIRET: We started out with about 100 data elements in our dictionary, and it's grown ever since then because of our approach. When a system

construction project starts, they must define their terms in the dictionary
if they're not already there. If they're there, they must use those terms.
That was the method of achieving standardization throughout the development
process; we've been doing that since 1967. There is a corporate policy
that all data processing systems construction must use the corporate
dictionary.   There is a constant problem of trying to manage duplication.
There is the problem caused by someone looking in the dictionary, deciding
his data is not there. He then writes out a definition and sends it in.
Then the data analyst analyzes it in detail, and finds out that it is
indeed present. To help solve that problem, we've developed a full context
reverse word order term name. We start with the basic entity and we start
adding qualifiers, and we keep going until we get it to the point where
there is no ambiguity. We construct a key-word-in-context list, so that
the data analyst can analyse the new definition until he gets to the point
where there's a few items that may be the data.   Then he goes back and
questions the analyst. We need better tools in that area. Right now our
dictionary is approaching 10,000 defined terms.

BRAWLY: Could you relate the data systems department managers to the
enterprise, data base, and application administrators.

MAIRET: Right now, the data systems department is involved in all three
roles.   We generate the logical view for the applications from the data
dictionary directory. We perform the data definition process, manage the
data dictionary-directory, the data base design, and the performance
monitoring and fine tuning of it. Some of those roles, particularly as
they relate to the applications area, are starting to be decentralized into
data base administration groups in the units. A common question is whether
the data administration function will be in the data processing department
or outside it? My reponse to that is: it depends on how broad is the scope
of the charter of the data processing organization. Our's is called
business systems, not data processing, and it's defined with a fairly broad
charter which includes the data administration function. If your charter
is just EDP, then I think data administration will probably evolve outside
that department.

VIEWS ON DATA

D. Tsichritzis and F. Lochovsky
Department of Computer Science
University of Toronto, Toronto, Canada M5S 1A7

Introduction

There is currently a debate among DBMS professionals concerning the advantages of different DBMS approaches [Canning, 1972; Ashenhurst, 1974; Bachman, 1974; Codd and Date, 1974; Date and Codd, 1974; Sibley, 1974; Steel, 1975]. The debate concerns not only specific, desirable features for a DBMS, but also the possibility and desirability of a standardization. The different positions in this debate can be summarized as follows:

1. A group of proponents of network systems want a specific proposal [CODASYL DBTG, 1971], with possibly some modifications, to become a standard. Such standardization, they argue, will have the same beneficial effect on DBMS's as the standardization of COBOL had on EDP.

2. A group of independents strongly oppose any effort at standardization. They claim that it is too early to impose a standard in an area as rapidly developing as DBMS's. They would like to postpone any standardization effort. They believe that the development of DBMS's should not e interfered with. In this way a successful commercialDBMS may become a de facto standard.

3. Some people prefer the relational data model as the basic data model for DBMS's. They cite as advantages simplicity, data independence, etc. They do not disregard hierarchies or networks for implementation, but simply prefer the end user interface to be relational. Although they do not push for standardization, they would like DBMS development to be heavily influenced by the relational data model.

4. Some people propose that a different, more flexible data model should be the basis for DBMS's. It is proposed as a compromise beteen the hierarchical, network and relational approaches, being identical to none, but able to accommodate all.

In this paper we will present and compare the three main approaches to DBMS data organization. We will try to avoid taking a particular position. We have our own prejudices which may show. However, we think that the differences between the approaches have been overemphasized. We hope that time and maturity will eventually minimize the differences. At least the air will be cleared of misunderstandings, misconceptions and differences of terminology which generate much of the controversy. In reality, the approaches are not really all that different [Stonebraker and Held, 1975].

The debate will probably end up as an argument between efficiency (potential network advantage) and ease of programming (potential relational advantage). As such, it reminds one of the old controversy on the merits of assember language versus high level language programming.

2. Data Relationships

Data can be viewed at several levels [Mealy, 1967; Engles, 1972; Schmid and Swenson, 1975]. At one level, people logically organize their perceptions of the real world. At another level, they interpret (give meaning to) the real world. Finally, they describe and record the ideas about the real world as data in their computers or, perhaps, in some other physical medium.

When considering the real world, one can identify many classes of objects, e.g., "house", "car", etc. In order to understand the real world it is necessary to place a certain interpretation on the objects. For example, it is necessary to decide whether some objects will exist independently or only to characterize other objects. When giving meaning to the real world, independent objects are interpreted as sets of entities or entity sets. Entity sets correspond to objects that have an independent existence and can be meaningfully considered by themselves. For example, the object "house" can be interpreted as an entity set house.

An entity set is meaningfully described in terms of its attributes. For example, the entity set house is described by attributes such as address, colour and style. Notice that in this interpretation of the real world, the object address has been interpreted as a characteristic of the object house and is therefore an attribute of the entity set house.

Although there may be a real distinction between objects and characteristics in the real world, this distinction is sometimes blurred when representing ideas about the real world by attributes and entity sets. For example, address can be interpreted as an attribute (as in the entity set house) or as an entity set by itself. In the latter case, address has an existence of its own apart from any other entity set. At any one time, an object can be interpreted as an independent object or as a characteristic of another object, but not as both. However, the interpretation can be different at different times or change with time.

For each entity set, its attributes have certain values. For example, the colour attribute has values such as red, green and blue. The set of possible values of an attribute is called the domain of the attribute. It is possible for different attributes to share a single domain. For example, the attributes house size and lot# both assume values from the domain called non-negative-integers.

Data values, by themselves, say nothing meaningful. A given set of house address values and another of colours, does not really communicate anything, except perhaps, that the addresses and colours exist somewhere. However, if one is informed that the house at 125 Evelyn Ave. is painted red, the house at 4 Bridgetown Dr. is painted blue, etc., the two sets of values immediately convey some information. This information is available because a relationship has been established between the values of address and colour.

A relationship is a correspondence, or mapping, between the members of two sets. There are many relationships which can be identified in our perception of the real world. For instance, each of "father of", "age of" and "residence of" define relationships between a person and, respectively, a person, age and address. A relationship may be a 1:1, 1:N or N:M correspondence between the members of two sets. A 1:1 relationship, for example, is the relationship between an employee's personnel number and social insurance number. Each employee has only one unique personnel number and one unique social insurance number. The relationship between an employee's personnel number and salary history is, in general, 1:N. An employee has only one unique personnel number, but may have had several different salaries. Finally, an N:M relationship is that between house colour and house price. That is, houses with a certain colour may sell at different prices and, similarly, houses at the same price may have different colours.

It is useful to distinguish between two types of relationships. The

difference between them can be explained by the following examples [Schmid
and Swenson, 1975]. A person's name and social insurance number are
usually considered characteristics of the object "person". They are
characteristics since they usually describe a person and are of interest
only so long as the person they describe exists. Therefore, a person's
name and social insurance number are attributes of the entity set person.
In this case, the relationship between name and social insurance number
defines an attribute relationship, i.e., a relationship between attributes
of an entity set.

On the other hand, suppose that a person is the owner of a house. The
house and the person each exist independently, whether or not the house is
currently owned by the person. If the person sells the house, both the
house and the person still exist although the relationship between them has
changed. Therefore, in this interpretation of the world, house and person
are considered entity sets. In this case, the relationship between house
and person defines a relationship between entity sets. Such a relationship
is called an association [Schmid and Swenson, 1975]. Associations, since
they are themselves relationships, can be 1:1, 1:N or N:M.

Associations are not very different, syntactically, from attribute
relationships. Sometimes, it is difficult to differentiate between
associations and attribute relationships. For instance, the relationship
"married to" can be considered as an association between two independent
entity sets men and women. Alternatively, a person entity set can have a
spouse attribute. Thus, the relationship "married to" is represented as an
attribute of a person. In any particular situation, people perceive a
relationship either as an attribute relationship or as an association.
However, this perception can change with time or if a different point of
view is taken. After all, the difference between an attribute relationship
and an association is subject to interpretation, and interpretations are
not static.

When storing data in computers, we usually organize the data according to
some pattern that represents entity sets and the relationships between
them. A data model is a pattern according to which data is logically
organized. It consists of named logical units of data and expresses the
relationships among the data as determined by the ideas of the world.

The data models used by DBMS's can be distinguished mainly as to how they
represent relationships among data. Most data models handle attribute
relationships in similar ways. However, associations are handled in
different ways. There are two main approaches: the network approach and
the relational approch. The rest of this paper will present the details of
these two approaches. The hierarchical data model will be presented as a
special case of the network approach. It should be noted that there are
other, very important, data models proposed in the literature [Kerschberg
et al., 1976]. However, in this paper only the network, hierarchical and
relational data models will be discussed.

3. The Network Data Model

The network data model is a formal model for representing attribute
relationships of an entity set and the associations between the entity
sets. The data model consists of record types and connections among them
which we will call links [Tsichritzis, 1975a]. Record types are used to
represent the relationships among the attributes of an entity set. Links
are used to represent the associations between entity sets.

A record type is defined, in the usual manner, as a collection of data
items. A data item is the smallest unit of logical data. Record types are
generic since they represent a set of record occurrences consisting of data
item values. For instance, the record type EMPLOYEE can consist of the

data items NAME, ADDRESS, AGE, SALARY and SKILL. A particular record occurrence of the EMPLOYEE record type represents a particular employee. Such a record occurrence can have data item values ´Smith´, ´190 St. George St.´, ´33´, ´10.00´ and ´Electrician´ corresponding to the data items of the EMPLOYEE record type.

In the network data model, associations are usually effected by explicit mappings between different record types. A link is defined as the representation of an association. In the same way that a record type represents an entity set, a link represents an association between entity sets. While an association is an abstraction corresponding to a perception of the world, a link is a concrete object representing the association in the network data model. For example, the association "owner" between the entity sets person and house can be represented by a link, OWNER, between the record types PERSON and HOUSE. The link represents the two mappings which define the association between the entity sets house and person. One mapping maps house to person while the reverse mapping maps person to house.

Links, since they define relationships, can be 1:1, 1:N or N:M. For instance, a link LIVING IN between the record types PERSON and HOUSE is usually 1:N. A link OWNER between the record types PERSON and HOUSE is N:M if the possibility of joint ownership is considered. That is, each person can own many houses and each house can be owned by many persons. A link BUILT ON, between the record types HOUSE and LOT, is usually 1:1. That is a house occupies one lot and each lot has only one house.

Two kinds of links can be distinguished: information carrying and non-information carrying [Metaxides, 1975; Tsichritzis, 1975b]. An information carrying link represents an association which cannot be expressed as a closed form property between the attributes of the entity sets. For instance, consider the record types PERSON and HOUSE. Suppose that there is no data item in the HOUSE record type the value of which identifies the persons that own a house. Therefore, a link OWNER between the PERSON and HOUSE record types is information carrying since it is the only means of identifying the persons that own a house. That is, the link encodes some extra information not present in the data items of the record types. On the other hand, suppose there is a data item in the record type HOUSE the value of which can be used to identify the persons owning a house. In this case, a link OWNER between the PERSON and HOUSE record types is non-information carrying. It carries no information since the ownership information is available directly from the HOUSE record type and can be used to identify PERSON records. The link OWNER is merely a convenient way of relating houses (HOUSE records) to their owners (PERSON records).

Information carrying links are usually constructed manually by selecting records and explicitly connecting them. Non-information carrying links can be constructed algorithmically, once the user specifies the property among the data items which defines the link. Such links are also called automatic because they can be algorithmically constructed and then maintained automatically.

Consider the relationship graph shown in figure 1. The nodes represent record types and the arcs represent links. All record types and links are explicitly named. In this way, more than one link can be defined between the same two record types. The links, in general, represent N:M relationships and form a network connecting the record types. For instance, the N:M relationship concerning the registration of companies in states can be represented by a link between the STATE and COMPANY record types.

In a general network data model, there are no restrictions on the relationships represented by the links. They can be 1:1, 1:N or N:M.

However, if links correspond only to 1:N relationships, then the arcs in the graph can be directed. The direction of an arc encodes the information about the 1:N (tail:head) direction of the relationship (figure 2). For instance, if a person can be a citizen of at most one country, then the link CITIZEN OF is 1:N from COUNTRY to PERSON. This implies that the link in the opposite direction is functional; each person is a citizen of at most one country. Such a directed graph, representing record types and links, is often called a data structure diagram. It displays permissible connections between records of different record types.

In general, a link can connect a record type with itself. For instance, a link MANAGED BY can connect occurrences of a record type EMPLOYEE with itself. Such links are sometimes called recursive links. In some systems recursive links are prohibited [CODASYL DBTG, 1971]. The reason for this restriction is that when selecting records according to the connections defined by a recursive link, additional context is needed to determine how to follow the connections. For instance, in our example we can follow the MANAGED BY link in two ways. In one way we will obtain all persons managed by a particular person. In the other way, we will obtain a hierarchy of managers, e.g., the line management of a person.

The network data model is very widely accepted. It corresponds to the data model proposed by the DBTG [CODASYL DBTG, 1971]. In fact, the DBTG data model is the network data model described in this section with two restrictions:

1. All links are 1:N (This corresponds to the DBTG rule that no record occurrence can participate in more than one set occurrence of the same type.)
2. No recursive links are allowed. (This corresponds to the DBTG rule that owner and member records of a set have to be of different types.)

There is also some difference in terminology. For instance, links are called set types by the DBTG. In addition, the DBTG proposal includes some other features, e.g., aggregates, multi-member set types, etc. However, the DBTG proposal is, in essence, the network data model.

Consider now a data base organized according to the network data model, i.e., consisting of record types and links. To query the data base and select appropriate data a user typically traverses the data base according to the connections defined by the links between the record types. This traversal is called navigation [Bachman, 1973]. The user selects a record occurrence using some qualification, moves to another record occurrence following a connection according to a link, perhaps keeps some data item values, follows another connection, and so forth. The system keeps track of the record occurrences the user visits by maintaining pointers, called currency indicators, to the record occurrences. The currency indicators are implicitly or explicitly manipulated by the user. In the implicit case the user navigates through the data base and the system automatically updates the currency indicators. In the explicit case the user can move values between different currency indicators, i.e., change pointers. However, in both cases the user cannot arbitrarily manipulate these pointers, but must set pointers according to well defined rules. Most data languages for network systems implement some sort of navigation with either explicit or implicit currency indicators.

4. The Hierarchical Data Model

Consider the special case where the data structure diagram representing a network of record types is an ordered tree with the direction of the arcs away from the root as in figure 3. In addition, between any two record types there can be at most one link; hence, the arcs do not need to be labelled. Furthemore, each link, which represents an association, is not only functional, but it is totally functional. Such a restricted data structure diagram is called a hierarchical definition tree. The hierarchical definition tree specifies what record types are allowed in the data base and the permissible links between record types. It is a template for the actual data base.

An instance of an actual data base for figure 3 may appear as in figure 4. The data base is a collection or forest of trees called data base trees with record occurrences as nodes. All trees are constructed according to the links permitted explicitly in the hierarchical definition tree. That is, each COUNTRY record occurrence can have many STATE record occurrences connected to it, each of which may in turn have many CITY record occurrences connected to it, etc. Each CITY record occurrence, however, has exactly one parent record occurrence STATE and one grandparent record occurrence COUNTRY.

Two things should be noted in figure 4. First, there can be a varying number of occurrences of each record type at each level. Second, each record occurrence (except for a root record occurrence -- record type COUNTRY) must be connected to an ancestor record type as constrained by the hierarchical definition tree. There can be no "independent" record occurrences of record types STATE, TERRITORY, CITY or TOWN.

In a hierarchical data base, parents and children, ancestors and descendants among the record occurrences can be identified in a natural way. Once a record occurrence has been specified in the data base, then unique ancestors for that record occurrence can be identified but in general, no unique descendants. The process of going up a data base tree and determining an ancestor is called upward normalization. Going down a data base tree and determining the descendants is called downward normalization [Lowenthal, 1971].

The hierarchical data model provides no means for implementing direct N:M relationships between record types. Such a relationship can only be effected within a record type. However, most hierarchical systems provide the ability to handle many hierarchical definition trees. By using data duplication, one can represent an N:M relationship as two definition trees each representing a 1:N relationship. For instance, in the example of figure 1 the STATE and COMPANY relationship would be handled by two definition trees, one with root STATE, the other with root COMPANY. Some hierarchical systems have separate features that allow different hierarchical data bases to be connected and in this way N:M relationships can be implemented [IBM, 1971; MRI, 1972].

To summarize, a hierarchical data base is a set of records and connections among the records which are defined, respectively, by record types and links as follows:

1. A set of record types {R1, R2, ..., Rn};
2. A set of links Lij connecting all record types in one hierarchical definition tree;
3. At most one link Lij between any two record types Ri and Rj;
4. No Lii defined for any i. That is, we do not allow links connecting occurrences of the same record type;
5. Each Lij is totally functional in one direction. That is, for every Rj record occurrence there is exactly one Ri record occurrence connected to it (Ri is the parent of Rj);
6. A distinguished record type called the root record type which does not have a parent record type.

Given a hierarchical data base, how does one traverse (navigate) the data base and select pertinent record occurrences? One way of navigating a hierarchical data base is to select record occurrences one at a time according to a specific ordering. A preorder data base tree traversal is one method of ordering the record occurrences in a hierarchical data base [IBM, 1971]. For example, for the data base tree given in figure 5, a preorder data base tree traversal would visit the records in the order indicated. Individual occurrences of the data base trees given in figure 4 are imagined to be connected to an imaginary head record thus forming a single data base tree. In this way it is possible to visit all data base trees. The traversal need not visit every record in the data base tree since records may be skipped by qualifying the record occurrences to be visited. In addition, only records of a certain type, or descendants of a given record, can be visited.

Another method of traversing a hierarchical data base is to select a record occurrence and then either isolate one ancestor, by its type alone, or select a subset of descendants by their type and some qualification [Bleier, 1967; MRI, 1972]. Using figure 5 as an example, suppose one is at an occurrence of record type STATE. One can select the unique occurrence of the COUNTRY record type ancestor simply by specifying that one wants the record type COUNTRY. On the other hand, one can select the TOWN record occurrences connected to the STATE record occurrence by specifying the record type TOWN. In addition, the particular TOWN records selected may be restricted to a subset of all the TOWN record descendants. The selection can be effected by qualifying the record occurrences, e.g., by the value of a data item within the record occurrence.

Hierarchical data languages enable the user to traverse the data base trees either explicitly or implicitly. In the explicit case the user controls the traversal using some method of ordering the records as outlined previously. In the implicit case the user exploits the relationships among the data items in a hierarchical definition tree. The system then uses the structure of the data base trees to traverse the data base and select the data.

5. The Relational Data Model

The relational data model is a formal model for representing relationships among attributes of an entity set and the associations between entity sets [Codd, 1970]. Consider a set of domains S1, S2, if it is a set of n-tuples or simply tuples each of which has its first element from S1, its second element from S2, and so on. More concisely, R is a subset of the Cartesian product S1 x S2 x ...x Sn. The set Sj will be referred to as the j-th domain of R. As defined above, R is said to have degree n. Relations of degree 1 are often called unary, degree 2 binary, etc. The following table illustrates four relations, of different degree, corresponding to the entity sets course, person and house, and the association owner between person and house.

Unary	relation	COURSE(SUBJECT)
Binary	relation	PERSON(NAME, ADDRESS)
Ternary	relation	HOUSE(ADDRESS, PRICE, SIZE)
Binary	relation	OWNER(PERSON NAME, HOUSE ADDRESS)

A relation represents an entity set both in terms of its intension, i.e., the entity set name, its attributes and their properties, and in its valid extension, i.e., the possible values that the attributes may have. In addition, a data base relation is time-varying. For instance, the entity set which the relation represents normally changes over time since entities are inserted, deleted and modified. The time-varying nature of data base relations is one important aspect in which they differ from mathematical relations.

An n-ary relation can be represented as a table [Codd, 1970; Date, 1972]. Each column of the table, called an attribute, correspond to a domain of the relation. Each row corresponds to an n-tuple. For instance, if a relation represents an entity set, each column will correspond to an attribute and each row to an entity of the entity set. In addition, the ordering of the rows is immaterial and all rows are distinct, i.e., an entity's representation as a tuple cannot appear more than once in the table. These properties are an immediate consequence of the fact that a relation is a set. Normally the ordering of columns is significant, representing as it does the ordering of the underlying domains. However, if each column is labelled with the name of its corresponding domain and referred to by this name, rather than its relative position, then the ordering of the columns is also insignificant.

To ensure unique identification of an attribute (column), attribute names within relations must be unique. However, a difficulty arises when two or more attributes of a relation take their values from the same underlying domain. In the resulting relation, two or more attributes then have the same name. In such a situation the distinct roles played by each attribute can be distinguished by prefixing each appearance of the common attribute name with a distinct role-name. In this way, attribute names of the relation remain unique. For example, consider the relation:
   BUILDINGS(ADDRESS, MORTGAGE, MORTGAGE).
The meaning of BUILDINGS(X, Y, Z) is that the building at address X has two mortgages on it -- a first and a second mortgage. The names FIRST and SECOND can be prefixed to MORTGAGE to form the relation:
   BUILDINGS(ADDRESS, FIRST MORTGAGE, SECOND MORTGAGE).
The prefixes identify the roles played by MORTGAGE in its two distinct appearances.

Normally the values of some subsets of the attributes of a relation uniquely identify each tuple of that relation. A key, K, of a relation, R, is a subset of attributes of R with the following time-independent properties [Codd, 1972a]:
   P1. Unique Identification. In each tuple of R the value of K uniquely
       identifies that tuple.
   P2. Non-redundancy. No attribute in K can be discarded without
       destroying property P1.
An association can be viewed as a relation in the same way that relationships among attributes are viewed as relations. For example, consider the association "owner" between the entity sets person and house. The entity sets person and house can be represented by the relations PERSON and HOUSE respectively. The association "owner" can be represented by another relation as follows. Two keys can be isolated from each of the relations PERSON and HOUSE. Let PERSON NAME and HOUSE ADDRESS, respectively be the two keys. These attributes can now be used to form another relation, OWNER, which represents the association between the entity sets person and house. The tuple (John Smith, 111 Main St.) in the new relation OWNER defines an association between a person and a house that the person owns.

In the relational data model all attribute relationships and all associations are represented as relations. There is no distinction, at least at the data model level, between different kinds of relations. Syntactically, all relations are the same. However, the data model does not preclude the introduction of additional semantic information to distinguish different relations according to their semantic properties.

In a relational system, relations can already exist in the data base, or they can be generated (created) from existing relations by using relational operators. Both the operand(s) and the result of a relational operator is a relation. A new relation, generated by relational operators, represents a subset of the relationships among the data in the data base. For instance, there may be a relationship between PERSON, HOUSE and COMPANY relations expressed as "the houses of persons working for a company". Such relationships are expressed again as relations. In this particular example, the new relation is the result of a definition which relates the original three relations by the use of relational operators. The fact that the result is expressed again as a relation should not be surprising. Afterall, a relation can express any relationship.

The relational operators can be described using either the relational algebra or the relational calculus [Codd, 1972b]. The relational algebra is a set of operators which constructs the required relation from given relations. The new relation is obtained by combining and subsetting the given relations and any intermediate relations that result. The relational calculus gives a definition of the desired relation. The definition is in the form of a predicate which is the set of conditions that determines the shape and the membership of the resulting relation [Meltzer, 1974]. Relational data languages provide either algebra, calculus or equivalent facilities to define and generate new relations which select the data a user wants.

6. Concluding Remarks

DEMS's handle attribute relationships in similar ways, through record types or relations. However, the associations among entity sets can be handled with different mechanisms. These mechanisms are used to distinguish among data models, i.e., the network, hierarchical and relational data models. DBMS's are characterized according to the features offered for representing associations. There are two main approaches, the network approach and the relational approach. In the network approach, there is an explicit mechanism, links (DBTG sets), for representing associations. This approach appears in most existing commercial systems [CODASYL DBTG, 1971]. An historic reason for its widespread use is that it evolved quite naturally from files representing record types and the ability to crosslink them.

The network approach can further be divided according to the restrictions on links. In almost all commercial network systems, the links are functional, at least in one direction. That is, the links are restricted to be 1:N. However, for many systems further restrictions are imposed which enable the links between record types to be structured in a hierarchical fashion. Such systems are called hierarchical systems. The other network systems, follow mainly the proposal of the DBTG [CODASYL DBTG, 1971].

The relational approach uses relations to represent both attribute relationships and associations among entity sets. Relational systems themselves may use different mechanisms to implement different relationships, but such differences are transparent to the user. The user sees only relations although, semantically, they may represent quite different relationships.

DBMS's have developed mainly along these three approaches. There are hierarchical systems, e.g., IMS [IBM, 1971], GIS [IBM, 1970], TDMS [Bleier, 1967], SYS2000 [MRI, 1972], IDMS [Cullinane, 1975], DMSII [Burroughs, 1975], PHOLAS [Phillips, 1974]. Finally, there are relational systems, e.g., XRM [Astrahan and Chamberlin, 1975], TYMSHARE [Codd, 1975], INGRES [Held et al., 1975]. There has been much debate concerning the different approaches and their relative merits and drawbacks. The question is, how different are they really?

The approaches differ according to three distinct coordinates:
1. Terminology -- syntactic sugar of languages and names of concepts;
2. Attitude -- what they are trying to provide to the user;
3. Essential features -- things which are both important and different.

A very confusing terminology has developed historically in DBMS's. The
same name is used in different ways. For example, the word key means an
inverted data item in SYS2000, but a unique tuple identifier in relational
systems. In addition, different names are used for the same concept. For
example, segments in IMS and records in DBTG systems are essentially the
same. The following terms are used in approximately the same fashion
according to the three approaches: hierarchical, network and relational.
  Segment type - Record type - Primary relation
  Segment occurrence - Record occurrence - Tuple
  Field - Data item - Attribute
  Parent-child relationship - DBTG set - Join
The three approaches differ in attitude. Hierarchical systems were
developed mainly with implementation in mind. They provide the features
that people initially knew how to build. Network systems were developed
with the DBA and sophisticated user in mind. They provide many features
and options to optimize the structure and operation of the DBMS. Finally,
relational systems were developed with the casual user in mind. They
provide features which are natural for a broader class of users to use.
The three approaches differ in some essential features. The most
important difference is in the way they handle associations. All systems
group attributes of the same entity set in either segment types, record
types or relations. However, they use different mechanisms for relating
the different entity sets. Hierarchical systems use parent-child
relationships in a hierarchical definition tree. The relationships are
very restrictive and they follow some very rigorous rules. Network systems
use DBTG sets between owners and members. They offer many options to
handle very different relationships. As a result, these relationships have
many complex characteristics. Finally, relational systems use relational
operators, like joins, to connect different relations. The access paths
are invisible to the user according to the relational data model. However,
in implemented relational systems, some joins are more permanent than
others and the user knows it, e.g., the net facility in SEQUEL [Boyce and
Chamberlin, 1973; Chamberlin and Boyce, 1974].
What do we expect to happen in the future with respect to these
differences?
First, in a few years a common terminology will emerge. Numerous books
and papers are being produced. The most popular of these will establish a
common terminology. Commercial systems will still have their own
terminology, but there will be no basis for argument. Everybody will
understand everybody else. (This does not seem to be the case now.)
Second, attitudes will change and mellow. We see signs of this trend
already. Hierarchical systems are trying to expand their horizons by
offering new, fancy features. Network systems do not always implement the
full DBTG proposal. Hence, network systems are losing some of their very
fancy features. Finally, the implementation of relational systems, faces
exactly the same problems as other systems. As a result, for the time
being, some of the purity of the relational data model is being sacrificed
for implementation and efficiency considerations. We expect the different
attitudes to converge in a few years.
Finally, the difference in essential features, such as the handling of
associations, will become a non-issue. Eventually all systems will deal
with the problem in essentially the same manner. Hierarchical and network
systems will have to build higher level, relational-like interfaces to
accommodate end users who do not understand trees and networks. Relational
systems will have to use mechanisms, underneath the relational interface,
which resemble hierarchies and networks [Tsichritzis, 1975a; Tsichritzis,
1976]. Hence, all three approaches will have both visible and invisible

access paths at different levels. The levels will provide an architecture, like for instance, the one proposed by ANSI/SPARC [ANSI/X3/SPARC, 1975]. In such an architecture the different approaches can coexist as different schemas.

So who can be considered the potential winner among the three approaches? All of them together. From the point of view of the casual user, the systems will probably look relational. For DBA's, sophisticated users and implementors the systems will probably look hierarchical or network.

Of course, the salesmen will still argue about the merits of different systems. But the professionals, who design and build DBMS's, will not be arguing about data models. Future systems will use the important ideas from all approaches. In addition, the success of a system will depend mainly on features, ease of use, reliability, efficiency and all the other classical, but forgotten, issues which make a software product really good.

References

ANSI/X3/SPARC. [1975]. Study Group on Data Base Management Systems Interim Report, FDT 7, No. 2.

Ashenhurst, R. [1974]."A Great Debate," CACM 17, No.6 (June), 360.

Astrahan, M.M., and Chamberlin, D.D. [1975]. "Implementation of a Structured English Query Language," CACM 18, No. 10 (Oct.), 580-588.

Bachman, C.W. [1969]. "Data Structure Diagrams," Data Base 1, No. 2, 4-10.

Bachman, C.W. [1973]."The Programmer as Navigator," CACM 16, No. 11 (Nov.), 653-658.

Bachman, C.W. [1974]. "The Data Structure Set Model," Proc. ACM SIGMOD, Data Models: Data-Structure-Set versus Relational, Rustin, R., (ed.), 1-10.

Bleier, R.E. [1967]. "Treating Hierarchical Data Structures in the SDC Time-shared Data Management System (TDMS)," Proc. ACM National Conference, 41-49.

Boyce, R.F., and Chamberlin, D.D. [1973]. "Using a Structured English Query Language as a Data Definition Facility", Technical Report RJ1318, IBM Research Lab.,San Jose, Calif., (Dec.).

Burroughs Corp. [1975]. DMSII Host Language Interface Reference Manual, 5001092.

Canning, R.G., (ed.). [1972]. "The Debate on Data Base Management," EDP Analyzer 10, No. 3 (Mar.).

Chamberlin, D.D., and Boyce, R.F. [1974]. "SEQUEL: A Structured English Query Language," Proc. ACM SIGMOD Workshop on Data Description, Access and Control, 249-264.

CODASYL DBTG.[1971]. CODASYL Data Base Task Group Report, Conference on Data Systems Languages, ACM, New York.

Codd, E.F.[1970]. "A Relational Model of Data for Large Shared Data Banks," CACM 13, No. 6 (June), 377-387.

Codd, E.F.[1972a]. "Further Normalization of the Data Base Relational Model," Data Base Systems, Courant Computer Science Symposium 6, Rustin, R., (ed.), 33-64, Prentice-Hall, Englewood Cliffs, New Jersey.

Codd, E.F. [1972b]. "Relational Completeness of Data Base Sublanguages," Data Base Systems, Courant Computer Science Symposium 6, Rustin, R., (ed.), 65-98, Prentice-Hall, Englewood Cliffs, New Jersey.

Codd, E.F. (ed.). [1975]. Implementation of Relational Data Base Management Systems, Panel Discussion National Computer Conference.

Codd, E.F., and Date, C.J. [1974]. "Interactive Support for Non-programmers: The Relational and Network Approaches," Proc. ACM SIGMOD Data Models: Data- Structure-Set versus Relational, Rustin, R., (ed.), 11- 41.

Cullinane Corp. [1975]. Integrated Database Management System (IDMS) Data Manipulation Language Programmer's Reference Guide, Release 3.1.

Datapro Research Corp. [1972], "Total, Cincom Systems, Inc.," Datapro 70, (Dec.).

Date, C.J. [1972]. "Relational Data Base Systems: A Tutorial," Proc. Fourth International Symposium on Computer and Information Sciences, Plenum Press, New York, New York.

Date, C.J., and Codd, E.F. [1974]. "The Relational and Network Approaches: Comparison of the Application Programming Interfaces," Proc. ACM SIGMOD, Data Models: Data-Structure-Set versus Relational, Rustin, R., (ed.), 83-113.

Engles, R.W. [1972]. "A Tutorial on Data-Base Organization, Annual Review in Automatic Programming 7, Part 1, 1-64.

Held,G.D., Stonebraker, M.R., and Wong, E. [1975]. "INGRES --A Relational Data Base System," Proc. AFIPS 44, NCC, 409-416.

Honeywell Information Systems.[1969]. Integrated Data Store, BR69.

IBM. [1970]. Generalized Information System GIS/360, Application Description Manual (Version 2), GH20-0892-0.

IBM.[1971]. Information Management System IMS/360, Application Description Manual (Version 2), GH20-0765-1.

Kerschberg, L., Klug, A., and Tsichritzis, D. [1976]. A Taxonomy of Data Models., Technical Report CSRG-70, Computer Systems Research Group, University of Toronto.

Lowenthal, E.I. [1971]. "A Functional Approach to the Design of Storage Structures for Generalized Data Management Systems", Ph.D. thesis, University of Texas at Austin.

Mealy, G.H.[1967]. "Another Look at Data," Proc. AFIPS 31, FJCC, 525-534.

Meltzer, H.S. [1974]. "Relations and Relational Operations," GUIDE 38.

Metaxides, A. [1975]. "'Information bearing' and non-information bearing' Sets," Data Base Description, Douque, B.C., and Nijssen, G.M., (eds.), 363-368, North-Holland, Amsterdam.

MRI Systems Corp. [1972]. System 2000 General Information Manual.

Phillips-Electrologica B. V. [1974]. Phillips Host Language System (PHOLAS) System and Operations, Pub. no. 5122 991 26071.

Schmid, H.A., and Swenson, J.R., [1975]. "On the Semantics of the Relational Data Model," Proc. ACM SIGMOD, 211-223.

Sibley, E.H.[1974]. "On the Equivalence of Data Based Systems," Proc. ACM SIGMOD, Data Models: Data-Structure-Set versus Relational, Rustin, R., (ed.), 43-76.

Software AG. [1973] ADABAS General Information Manual.

Steel,T.B. [1975]. "Data Base Standardization: A Status Report," Data Base Description, Douque, B.C., and Nijssen, G.M., (eds.), 183-195, North Holland, Amsterdam.

Stonebraker, M.R., and Held, G.D. [1975]. "Networks, Hierarchies, and Relations in Data Base Management Systems," Proc. ACM Pacific 75, 1-9.

Tsichritzis, D.C. [1975a]. "A Network Framework for Relational Implementation," Data Base Description, Douque, B.C., and Nijssen, G.M., (eds.), 269-282, North Holland, Amsterdam.

Tsichritzis, D.C. [1975b]. Features of a Conceptual Schema, Technical Report CSRG-56, Computer Systems Research Group, University of Toronto, (June).

Tsichritzis, D.C. [1976]. "LSL: A Link and Selector Language," ACM SIGMOD, 123-133.

DISCUSSION

KENT: When you talk about co-existence in continuing to support all these data models simultaneously, does that imply you're talking only about the external model?

TSICHRITZIS: The problem is not so much to give the different views of the different models to the outside world. The problem is to do it efficiently, which means that somewhere in the system you have to have some facility to accommodate the different models. If you take one data model and impose another data model on it, you will find a very weird situation whereby you do something underneath, then you cover it with something else, and then you unearth it higher up.

SENKO: I'd like to ask a question on the nature of the conceptual model. The conceptual schema will have to be written in terms of some data model (in the broad sense of the term). In a given installation you don't have the option of supporting many different models at the conceptual schema level because what you want to do is make many different models available to the end users, and you want to map it to some common canonical description. This suggests that even though you've got the option of not having to choose only one view at the external level, at the conceptual level you have the original problem of choosing one. Do you have any feeling for whether any of the three models you described are appropriate candidates, or, do we have to look for some other model appropriate for canonical description at the conceptual level.

TSICHRITZIS: I think that it's perhaps too early to settle that question. My preference would be, obviously, a relational model, but I don't want to give a definite answer on that. On the other hand, there are many people trying to pick a data model able to accommodate many of the others. We may find this new improved data model may be the final answer. Probably the relational model is the best candidate among the three, because it is at the more appropriate level, but again there may be another one among the rest which may be the most appropriate of them all.

SENKO: With regard to the great debate, I think there is still a debate because there has to be one model at the conceptual level. We looked at this in a fair amount of detail and the closest to what seems to be realistic is the modelthat Dennis [Tsichritzis] showed earlier of houses and other objects with arrows between them. [the generalized network model] I would disagree with some minor aspects, but essentially a model that accommodates sets of entities and relationships between entities seems to be the most appropriate one. The other models, of which you mentioned three, all have some data representation aspects in them. We again looked at those in considerable detail with regard to representing strings in the DIAM model, and I think they can be mapped in both directions. Mapping to external models is very similar to the mapping to data representations, where you want hierarchies and networks, etc., for efficiency considerations. We've looked at that and at the problem of finding optimum paths and it seems feasible. The mapping to the external view is just a subset of that, so you can provide these as well.

TSICHRITZIS: I agree with you, and I think that something having to do with record types and links among them is probably the appropriate model at the conceptual level. One of the reasons I didn't want to give a definite answer about the conceptual data model is because there is room for improvement. However, I would like to suggest that from now on it's not going to be a great debate, it's going to be a small debate, which will affect a smaller set of people and will affect them less. For a small subset of people who are seriously building system,s I think there is still a great deal of room for improvement, so the debate is still going to go on.

NELSON: I don't think that three models are nearly enough and I think that the issue is not what's pleasing to people who design data base management systems, and I don't think that the idea of selecting a single model and presenting that to the user, especially at the conceptual schema interface, is doing the user justice. We're trying to decide that there is a particular universal comprehensive data model which we'd like to work on as developers and designers, and we're going to require the users to deal with that. I think the data model should match as closely as possible the data that's being decribed, and if there is some natural inherent structure in an information system, or if there is some natural inherent structure in the way data is being managed by the end users of that data, then we ought to have a data model that caters to that. The architecture and facilities in the data model ought to help the user faithfully to represent the conceptual relationships and the type of data.

TSICHRITZIS: The art of designing the right data model is trying to come up with something which is conceptually simple. It would be a noble goal to support as many data models as possible, but, as I mentioned, there are twenty-three of them, and they are still coming.

NELSON: I don't think that even twenty-three are enough. In a sense, we can support all of these, or as many as the trade-off allows between having too many models and having the right model for the right problem. It is possible to map data models onto existing data base management systems that weren't intended to support that data model. It's going to be relatively inexpensive to take a useful data model and map it onto another implementation of the data model that might be quite different in the way it handles data. If I'm interested in representing a description for a power network, I'd rather not have to do that with a relational model.

TSICHRITZIS: This is an argument for supporting two or three data models, but not an argument for supporting twenty. We are at the stage where we can think of supporting more than one data model, but I don't think we're at the stage of supporting a multitude of data models.

STEEL: It appears to me that it is possible, and some work has been done in this area, to develop a mechanism for describing the conceptual schema in any way you want to. I'm essentially taking issue with Mike Senko's remark that we have to pick a model for the conceptual schema. I think that's wrong. I think we can develop a way of writing conceptual schemas where you can choose your model. In any particular instance one will have to pick a model, but I do not think it is necessary to predetermine in advance what the data model is for a conceptual schema. I think that can be left to the choice of the enterprise.

TSICHRITZIS: You could have a data model which is able to handle more than one. Many people have built data models which have facilities to represent, say, networks, and have facilities to represent something else too. An appropriate data model of this kind may be found, which has inherently the capability of describing most of the others.

SENKO: The reason for choosing one data model is not simple, but is perhaps understandable. The various data models each have a certain set of properties, and you have to decide which properties you want overall. Now, one thing that ANSI/SPARC has asked for is a canonical model, that is, a model in which there is one and only one place for a fact. If you look at this problem in detail, you find out that you cannot get that with a network model, or a relational model, or a hierarchical model. If you want some decent properties, then you must think a little about how you construct the model, and construct it in a neat fashion. It turns out that the general network model allows you to do that. It also allows you, probably in the easiest fashion, to map to these other models. But these other models should not be at the conceptual schema level. They should be at the external schema and at the internal schema, and we can support ten, twenty, thirty, one hundred thousand, if you like. Recognize, however, that they should be mapped from a model which allows you to describe the corporation in the simplest fashion possible, and which has one place for facts.

THE ROLE OF THE EXTERNAL SCHEMA

Dr. David K. Jefferson
Code 188A David W. Taylor Naval Ship R&D Center
Bethesda, Maryland 20084

INTRODUCTION

The ANSI/SPARC/DBMS Report[1], hereinafter referred to as the DBMS Report, describes a generalized model of a data base management system, with particular emphasis on interfaces. A reasonable familiarity with the objectives, terminology, and general conclusions of the DBMS Report is assumed in this presentation. However, since the DBMS Report is quite long and complex, it is prudent to state the following interpretations of three key concepts:

. The conceptual schema. As a repository of information about the entire data base, the conceptual schema serves as a means of communication among the enterprise administrator, the date base administrator, and the application administrators. Through centralized privacy and integrity controls, it coordinates the activities of the various applications. It provides a degree of independence between an application and the internal schema, and hence between an application and the hardware, software, and other applications.

. The external schema. As a repository of information about a particular application, the external schema serves as a means of communication among the application administrator, the application programmers, and (possibly) the users. It provides mechanisms for access control, validity checking, and so on, within an application area. It also provides a facility to accommodate application or language-dependent naming conventions and structuring rules.

. The data dictionary/directory. This concept seems to be a catch-all for valuable information not stored elsewhere. It includes cross references, statistics, and program descriptions.

A minor change in terminology is convenient: all information about a particular application area, or about the enterprise as a whole, will be referred to as if it were part of the relevant schema, rather than a part of the data dictionary/directory. For example, the frequency of a given query, or a description of a given program, would be considered part of the appropriate external schema. The change in terminology has no real effect on the DBMS Report, since there is no change in either the total information content of the schemas and data dictionary/directory, or in the controls over access to that information.

Two substantive questions are addressed in this presentation:

. Should the conceptual schema be derived fromthe external schemas, rather than vice versa as in the DBMS Report? This question is addressed in the section entitled "Production and Modification of the External Schema."

. Should the external schemas, with the additional information from the data dictionary/directory, serve roles in the design, implementation, optimization, and/or maintenance of an information system, rather than serving primarily as interfaces for application areas? This question is addressed in the section entitled "Use of the External Schema."

The answer, in each case, is a tentative "Yes." However, the purpose of this presentation is to initiate thought and discussion, rather than to provide answers. Consequently, the arguments will be brief, informal, and, hopefully, provocative.

PRODUCTION AND MODIFICATION OF THE EXTERNAL SCHEMA

Let us first analyze four phases in the life cycle of an information system.

Phase 1: Identification of Needs
This phase is critical, yet is generally conducted by a systems analyst on the haphazard level of "what do you think you'd like?" or "here's what I think you should want (because its what I want to give you)". Hence, users find it difficult to communicate their needs. Furthermore, a series of experiments at the University of Minnesota [2] suggests that managers are frequently incorrect in assessing the relative value of different types and presentations of information. An additional problem is that information which is very desirable for a manager with one set of attitudes, abilities, and level of experience may be less desirable for another manager with a different set of attitudes, abilities, and level of experience who is engaged in similar work [3]. Much more experimentation is needed to provide a firm basis for identifying the different types of people and the information that they need and can be persuaded to use.

Phase 2: Requirements Analysis
This is (or should be) the translation of inconsistent and incomplete statements of "needs" into precise definitions of what must be done and what data must be involved. This phase requires a precise yet simple language for communicating between the designer (who proposes a system) and the user (who critiques it).
Substantial progress has been made in this phase. The Problem Statement Language/Problem Statement Analyzer (PSL/PSA) [4,5] and the Structured Analysis and Design Technique (SADT) [6,7,8] both recognize the need to describe hierarchically both processes (computer programs or manual procedures) and collections of data. That is, the top-level requirement, or goal, is divided into simpler requirements, which are in turn divided, and so on. A complete description at any level must include both processes and data.
Both PSL/PSA and SADT are oriented to the description of interfaces: a process is described by the collections of data which it uses or produces, or by the collections of data which control it, while a collection of data is described by the processes which produce or use it, or byprocesses which control its use. The determination of the sequence in which processes are performed will generally be unnecessary at this phase, and should be postponed.

Phase 3: Design, Implementation, and Testing
Sequencing should be introduced during this phase to determine when and how processes are to be performed and how the data are to be represented. Substantial progress has recently been made in this phase. The discipline imposed by structured programming, particularly top-down design and implementation, has demonstrated the practical advantages of combining what used to be three sequential phases (design, then implement, then test) into one essentially indivisible phase [9,10]. Abstract data types, which are defined by the operations to be performed on them, provide the data analog to the stepwise refinement process [11].

Phase 4: Operation and Maintenance
This final phase includes fine-tuning the system, using information about rates, volumes, and patterns of processing. The documentation produced during earlier phases must be clear and precise if errors are to be corrected and improvements are to be made. The only reasonable way to organize this documentation is by means of a top-down unfolding of detail; complex systems, as noted in the description of requirements analysis, must be divided into meaningful, manageable pieces if they are to be understood by people. Processes and data in an SADT model, for example, may be either described by a hierarchical decomposition within the model, or named and then described in some other model.

Top-down Schema Design
Although the precise content or boundaries of these phases may be the subject of some dispute, this rather extended discussion is necessary to provide an understanding of why external schemas should be produced before the conceptual schema, rather than after it. Essentially, current work in each of the phases implies the same rule: start with the problem rather than a currently available collection of solutions. In program production, the rule specifies top-down design and implementation. In schema production, the rule specifies that the first product to be developed is the application (the top), then the external schema (an amalgamation of applications), and finally the conceptual schema (the bottom). This might seem upside-down; one could argue that the conceptual schema represents the "big picture", or ultimate goals, while the application represents a much more detailed level of activity. If phase 1 of the system life cycle, the identification of needs, were a precise and reliable process which could be applied throughout the enterprise, this would indeed be the case.

However, in practice the only way to obtain information about the needs of an enterprise is to obtain information, which need be detailed only to the level of requirements analysis, about specific applications. Applications exhibiting common characteristics of data usage, subprogram usage, and programming language are then used to define the requirements of an external schema. External schemas are then used to define the requirements of the conceptual schema. The critical point is that the entire process of system production should be driven by the needs of the user; these needs can be determined precisely only through interaction between the user and the designer. It is completely unreasonable to suppose that any one individual could possess the knowledge, or have the time, to precisely formulate the information requirements of a large enterprise.

If the production of the conceptual schema precedes requirements analysis of the application, the resulting information system is apt to exhibit the following characteristics:
. Ineffectiveness. Building an application from existing programs and/or data will generally necessitate compromising the original requirements.
. Ineffficiency. The real goals of the system are obscured, so that it is impossible to determine the trouble spots or alternative solutions. The data base administrator may think that the system can be optimized, but it will merely produce the wrong information faster.
. Inflexibility. Bottom-up design and implementation inevitably lead to disaster when the bottom must be altered.

Conclusion
The process of schema production is not as strange and difficult as it might appear. The same process occurs in structured programming-- the design phase leads to new insights into the application, so that common problems can be solved by generalized program modules with well-defined

interfaces. The schemas are, similarly, high-level modules produced for
well-defined purposes, and should be much more stable than the applications
themselves.

In summary, it is critical that the most precise requirements, those
formulated for specific applications, should be the major influences in
system design. The least precise requirements, those formulated for the
enterprise as a whole, should be minor influences, used only in formulating
initial estimates of system costs, benefits, response times, etc.

Use of the External Schema
The external schema, as extended with information from the data
dictionary/directory, performs two functions: interfacing the application
program with the data base, and describing the applications system to
various people. Since the former function is reasonably straightforward and
is quite well covered in the DBMS Report, it is only briefly summarized in
this section. The latter function is discussed in detail in this section.

The External Schema as an Interface
As the interface between the application and the data base, the external
schema can provide the following features:
. Access control within that part of the data base known to the
application area.
. Application-dependent validity checking.
. Naming conventions appropriate to a given language processor.
. Data structures which can be manipulated in a given language.
. Data structures which are appropriate to the application area.

The External Schema as a Communications Medium
The features listed in the preceding subsection are primarily
conveniences - they eliminate or reduce some of the more mechanical
activities involved in the design and implementation of an information
system, but they do not provide new insights into the nature of the system.
The external schema, if properly structured, can provide such insights
through its descriptive function. The primary objectives are the following:
. Commonality. The external schema should provide a communication medium
common to the user, the various administrators, and the programmers.
. The external schema should provide descriptions to any required level
of detail.
. Simplicity. Information should be presented in pieces small enough to
be understood by everyone concerned with that information. Unwanted
information should be suppressed.
. Generality. Questions of what, how, when, and how much should all be
answerable. On basic descriptive mechanism should suffice for a wide
range of applications and programming languages.
To be more specific, the external schema should provide information to
the following people:
. The user.
The relevant information concerns what can be done by an application
and how much it will cost. Note that costs cannot be predicted from
data descriptions alone; both data and process descriptions are
required.
The application administrator.
The external schema provides the documentation of the application area.
It must be structured so that effective access controls can be readily
designed and implemented - e.g., the units of data to be protected must
be neither too large nor too small. The application administrator must
know what processes do and when they are performed, in order to

properly coordinate them, but the required degree of detail need not be very great.

. The enterprise administrator.

The requirements of the external schemas are used to design the conceptual schema, which is then used to design the details of the external schemas. Hence, the requirements of an external schema must be presented in a format which is understandable to the enterprise administrator, who is not necessarily an expert in the application area.

. The data base administrator.

Information regarding frequencies, volumes, and patterns of processing (how much and when) must be initially estimated during the design of an application, and then revised during actual operation. The external schema is the most appropriate repository for such information, since the information must be related to specific applications in order to determine appropriate scheduling, to predict the results of changes in the internal schema, and so on. Briefly, the external schema represents the only link between high-level descriptions of what needs to be done, and low-level measurements of activities. Effective optimization requires access to this link.

. The programmer.

The external schema provides complete specifications of the programmer's task (how) including the over-all purpose of the program (what) and any relevant time or space constraints (how much). The objective is not to make programming easier, but to make programs and systems more reliable and maintainable.

Conclusion

An information system can be far too complex for effective management by manual methods. A meta-information system must be devised to cope with this complexity; it is convenient to consider all information about a specific area to be consolidated within a single meta-data base, the external schema. Properly structured and presented, this information can be of great value in producing more effective, efficient, and maintainable systems.

SUMMARY

Extensions of the External Schema

This presentation suggests that the prospects are poor for finding individuals or groups who can fill the role of enterprise administrator as defined in the DBMS Report - the required amount of knowledge about the enterprise is both too broad and too deep. However, the prospects are good for effectively utilizing the external schemas to perform the same function, as well as other functions vital to improving information systems.

A Prototype System-Design System

The Information Systems Design for Navy Logistics Systems (ISDNLS) Research Project at the David W. Taylor Naval Ship Research and Development Center (DTNSRDC) is currently developing an integrated system-design system. The Project began in 1974 with primary emphasis on optimization of file structures, but has been devoting increasing attention to requirements analysis, and, most recently, to determination of needs. These latter areas seem to be the sources of most problems, and to promise the greatest pay-offs. Current plans call for the construction of a design data base essentially equivalent to the external schema described in this presentation.

REFERENCES

1. American National Standards Institute (ANSI) Study Group on Data Base Management Systems, "ANSI/X3/SPARC Interim Report on Data Base Management Systems", FDT (Bulletin of ACM-SIGMOD), Vol. 7, No. 2, pp. 1-140 (New York: ACM, 1975).
2. Dickson, G.W., J.A. Senn, and N.L. Chervany, "Research in Management Information - Decision Systems: The Minnesota Experiments". (Minneapolis: Management Information Systems Research Center, Graduate School of Business Administration, University of Minnesota, May 1975). MISRC-WP-75-08.
3. Chervany, N.L., and R.F. Sauter, "Analysis and Design of Computer-Based Management Information Systems: An Evolution of Risk Analysis Decision Aids". (Minneapolis: Management Information Systems Research Center, Graduate School of Business Administration, University of Minnesota, September 15, 1974). Monograph 5.
4. Hershey, E.A., III et al., "Problem Statement Language Version 3.0, Language Reference Manual" (Ann Arbor: ISDOS Research Project, Dept. of Industrial and Operations Engineering, The University of Michigan, May, 1975). ISDOS Working Paper No. 68.
5. Teichroew, D., and M. Bastarache, "PSA Outputs" (Ann Arbor: ISDOS Research Project, Dept. of Industrial and Operations Engineering, The University of Michigan, October 1974). ISDOS Working Paper No. 99, Preliminary Draft.
6. SADT is a Trademark of SofTech, Inc.
7. SofTech, "Structured Analysis Reader Guide" (Waltham, Massachusetts: SofTech, Inc., April, 1975).
8. Ross, D.T., "Structured Analysis: A Language for Communicating Ideas" (Waltham, Massachusetts: SofTech, Inc., December, 1975).
9. Wirth, N., "Program Development by Stepwise Refinement," Commun. ACM, Vol. 14, No. 4, pp. 221-227 (April, 1971).
10. Baker, F.T., "Structured Programming in a Production Programming Environment, Proc. 1975 Int. Conf. on Reliable Software, SIGPLAN Notices, Vol. 10, No. 6, pp. 172-183 (New York: ACM, June, 1975).
11. Liskov, B., and S. Zilles, "Programming with Abstract Data Types," Proc. Symp. on Very High Level Languages, SIGPLAN Notices, Vol. 9, No. 4, pp. 50-59 (New York: ACM, April, 1974).

DISCUSSION

NELSON: The material that you used to reach your conclusions was well drawn. I only disagree with the conclusions. I believe you should attempt to derive the external schema from the conceptual schema, for the reasons you gave, and I think that top-down design should be avoided for the reasons you gave, and I think that throwing out the data dictionary, scattering it to the winds, should be avoided at all costs, for the reasons you gave, and I think there is a reason why we disagree about this. I would put it to you this way. There are only two kinds of people in the world, the analysts and the synthesists, and you, sir, are an analyst, and I am a synthesist.

JEFFERSON: I don't believe that we are that diametrically opposed. I would think that the differences that you allude to are not differences that would affect us in practice. If we were to sit down and design an information processing system, I suspect we would probably do it in similar ways. We might call the steps by different names, and say we were doing different things, but the products at different points along the way, would probably be remarkably similar.

COLLINS: You seem to have said that you believe the collection of external schemas can produce the conceptual schema, but the opposite is just the point. The collection of particular application views, it seems, doesn't produce a coherent whole that can be a basis for evolution. The contrary of what you've proposed is, I believe, the primary point behind the SPARC report. The second point is this reference to project life cycle, pointing out the relationship of the external schema to project life cycle. However, it is depicted as the lifetime of an individual, not of a species. Until we start treating this as an actual species rather than an individual project, I don't think we'll get off first base. External schemas are my current view of the data, and consequently, are just the thing that are old at the end of a one individual's lifetime in the project life cycle. When I start on the next one, I may want to throw away the old external schemas and make some new view of the data based, perhaps, on what's in the conceptual schema.

JEFFERSON: I agree that the external schemas do not produce a coherent whole. Obviously they don't, because they are different points of view of something that hasn't been described yet. So you can't simply take a bunch of external schemas and jam them together into one data base. It requires considerable analysis. The point I'm trying to make is that the analysis must be based on facts, that is, the construction of a conceptual schema must be based upon facts. I believe that the best way of learning what is done in the enterprise is by looking at the external schemas, provided those external schemas can be described in a way which is humanly comprehensible. The process is to formulate the external schemas in a way in which they can be read easily, and from those unambiguous facts about your enterprise, you construct a first attempt at a conceptual schema. This won't be correct, and you'll have to go through some iteration. The alternative is to gather information about the enterprise in some other way. There should be an orderly way of gathering information about an enterprise, and if that information can be used to produce the conceptual schema, then I would contend that such information is really the composite of the external schemas.

COLLINS: Is there some way a global view can be brought to bear?

JEFFERSON: I'm putting a lot of information in the external schemas, everything that relates to particular application areas, so the only thing left is that which either relates to the internal representation, which has no effect on the conceptual schema, or those things which are not peculiar to particular application areas. If no application area uses a particular element of data, then why have it in the data base?

COLLINS: Why store the data, surely, but there's no harm in keeping track of the definition if you perceive this is a component of reality with which you want to be concerned later.

MOERKE: I also agree with all your premises, and disagree with nearly all your conclusions. We have experience in our shop with everything you've

been talking about. However, we have had success as measured by projects
in on time,on budget, and satisfying users, when we've started with
something like the conceptual schema, top down, if you will, rather than
bottom-up from a business function point of view. I maintain what you've
described is a bottom up approach. The kind of operating management with
which you're involved when you're trying to elicit these requirements is, I
agree, notoriously poor at identifying them.   However, it is also
notoriously bad at having the right view of what good business practice is.
Their view of good business practice is typically what they've always been
doing, or making small changes to do it better. I'm not going to say that
we can tell someone what's good business practice. There are ways in which
you can elicit what is good business practice. One of the best techniques
is to stop being concerned about reports and transmittals and current
procedures, and to get into the conceptual realm, if you can sufficiently
make it easy for him and define what are, in fact, the correct processes,
what is really happening in the business. After that's done, develop an
external schema view which describes how to make it work in this
organization. We've had experience at doing this, and I think it's very
good. You must develop the conceptual level first. If you develop the
external level first, you'll fall into the same trap we've been in for
years.

JEFFERSON: First off all, there seems to be some confusion about 'bottom-
up' and trees with a root at the top. It seems when you have a long-term
difficulty with this sort of concept. When I say top-down, I mean that you
start from the goal, and then you try to refine that goal into things that
will attain the goal. Our only real goals are providing information to
people, or possibly to other computers. The goal of satisfying the
enterprise is a derived goal. It is something that is not real.   If you
satisfy all the individual memebers of the enterprise, you satisfy the
enterprise, because there is no such thing as an enterprise, regardless of
what the chairman of the board claims as his prerogative. The only way to
determine what must be done is to look at the people who need to do it.   I
agree with the second point: that people don't know what is good business
practice. What you should do is ask them the question, "What are you
doing?", not, what data you need, or how do you fit into the enterprise,
but what are you doing, what decisions do you have to make? You then use
that information to formulate an external schema, not a conceptual schema.

YORMARK: I think there might be a misconception on your part as to the role
of the enterprise administrator.   In fact, we were realistic enough to
understand that the enterprise administrator was not, and did not have to
be, responsible for 10,000 data elements. The role of the enterprise
administrator in describing and defining the conceptual schema is in the
context of all the applications administrators for the various
applications. I strenuously disagree with your point that in order to
provide a conceptual schema that one must know the views of the data in
certain applications. The external schema is a view specific to an
application class, and a view of data is not, in fact, the entities of
interest to that application. The entities of interest are defined by the
applications administrator along with line managers and the enterprise
administrator. Were you aware, in reading the ANSI/SPARC Report, that the
enterprise administrator worked with the applications administrators in
defining the conceptual schema?

JEFFERSON: I was misled, I think, because one of the pictures showed data
flowing from the conceptual schema to the application administrator, but

not backward.

YORMARK: No, it's a double arrow. [see MAIRET, below]

PRATT: The question is whether it is valid to induce a conceptual schema. Let me give you an example. I'm in the manufacturing business. As soon as I say that, you can immediately come to a number of conclusions about my data processing organizations and the kinds of business functions that we support. I would like to define all those processes which are shared by all those business functions. If I define my system from a conceptual level I can immediately deduce that certain business processes will share certain business functions, and capture them at a conceptual level.

JEFFERSON: The conceptual schema is of tremendous value once it has been produced. I'm not claiming there is any reason why it should not exist. I'm merely suggesting a different way of producing it in the first place. It represents information of tremendous value about how the enterprise works. It represents the commonality among the different external schemas. It's necessary to develop the internal schema, it's necessary to make orderly modifications of the external schemas.

JARDINE: This whole argument was discussed some three hundred years ago. I think your view of the construction of a conceptual schema was identified by the philosopher John Locke, whose basic concept was that consensus constitutes truth, and that there exists a community of people among whom consensus is conceivable. This is widely used today, and is the philosophical basis of the Delphi method. There are a number of situations where problems are relatively ill-formulated, or where there is indeed no well-defined discipline, where such a technique is extremely useful. It suffers from a couple of fundamental problems. Firstly, there doesn't appear to be any well-defined mechanism within the philosophy of determining what constitutes relevance of the perception of reality. Secondly, it doesn't include, as far as I know, any mechanism of resolving a conflict. There are two areas where one might have conflict. One is a genuine lack of agreement, and that happens very often. Committees very often end up not agreeing. I believe that happened even in the SPARC Study Group. The other is that if one attempts to generate a model of reality by a consensual process, that there is no guarantee that one will have a mathematically consistent perception. It seems to me we are dealing here with a field that at least ought to be subject to the normal rules of mathematics. Any schema definitions and algorithms must have at least some rational basis in commonly accepted mathematical principles. There is another philosophy, of course, that forms the basis of the whole scientific method, the Liebnitzian philosophy, which assumes there is some innate a priori knowledge by which one could interpret one's perception. By analogy, there is an innate a priori knowledge of the realtionships among the entities in the enterprise that is not represented by, or perceivable from, the union of all the external schemata.

JEFFFERSON: I believe that your philosophy goes a great deal farther back. Your belief in the innate existence of a priori truths goes back to Plato. Let's look at the argument, and then start from the idea whether or not consensus should constitute truth. Clearly, consensus does not constitute truth. Something is not true because we all say it is, or a majority says it is. But, as far as our operational ability to do things is concerned, in a pragmatic sense, then consensus is generally our best bet. It comes closest to the truth. The real difficulty with running things by consensus

is this possibility of conflict which is difficult to resolve. The reason
why you do not have conflict if you do not have truth by consensus, is
because you have only one point of view presented. If that point of view
is incorrect, then no one knows. If someone formulates a conceptual schema
which is very oriented to a certain application area or a certain way of
doing things, then, not only will people suffer because they'll be working
with something that is not really tuned to their needs, but they won't even
know that they are suffering, because they have no basis for comparison.
So I would say that your problem of resolving conflict is basic to the
human inability to know everything, to be able to comprehend all of the
facts. To allow for variety, for change, we must have a mechanism for
resolving conflict.   It's inevitable in the nature of human interaction.
Finally, on the idea of whether there is a mathematical basis for doing
this, I think that you are reading something into my remarks, something
which I had not intended to be in them. I am not saying you can take the
external schemas and turn them over to somebody who understands very little
about any of them and expect a conceptual schema to come out. The best you
can do, probably, is to use the external schemas as guidelines or as means
for measuring the conceptual schema, so that as you generate different
conceptual schemas, you compare them against the various external schemas,
and you can determine then whether you are making progress or not. It's a
matter of a standard for comparison, which I think is a rather important
consideration. It goes back to the idea of conflict resolution.

MAIRET: When Bea Yormark was talking about the interactions between the
enterprise administrator and the applications administrator, she was
referring to the human-to-human communications. Then there was a reference
made to my diagram which showed a one direction arrow. I did not portray
any of the human-to-human communication paths in my diagram. I think the
reference was to the arrow between the conceptual schema processor to the
individual which indicates that he's retrieving information.   Obviously,
the enterprise administrator cannot do his job in a vacuum, but I did not
have any arrows that related to Bea Yormark's comments on my diagram.
Another observation is that the conceptual schema is not just for defining
data, it is also a very important control point for defining integrity
constraints and security provisions which I do not believe can be factored
out of what one application wants to view, and how it wants to treat the
data.

JEFFERSON: Let me apologize. My purpose was not really to criticize the
report.   In fact, I went to great pains to say that there were many things
in it which I admired, so I am quite relieved, really, to find out that
there is communication between the various administrators. That's the sort
of thing which I am advocating.

SENKO: Each side here is exaggerating their points a little bit. Nobody is
a pure synthesist and nobody is a pure analyst. We're usually half-way
between, and very frequently, to make a point, one tends to sharpen things
much more than one really believes. Neither the external schema nor the
conceptual schema is first. Obviously, no one decides on a conceptual
schema if he doesn't know what's going on in the corporation. Someone has
to tell them: how formally is not quite clear. You might decide that it's
just an informal discussion, you might make up a very formal external
schema. Difficulties in that situation cannot be resolved by mathematics,
because the difficulties have to do with very fuzzy things. They are
problems of classification, and mathematics, in spite of what everybody
tells you, never helped very much in classification. In effect, neither

the external schema or the conceptual schema dominates or is first.

JARDINE: The conceptual schema is a hypothesis about the behaviour of the enterprise in some sense. An external schema, together with its processing programs, is a piece of experimental evidence about the behaviour of the enterprise. Under those conditions, we can apply the normal techniques of the scientific method, as Mike Senko has just suggested, whereby the conceptual schema, that is, the hypothesis, will be modified in the light of the experimental evidence. We will also find, because the essence of the scientific method is not raw analysis of data, but the ability to predict, that one can then test the adequacy of the hypothesis in the conceptual schema against many remaining pieces of experimental evidence in the external schemata. To the extent that it predicts those, you're fine, and in the case where it does not predict, one is faced with the usual problem that either one has a bad theory, or one has a bad point of experimental evidence. We're going to find both. There are some external schemata which are irrelevant to the behaviour of the enterprise, as witnessed by the fact that most of the output produced by computers is never looked at by anybody.

JEFFERSON: I like all your points - especially the last one, and I think it is a very good analogy that you draw between the scientific method, and what we're trying to do. The question which arises, though, is at what stage is our science at present? Is it at the place where we're doing trial and error experimentation, or is it in a middle ground where we're doing a dance monitored by hypothesis, testing, refining, and so on, or are we farther along where we can really have a predictive ability. I think that in many cases we're still at the beginning where we're thrashing around: a lot more experimentation than theory.

COLLINS: With reference to the enterprise administrator, we're concerned not so much with his qualifications as his legitimacy. In other words, he serves a great portion of his function merely by existing as a single individual or a single point of view, doing his best to bind together what would otherwise be multiple points of view. If I'm permitted an historical parallel, this is what happened in England when kings disposed of claimants to their throne. This wasn't just an effort to protect themselves; they were fulfilling their social function. Part of the function of the King in England, was that there only be one King, because when there were multiple kings, everyone else suffered. Part of the function of the enterprise administrator is that there be one enterprise administrator.

JEFFERSON: I like your analogy to the King of England. I think another analogy is to honey bees. There the queen bee stings to death all her rivals. Now honey bees are noted for two things. One is that they have existed for a very long time; they are an extremely viable form of life. The other is that they are extremely stable - they don't have any change. That society has not changed for hundreds of millions of years. I don't think we can afford a system in which there is so much stability that we cannot change for hundreds of millions of dollars.

COMPTON: I'd like to direct a question to Bea Yormark. If the enterprise administrator develops his conceptual schema on the basis of the applications administrator's views, in what sense is the conceptual schema as stable as the enterprise as opposed to being as stable as the types and numbers of external schemas. Each time a new applications administrator comes in with his new needs and requirements, the conceptual schema may

have to be modified. The conceptual schema can be stable with respect to
minor changes, but I don't see how it can really be as stable as the
enterprise itself.

YORMARK: First of all, an applications administrator doesn't decide there's
a new application to be done. The enterprise determines whether or not a
new application area is needed which would result in a new applications
administrator being appointed.   In most cases, enterprises augment their
methods of operating. If an enterprise undergoes severe changes in the way
it operates, then certainly the conceptual schema would change to represent
the new views of the enterprise's goals. In most instances, an enterprise
augments its method of doing business, in which case this should not
severely impact other application areas.

JEFFERSON: Regardless of what sort of formalism or design system we have,
if we're not able to tell what applicatiion areas are affected by change in
another application area, then we're not doing our job properly.   The
important thing about these schemas is to tell very precisely what things
are affected by what other things.

COMBA: All the speakers stopped short of talking about the divine rights of
enterprise administrators.   I detect a very strong bias for a very
centralized data base administration, and we always talk of the conceptual
schema as though it were one. Would you comment on the distributed data
base, where there are really many enterprise administrators for example, at
the divisional level of a large company, and at the top there's a central
standard setting and co-ordination function.

JEFFERSON: I think it's an extremely important issue, and one that will
become more important in the future as we will have a great deal more
distributed processes. I would guess that it is going to make the role of
the enterprise administrator considerably more difficult.

STEEL: Speaking for the Study Group.   One of the intentions of the
conceptual schema is to be a central control point, to maintain consistency
across the various external schemas. Let me point out that the Study
Group's view of the conceptual schema is a model of the enterprise, a
description of the business functions, not a description of the data
processing.   It is not intended to be simply a union of the external
schemas.

MOERKE: I'd like to cite some experiences having directly to do with the
idea of taking a business function conceptual schema point of view, and
then implementing that in a decentralized situation. Experiences to date
are that this works very well as long as there is sufficient communication
and consensus among the participating decentralized units that we have, in
fact, correctly described a business function. The experience is that the
conceptual schema is the best way to reach that consensus. The conceptual
schema is very high level. We're a manufacturing firm, and our conceptual
schema starts by breaking down engineering and manufacturing, and financial
and accounting into two major categories. Our conceptual schema, as it
stands right now, is only four levels deep. At this point, we back up a
level and construct external schemas for each of the organizational units.
These don't describe a different business function, merely a different
materialization of a business function.   The interesting thing is that
we're able to define the same computer programs to serve those various
functions, and that's very cost-effective.

DELPORT: We have two approaches to the conceptual schema, because in a conceptual schema you have to consider not only data and relations among data, but also the procedures that operate on this data. The first approach, a more or less static approach, starts with an analysis of the activities in the university. Then we consider the objectives of the university, and from the objectives we define activities, from the activities, data, from data , another activity, and so on. Thus we construct our information flows. Now these activities [from the two approaches] must be the same. When we compare them, we have conflicts, and we have solutions and decisions. When we wish to implement procedures, we take a partial view of the conceptual data, and that's our external schema.

JEFFERSON: I would suspect that the reason this approach works, is firstly, the size that you're dealing with is reasonably limited, and secondly, it is probably reasonably homogeneous, so that you're really working with one application area.

DELPORT: It's a university of 17,000 students with 5,000 faculty and staff, 5,000 courses, and 1,200 buildings.

JEFFERSON: That is rather small.

END-USER INTERFACES FOR DATA BASE MANAGEMENT SYSTEMS

A.G. Dale   E.I. Lowenthal
Department of Computer Sciences   MRI Systems Corporation
The University of Texas at Austin   Austin, Texas

In this paper we focus on end-user interfaces to data base management systems (DBMS) that support a centralized conceptual schema, internal schema, and explicit user-oriented external schemas. These include systems constructed on the principles of the CODASYL DBTG proposals [1] or the ANSI/X3/SPARC Interim Report [2].

There are two aspects to an end-user interface in such systems: (1) the schema interface and (2) the data manipulation language (DML) processing interface. The schema interface conditions the user's perceptions (views) of the data base allowed by the system. The DML processing interface conditions the operations that can be invoked by the user on the data base, given the view of the data in his external schema. We shall consider problems involved in the design and manipulation of both types of interface.

End-User Categorization

The characteristics of a user interface must clearly reflect the characteristics of the end-user, so that it can provide an environment for interaction with the DBMS responsive to the user's established style of operation when engaged in information processing tasks. Styles of operation may be conditioned by established methods of information processing in a non-DBMS context, or by a variety of cultural and psychological influences in cases where the information processing activity is not a clearly identified and structured activity in some well- bounded work situation. In either case, the task of the system designer, at least in the near future, is to construct interfaces that provide the end-user with an acceptable transition from conventional methods of information processing to interaction within the discipline of a DBMS. The design must provide interaction contexts that utilize constructs with which the user is already familiar.

In this paper we exclude data processing professionals from the set of end-users of a DBMS. That is, we exclude professionals acting in the capacity of data base administrators, or application programmers accessing the system through host-language interfaces or through a system DDL and DML.

With respect to the non-data processing user, there are several categorizations that have been noted in the literature:

1. The non-data processing professional. The Data Base User Language Project of GUIDE [3] has characterized this type of user as follows:
   * His job may be associated with any job discipline; for example he may be an engineer, lawyer, nurse, clerk, scientist, secretary or manager.
   * He may work in any functional area within the company.
   * His job will involve problems or requirements which necessitate use of a data base.

* He may be at any level of the organization.
* His use of the computer, and of the User Language, will probably be
  an incidental part of his job.
* His requirements will vary from the simple to the very complex.
* He will not be required to know any other language.

This characterization is consistent with the one adopted by the CODASYL
End User Facility Task Group. The EUFTG in its June 1975 Progress Report
[4], defines for its purposes an end-user as a person
...engaged in a job that directs, or supports the direction of, one or
more of the activities which are necessary to operate any organization
that can perform useful work. Every end user is engaged in one or more
of the following activities:
(1) Planning...
(2) Direction...
(3) Execution...
(4) Monitoring...
(5) Evaluation...

Our End User is assumed competent in his job, without benefit of an
EUF. He may have a specialty occupation requiring extensive education or
training. We assume that his specialty is not data processing or related
specialties. An end user proficient in using this EUF is not expected to
become proficient in programming or any other data processing
specialty...
The End User has an established need to collect and manipulate data
that are directly related to his job requirements and experience. In
addition, the End User will make use of relationships that exist among
items of data...
Finally, we expect that the End User must be willing to understand that
his view of data is defined and that there is a finite set of operations
that he may invoke.
Within this general cateory of non-data processing professional users
we may distinguish two major subclasses:
1.1 Transaction-oriented user. This user repetitively invokes a limited
     number of pre-defined specialized processes with respect to a
     bounded set of data. A special case of the transaction-oriented
     user is the parametric user, whose in- put interaction is confined
     to supplying values in variable slots of a pre-defined input frame,
     either to initiate a process or to input data to the system.
1.2 Ad-hoc user, whose information processing activity cannot be pre-
     defined (i.e., is typically self-defined at the time of interaction
     with the system), and whose view of the data base may be less
     constrained than that of a transaction- oriented user.

2.   The casual user. A second major category of end-users comprises the
     casual user. We accept Codd's characterization, which he states as
     follows [5]:
       A casual user is one whose interactions with the system are
       irregular in time and not motivvated by his job or social role.
       Such à user cannot be expected to be knowledgeable about
       computers, programming, logic, or relations.

Although Codd has argued [6] that future growth in the casual user
population can be expected to exceed that for all other types of end-users
by a large factor, his speculative timetable for this development envisages
major impact after the mid-1980's. This reflects expectations regarding

the time-frame for development of suitable interface hardware, data bases of interest to the casual user, and problems of software interface design and development. Thus, although we consider that attempts to construct interfaces for the casual user, such as Codd´s Rendezvous system [5], or Waltz´s natural language front-end using prestored request networks [7] are of major potential interest, it is our view that solutions to the interface problems for the casual user do not have the immediacy of the requirements for the design and implementation of interfaces for the non-data processing professional end-user. For the remainder of this paper we therefore confine our attention to interfaces designed to support ad hoc user interactions with a DBMS.

Interface Design - General Considerations

   There is general agreement on the basic principles that must guide the design and implementation of interfaces for the processional end-user who is not a data-processing specialist:
   1. The interface should support interactive use off the system, partly because a large proportion of such users will be required, by the nature of their job activities, to have immediate access to the DBMS, and partly because user-system dialog may be a necessary condition for specifying system operations.
   2. The user language(s) must be simple, easy to use, and easy to comprehend (GUIDE Requirements). It should be adaptable (at least at the lexical level) to user terminology.
   3. The user language(s) must be sufficiently powerful to satisfy the end-user´s requirements.
   4. The interface must provide the end-user with data independence on two levels: Logical data independence (data structure independence) in the sense that the user is insulated from the need to know details of the logical structure of the data base as embodied in the conceptual schema, and thus is free to view the data within a subjectively acceptable conceptual framework. A consequence of this requirement, apart from the necessity to support multiple specialized views, is that these views should continue to be semantically valid (as a reference frame for user-initiated operations) under conditions where the conceptual schema may be reorganized.
      Physical data independence (storage structure independence) in the sense that the user is insulated from the need to know details of the physical organization of the data base, including data location and access paths. A consequence of this requirements is that changes in physical organization of the data base should be transparent to the user, and that user-defined processes should continue to execute successfully on the transformed physical structure without modifications at the user interface level.

   The problem of achieving logical data independence is the more difficult because, in general, it is not possible to bound or predict the manner in which the conceptual schema might change. With respect to physical data independence, however, the necessary and sufficient condition for independence is that the DML not refer to storage structure, but to the conceptual schema or its derived external schemas. If the external and internal schemas are separated, (as contemplated in the ANSI/X3/SPARC report), the necessary system mappings are defined, and a finite but reasonably flexible set of alternative internal schemas is allowed, then complete physical data independence can be achieved. The problem of physical data independence is further bounded by the fact that internal schema modification is constrained by the configuration of the associated conceptual schema.

Data independence is thus related to (a) the characteristics of the DML, (b) the schema architecture of the DBMS -- that is the separation of internal, conceptual, and external schemas, and (c) the existence of appropriate system mappings that permit internal and conceptual schema modifications to occur without disturbing existing external schemas or existing operations defined on the external schemas via the DML.

While these three factors are highly interrelated it is convenient. to consider them in more detail by viewing the end- user interface as comprising:

1. A schema interface, comprising a DDL, and system mappings between various schema levels.
2. A processing interface, comprising a DML and additional mappings supporting data independence.

We shall consider data independence requirements and some proposed solutions in this framework in the remainder of the paper.

The schema interface

1. End-user DDL design considerations

The preceding characterizations of the professional end-user who is not a data processing expert do not provide a framework that is operationally useful for the design of a schema interface. We take the view that was expressed by several participants at the 1973 SHARE DBMS Working Conference [8] that it is necessary to consider the development of specialized interfaces for more precisely defined classes of users.

The most comprehensive current effort of which we are aware is being undertaken by the CODASYL End User Facility Task Group. The following comments are based on the June 1975 Progress Report of the Group [4], which is charged with describing and defining an end-user facility for a "complex structured data base." So far, the EUFTG has emphasized work on a relevant data description facility, and not on a DML.

The group has adopted the position that an important class of end-users comprises users accustomed to conceptualizing and perceiving data in the framework of two dimensional forms, and that a DBMS must therefore have, as one of its interfaces, a forms-oriented view of the data base and a forms-structured framework for defining operations on the data.

Three types of form are postulated:

Perception form, in which data structure and relationships are presented to the end-user. The maximum complexity of a perception form (as for other types of form) is a simple hierarchy, following the observation that this is a widely understood and accepted basis for organizing data in two dimensional forms. Construction of a perception form requires a mapping from the conceptual schema. Thus, perception forms are defined by the data base administrator, not the end-user, because the DBA is in charge of the conceptual schema and the end-user is not expected or required to know about the conceptual schema.

User form, which is mappable from the perception form. Since user forms are derived from perception forms, their construction does not require knowledge of the data base structure (conceptual schema). Therefore, they may be defined either by the DBA or the end-user.

Worksheet is a scratchpad form, defined by the end-user, as a framework in which to extract data from user-form instances and as an environment within which operations on the data can be defined.
It is important to note two implications of this external schema architecture.
1. There can be a number of forms of each type for each user or for different users (i.e., multiple user views can exist).
2. It is intended that user views may differ significantly from the conceptual schema -- that is the user should not be restricted to views that are merely simple subsets of the conceptual schema.

The EUFTG schema interface is shown in the following figure.

Figure 1

EUFTG Schema Interface

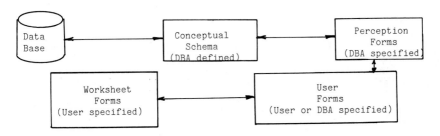

(Adapted from EUFTG June 1975 Report)

Note that this multi-layered interface requires several schema mappings. These mappings must support the definition of external schema structures that differ from those embodied in the conceptual schema (i.e., support multiple user views). This is one aspect of logical data independence. The mappings must also define the set of derived external schemas that can continue to be used as a frame of reference by the end-user even though the conceptual schema is modified. This is the second aspect of logical data independence.

The data constructs available to a user at the schema inter-face are shown
in Figure 2.

Figure 2

EUFTG Schema Constructs

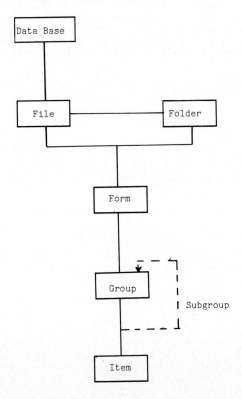

Source: EUFTG June 1975 Report

Item is a named data element, which exists explicitly in the data base or
may be derived from other item values.
Groups consists of one or more groups (i.e., subgroups) and/or items
appearing on a form.
Form consists of one or more groups and/or items.
Folder consists of instances of one or more form types.
File consists of instances of either a form or a folder of one type only.

These constructs present the user with a hierarchical view of data at the schema interface. The internal structure of a form, as mentioned previously, is restricted to a hierarchy. The interface also permits aggregating data into groups and form instances into folders or files. However, it should be stressed that the conceptual schema (transparent to the end-user) need not be a simple hierarchy. In fact, the EUFTG assumes that the data base could be of the DBTG type for which the conceptual schema may be a network.

We also note in passing that the restrictions of end-user views to hierarchies embedded in a forms context is very similar to the constructs used in the CONVERT system [10], an experimental facility designed for the manipulation of hierarchical structures.

In summary, we believe that the EUFTG work is representative of the type of effort that, at the present stage of DBMS technology, is a high-priority activity. At this juncture it is essential to place emphasis on the design of specialized schema (and DML) interfaces that match the needs of operationally defined classes of end-users.

The EUFTG has adopted an operationally useful definition of a particular class of end-user. But clearly there are other identifiable classes of end-user for which appropriate interfaces need to be built. For example, there is a large class of end-users whose primary concern with a DBMS will be as an environment for document generation. If one examines a stand-alone document production system such as XOFF for example [11], it is evident that both the schema and DML interfaces to a generalized DBMS supporting this class of user would be radically different from the EUFTG interface design.

2. The schema interface and data independence

The EUFTG has noted that among the technical areas requiring work to support the implementation of the proposed external schema architecture is definition of permissible mappings that will be necessary to relate the various objects of the EUF within themselves and to the conceptual schema. The EUFTG has not yet reached the point of defining the mappings. However, an example of recent relevant work is contained in two papers by Dale and Dale [12, 13]. This work is relevant for considering 1) mappings between perception forms, user forms, and worksheet forms, where the maximum structural complexity is a simple hierarchy; and 2) mappings to/from the conceptual schema if it is restricted to a hierarchy.

In [12] transformation rules for permissible rearrangements of hierarchically structured schemas at the inter-record relatiionship level are identified, such that DML statements defined against an initial conceptual schema will continue to execute successfully against a data base restructured to conform to a rearranged conceptual schema.

In [13] the question of interaction between schemas is investigated in the following framework: Given a hierarchically structured conceptual schema for a data base, what derived external schemas are permissible such that DML statements defined with respect to an external schema will produce expected results?

It is shown that three classes of consistent schemas can be derived from a given hierarchical schema. These are termed subschemas, ancestor schemas, and descendant schemas.

A hierarchical schema consists of a set of record types. A given record type, Ri, is connected to ancestor record types and descendant record types.

A schema S2 is a subschema of a hierarchical schema S1 if:
1. The set of record types in S2 is a proper subset of the set of record

types in S1, i.e., there are fewer record types in S2 than in S1 and
every record type Ri in S2 is also in S1.
2. For every record type Ri in S2:
    a. Every record type that is an ancestor of Ri in S2 is either an
       ancestor or a descendant of Ri in S1.
    b. Every record type that is a descendant of Ri in S2 is either an
       ancestor or a descendant of Riin S1.
For example, suppose we have the following record type hierarchy in a
schema S1:

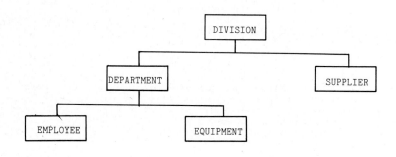

Subschemas of this schema might be:

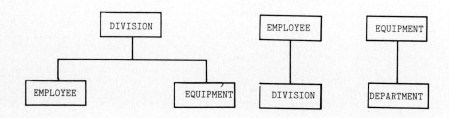

An ancestor schema S3 of a hierarchical schema S1 is a schema such that:
1. S3 is the same set of record types as S1.
2. For every record type Ri in S3 the same conditions regarding ancestor
    and descendant record types holds as in the definition of a subschema

given above. Note that this condition allows the set of ancestor and
descendant record types of Ri in S3 to be a proper subset of the set
of ancestors and descendant record types of Ri in S1.
Some example ancestor schemas of S1 would be:

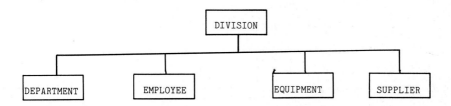

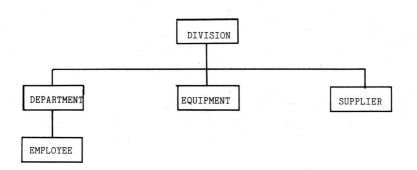

A descendant schema S4 of a hierarchical schema S1 is a schema such that:
1. S4 contains the same set of record types as S1.
2. For every record type Ri in S1,
    a. Every record type that is an ancestor of Ri in S1 is either an
       ancestor or a descendant in S4.
    b. Every record type that is a descendant of Ri in S1 is either an
       ancestor or a descendant in S4.
Note that the set of ancestor and descendant record types related to Ri
in S1 may be a proper subset of the set of ancestor and descendant record
types related to Ri in S4.
Some example descendant schemas of S1 would be:

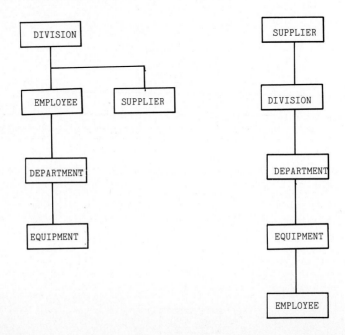

These are not useful examples of the pragmatic value of descendant
schemas (it is unlikely that anyone would want to relate equipment and
employees for example). However, it might be useful to derive a subschema
from the second example:

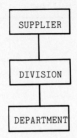

It is shown in [13] that DML processes definable on derived schemas satisfying these transformation rules can be directly executed on a data base corresponding to the S1 schema (termed the reference schema) or on a definable run-time transformation of the data base. In the context of the EUFTG end-user interface architecture this work allows a precise statement of the limits of logical data independence if the conceptual schema or perception forms comprise a hierarchy. It defines what derived external schemas (user forms) are permissible so that DML statements framed in the context of an external schema will produce expected results when executed against the data base.

The Processing Interface

Any thorough discussion of what constitutes the "best" data manipulation language for the class of user under consideration would have to encompass several wide-ranging aspects of system design. Other studies have concentrated primarily on the desirable syntactic and mechanical facets of the user language and the system which processes this language [3,5,7,9,14]. They emphasize "human engineering" -- familiarity of vocabulary, simplicity of grammar (or request format), effective system/user interaction and so forth. We have chosen to focus on certain fundamental semantic aspects of the user interface, such as the information content or meaning implicit in a user request as contrasted with the information that must be explicitly known to and supplied by the user. As an essential consequence of this decision it has been necessary to examine both parts of the user interface. The meaning of a request stated in the DML depends as much upon the data context (i.e., external schema) as it does upon the arrangement of symbols in the request itself.

The main conclusion of this section is that the simpler the underlying external data model, approaching a linear file at the extreme, the more likely is it that a DML defined over such a model will exhibit certain very desirable properties. One implication of this conclusion is that whatever may be viewed as the requirements for a conceptual schema, the external schema should not be standardized along the lines of any one model. Rather the intrinsic tradeoffs associated with each approach should be recognized by proposing a system that effectively offers each user the type of external schema (and DML) that best suits his individual needs.

1. High Level Data Manipulation Languages

It is clearly understood that an exceptionally high level DML is required for the end-user. That is to say, the language should be more declarative than procedural, permitting the user to state what he wants in problem-oriented terms rather than how results are to be obtained. The user language should avoid imposing programmer techniques upon the end user and whenever possible such techniques should be implicit in the user's request. [3] The motivation for stressing high level languages can be viewed as applying established software engineering principles to the case of user language "programming". Requests framed in a higher level DML are easier to create, understand, and modify than requests composed in a lower level DML; they are also more concise because of the power of individual statements. There are additional advantages for the end-user which are not generally considered in the case of the application programmer. The user sitting at a terminal wants to state his problem using the fewest number of typed characters, so it is important that each term (verb, operator, etc.) mean as much as possible. Furthermore, in an interactive environment it is practically essential that typical programming techniques such as branching and looping be avoided. Each statement should be self-contained, with alllooping, testing and branching accomplished by the DBMS. In particular it is evident that the recpord search and selection function should be generalized in any worthwhile use level DML. This need is recognized in various requirements statements [3,9]. Indeed most query systems do incorporate some facility for expressing "predicates" composed of relational conditions and logical connectors, for example, "Produce a count of employees who are in the personnel department and make over $10000.00 or have been with the company at least six years and...". If it is desirable to permit the applications programmer to manipulate sets of records in this fashion [6], then it is crucial in the case of the end-user. Simply working with one record at a time (navigation) is not adequate.

There are several other types of commonly used functions that are frequently generalized, such as brief statements for producing entire reports, producing tables or sorting sets of records. One objection that is often levied against generalizing procedures is that it ususally results in inefficiency. The typical analogy is made with a comparison between FORTRAN and assembly language. A procedure expressed in the higher level language will usually result in less efficient code than one which is semantically equivalent but produced by a skilled assembly language programmer. The analogy does not precisely hold because the vital resource with respect to data base management is more often response time rather than central processor time. In fact, a DBMS which supports a higher level DML has much more opportunity for I/O optimization than other- wise, since the system can predict ahead off time what disk activity is required. For example, if an entire conditional expression is presented to the DBMS at once, then the system cna rearrange theindividual conditions to minimize the number of records that need to be tested. Furthermore, in an interactive environment the use of a high level DML will result in fewer messages sent to the computer from the terminal, less intermediate data sent back to the terminal, less swapping activity and hence more acceptable response times.

The potential disadvantage of a high level DML is not inefficiency but inflexibility. The user has les control over the details of execution since the DBMS is essentially making standard decisions on his behalf. One solution to this problem is to provide multiple languages, or successively lower levels of language, each of which is more complex than the higher level facility but offering the sophisticated user more precise control over execution. The user who is satisfied with a certain level need not learn the more complex lower level dialects. SYSTEM 2000, for example, provides the user with three alternatives to producing a report from a terminal. The highest level DML permits the specification of a report using a single statement, usually less than 100 characters. At the other extreme is a formal report definition language which requires several statements to produce the same report. However the user has greater control over editing, sorting, selection, page formatting, etc. [15].

2. Ease of Use

Once again we are not concerned with those qualities of simplicity that have to do with the syntax, format, or style of the query process. Considerable progress has been made in this direction. Semantic simplicity is the issue here -- the user should have to supply only as much information as the DBMS needs to interpret his request correctly and unambiguously.

The user should never have to qualify beyond the level required to solve

ambiguities. [3] Now it appears to be the case that if the level of the DML
is held constant, then as the complexity of the underlying external schema
model increases, the necessary complexity off the associated DML also
increases.   That is, the less information there is in the external schema
(in the sense of there being more degrees of freedom in the way the schema
is constructed) the less information is implicit in a given DML statement
type, and therefore the more information must be explicitly provided by the
user.   The "theorum" can be stated in another way.   A given request against
a data base must be accompanied by a certain amount of user supplied
information in order to make sense and have a unique meaning.   Either that
information must be supplied entirely with the DML request,   or
alternatively all or some of it can be embedded in the external schema by
making that schema somewhat more precise than the conceptual schema.   A
simple example will serve to clarify this notion.

Suppose that the conceptual schema is network structured as follows:

CONCEPTUAL SCHEMA

The DIVISION record type includes an item called DIVISION-NAME.   The
OUTSIDE-COMPANY record includes an attribute called COMPANY- NAME. Each
instance of an OUTSIDE-COMPANY record corresponds to a supplier
and/orcustomer of some DIVISION depending upon whether the relationship is
by way of an intervening VENDOR or CUSTOMER record respectively.   These
"linkage records" contain attributes such as SUPPLY-ON-ORDER, EXPECTED-
SHIP-DATE, STATUS, etc.

Consider these two external schemas which are both straightforward subschemas of the conceptual schema:

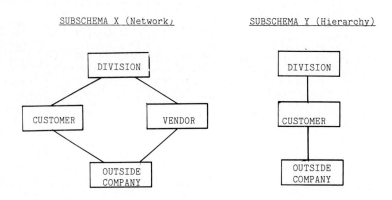

Now consider the following query:
Query 1: DISPLAY COMPANY-NAME FOR DIVISION-NAME = ´MANUFACTURING´ This
query is unambiguous in the context of the hierarchical sub- schema Y. It
can reasonably be interpreted to mean "produce a list of company names from
OUTSIDE-COMPANY occurrences which are linked to CUSTOMER records that are
linked to any DIVISION record containing "manufacturing". The query is
ambiguous in the context of the richer subschema X since it is not clear
whether the user is interested in the manufacturing division´s customers,
vendors or both. The problem could be resolved in a number of ways, all of
which require the user to introduce information sufficient to qualify which
path is desired. Using the RENDEZVOUS approach [55], the DBMS would enter
into a "clarification dialogue" perhaps asking the user to specify whether
he is interested in the VENDOR relation or the CUSTOMER relation. Or
perhaps the DML rules would preclude ambiguity from the outset by requiring
precision in any query.

Query 2: DISPLAY COMPANY-NAME OF OUTSIDE-COMPANY IN CUSTOMER AND CUSTOMER
IN DIVISION FOR DIVISION-NAME = ´MANUFACTURING´ Query 2 is rather complex
but unambiguous with respect to subschema X. It produces the same result
as query 1 on subschema Y. Thus the user whose data context is a network
rather than a hierarchy must be more aware of the external view and will
more frequently have to use that knowledge in constructing meaningful
queries. This is true whether the vehicle is a precise query language or a
more "friendly" clarification dialogue.

There is a corollary to the rule-of-thumb governing the tradeoff between
external schema richness and the semantic simplicity of the associated DML.
As the level of the DML increases and the complexity of the external schema
decreases, the higher is the probability that a given statement expressed
in the DML need not include names of record types and relations between

record types, but can refer exclusively to names of elementary items. This is certainly the case when the external schema is restricted to a single record type; there would be no reason to explicitly refer to this record type by name since there is no alternative, and there are simply no relations to refer to. A hierarchical schema is more complex but even here the need toinclude in DML statements the names of schema objects other than items would turn out to be very infrequent on a statistical basis. Query 1 above, which refers only to item names, is well formulated and unambiguous with respect to the hierarchical external schema but not the network external schema. Hierarchies and networks can be considered as two points on a continuum of possible external schema models. One can postulate models more complex than hierarchies but not as rich as networks for which Query 1 would continue to be unambiguous. The point is simply that there is a very good argument for offering a wide spectrum of external schema models and associated DML levels. Those users who could live within the constraints of a hierarchical model would enjoy the two-fold benefit of a simple view of his data and a semantically simply DML which necessitates only that items names be known, understood and referred to. Note, by the way, that this possibility can be exploited only if item names are required by the external schema DDL to be unique across the entire schema -- not just within record type.

3. Logical Data Independence

Data independence is rarely considered in discussion of data base interfaces for end-users. This is sopresumably because such users are not thought of as writing programs which must be protected from modifications to the conceptual schema. In fact many users do write "programs" in the user language, particularly when the DBMS allows a frequently used sequence of DML statements to be catalogued as a single statement, as recommended by Guide [3]. Other users develop habits and expectations that might suddenly become invalid in the face of schema evolution. It is not clear that these users require less protection from change than programs written by the technical staff.

With respect to logical data independence it has already been established that the schema interface participates in terms of the separation of the external schema and conceptual schema and the types of schema mappings that are supported. The DML also plays a vital role that tends to be overlooked. By not embedding references to a schema object within a DML statement, the meaning of this statement can be preserved even if the schema object is modified or deleted. In particular, if a DML statement refers only to item names, then it is possible to modify record relationships and to move items among record types without disturbing the meaning of the statement. For instance, observe that Query 1 is not sensitive to the actual relationship between COMPANY-NAME and DIVISION-NAME. For purposes of this query it is immaterial whether these two items are defined for the same record type or whether they are separated by six levels of record types. This is evidently not the case with Query 2. This query would hardly make sense if, say, the OUTSIDE-COMPANY record type were eliminated and all its items (including COMPANY- NAME) were moved into the CUSTOMER to DIVISION) would have to be simulated somehow. Thus the benefit of adopting the simplest possible user view is not only a simpler DML but therefore one which exhibits a greater degree of data independence.

Conclusion

The treatment of semantics has admittedly been informal and somewhat

intuitive, but we hope that this does not detract from the usefulness of the conclusions which are summarized here.
1. The Schema Interface
    Regardless of what model is used for the conceptual schema, the external schemas supported by the DBMS should comprise a range of models with the simplest being the hierarchy, if not the single record schema. If a user or a class of users requires a network external schema, then this should be made available to them. However there are strong incentives for using a hierarchy if it can be accommodated.
    . A hierarchy -- particularly one disguised as a form -- is easy to understand. It may be the most complex structure many users will feel comfortable with.
    . The schema mapping problem for hierarchies has been solved for most cases. [12]
    . A DML can be devised for a hierarchy which offers the greatest promise for simplicity and logical data independence.

2. The Processing Interface
    Again there should be not one DML but a range of compatible dialects. The lowest level DML would provide the user with greatest degree of control. However, the user would be motivated to employ the highest level DML for traditional reasons and because such a language best realizes the potential for simplicity and data independence in the framework of the hierarchical schema.

REFERENCES

1. CODASYL, Data Base Task Group Report, April 1971.
2. ANSI/X3/SPARC, Study Group on Data Base Management Systems, Interim Report, 75-02-08.
3. GUIDE International Corporation, Requirements for a User Language,(Revised), 19 August 1974.
4. CODASYL, A Progress Report on the Activities of the CODASYL End User Facility Task Group, June 1975.
5. E.F. Codd, Seven Steps to Rendezvous with the Casual User, IBM Research Report RJ 1333, January 17, 1974.
6. E.F. Codd and C.J. Date, Interactive Support for Non- Programmers: The Relational and Network Approaches, IBM Research Report RJ 1400, June 6, 1974.
7. D. Waltz, Natural Language Access to a Large Data Base: an Engineering Approach, in Advance Papers of the Fourth International Joint Conference on Artificial Intelligence, Tbilisi, September 1975.
8. Ed. Donald A. Jardine, Data Base Management Systems, North- Holland Publishing Company, 1974.
9. CODASYL End User Facility Task Group, Revised Results of Task 5 Perception Objects DDL, 20 February 1976.
10. Nan C. Shu, Barron C. Housel and Vincent Y. Lum, CONVERT: A High Level Translation Definition Language for Data Conversion, CACM, Vol. 18, No. 10, October 1975.
11. J. Newcomer, XOFF: A System for Generation of Documents, Carnegie Mellon University, 6 September 1974.
12. A.G. Dale and N.B. Dale, Schema and Occurrence Structure Transformations in Hierarchical Systems, Proc. ACM SIGMOD International Conference on Management of Data, June 1976.
13. N.B. Dale and A.G. Dale, Main Schema - External Schema Interaction in Hierarchically Organized Data Bases, Department of Computer Sciences,

The University of Texas at Austin, April 1976.
14. M. Zloof, Query By Example, Proceedings of the 1975 National Computer Conference, AFIPS.
15. MRI Systems Corporation, SYSTEM 2000 Reference Manual.

DISCUSSION

SHEEHAN: What you've said today doesn't address the twelve to fifteen items which make a user language more usable; moreover, you've also opened up other problems, one of which is trying to define an external schema for any approach that someone might take through the DML. You appear to be using external schemas to provide a language, which is not meaningful except in a transaction oriented environment. It would take a good applications analyst to figure out each reasonable path that a casual user might take through the data base, and provide a schema for it. When we talk about casual users, we're talking about going right back to the conceptual schema. That is the point at which a casual user could get into the data base without caring whether it was a hierarchy, or a network or a relation, etc.

LOWENTHAL: The real trade-off is the flexibility or richness of the data structure in the external schema versus the simplicity of the data manipulation language. The whole point of the EUFTG is that the user sees an external schema. He sees virtual filing cabinets with folders and tabs on them, and little pieces of paper in them called forms, but he really is thinking in terms of a hierarchical data structure. He doesn't ever have to know that it's a hierarchy. You cannot get by with saying that the end user is not going to know what data is around, or that he has no structure to work with. At least, he must know the items and some structure that binds these items together. The true casual user, in the Codd definition, is not going to be happy with anything less than the full richness of some semantic network. He doesn't know about the forms or anything, he just wants to ask questions. I'm divorcing myself from that problem, because frankly, it gives me a headache. However, someone who is a professional in the organization can find the hierarchy, if it's expressed properly, very familiar and very comfortable. I'm claiming, that for a large number of users, the hierarchy is rich enough.

ROBERTS: I am particularly concerned if this is leading to some kind of. standardization. Standardization implies that we know enough about our activities to be comfortable with doing them the same way for a while. Now is no time to define an end user facility that is very much attuned to an historical transactional approach. I'm even bothered about your definition of the end user. Typically, the end user that we're discussing is bi-modally distributed. One kind is a first line supervisor or junior manager who wants access to data. He knows a lot about the structure, because it is his data. We don't have to worry much about his end user facility because the degree of richness is essentially specified in advance. The other kind is the Codd casual user. Typically, he is not knowledgable about the data structure. He has an assignment to get an answer that's expressed in enterprise terms, such as return on investment on some set of assets. He needs a very rich, very powerful, highly interactive facility that allows him to work through the problem, and allows him to examine the structure selectively and iteratively. You cannot possibly develop a facility that deals with both of those examples in the manner you described.

LOWENTHAL: I'm not trying to adjust to the problems of the casual user.
Definitely, I agree, it's not the solution for him. What we're really
arguing about is whether there is a definable user class, that needs and
would be happy with an end user facility that has, as its basis, the
hierarchical model.

GRIMES: I'm a member of the End User Facility Task Group, and I'd like to
clarify some of the discussion. We are not in any final state, we don't
claim to be, and we have made progress since our last report.   Prior to
pursuing the forms approach, we analyzed different approaches, including
query, query update and a report writing facility.   We have chosen the
forms approach.   We spent much time analyzing who was the target class of
end users. That's outlined in the report and summarized in the paper.   We
feel that the familiarity of the forms and folder concept is a significant
breakthrough. It's dealing with the user's terms as opposed to the data
processing terms.   It is the data base administrator's job, we believe, to
define the perception objects, which include perception forms, and to
define the mapping between those and the data base.   Then the user can map
from these perception objects, which would be a structure familiar to him,
to other forms which he can deal with and operate on.   One of the questions
is whether a hierarchy is appropriate for end users, or is it the approach
for the conceptual model?

LOWENTHAL: I don't believe that the conceptual schema should be limited to
hierarchies. The only advantage of doing that is that it permits automatic
provision of the external conceptual transformer.

MOERKE: It's not clear to me there is sufficient built-in quality control.
I'm not confident that somebody walking up to a terminal is going to
necessarily get the information they thought they were going to get. As a
manager, I'm not sure I would use a terminal myself, even though I can
perhaps do it faster than one of my staff people.   Generally speaking, I
don't need the specific answer that soon, and I would just as soon have
someone else get it, look at it, put their own quality control perspective
on it, and come back to discuss the answer with me. I don't really see the
desirability of taking the professional out of the loop in many of the ad
hoc queries.   Now that doesn't hold for parametric users. In that case,
the problem has been well defined. I will do my own parametric queries, and
I think that's very easy because it's well understood by the user. I cite,
as one more parallel, that even though we might be very confident in our
ability to correctly modify a contract with a client, we still go through
the legal department.

KIRSHENBAUM: The data structure that is the best for any given user to use
is the one with which he is most familiar. In different professions,
different types of users are familiar with different data structures and in
end user query facilities, we need a more pluralistic approach. Any data
structure that's available in a data base management system should be made
available if the user wants it. Obviously there should also be a highly
structured set of defaults that he can fall back on, or use as his entry
set.   The ad hoc user does have bounds to his queries, determined by his
rights to the data, who he is, or whose surrogate he is.   Those bounds
should be taken care of, in my opinion, by the external schema. The ANSI
Study Group discussed, but never explicitly stated in the Study Group
reports, the possibility of nested external schemas, which I think you're

alluding to both in your subschema and your parametric form. The subschema or nested schema is bound to the larger schema which eventually gets bound to the conceptual schema. I think that that's necessary because it provides a mechanism of delegation of data authority as well as bounding the rights of the user.

LOWENTHAL: I quite agree that there will be multiple end user facilities depending upon the particular world in which the end user operates. Perhaps what is really needed is a series of classes of external schemas, ranging let's say, from flat files all the way up to the user view being as complex as the corporate data base. Of course, that is very difficult to implement, but it might be the only acceptable solution for a wide class of applications.

COMBA: I think there is a very serious implication in providing only a hierarchical view. If the user knows only one association between two entity types, the association need not be named. By not naming it, you effectively do not define the semantics. Specifically, by not naming the links, it is very possible to introduce semantic ambiguity, which should be avoided.

THE CODASYL DATA DESCRIPTION LANGUAGE:
STATUS AND ACTIVITIES, APRIL 1976

Frank A. Manola
Information Systems Staff
Naval Research Laboratory

1.0 Introduction

The CODASYL Data Description Language Committee (DDLC), which held its first meeting on November 30, 1971, was instituted to take the work done by the CODASYL Data Base Task Group (DBTG), as reflected in its April 1971 Report [1], as a base and to develop from it the specifications for a host-language independent data description language (the schema DDL). In addition, the DDLC formulated objectives to investigate certain related areas, such as the relationship between the schema DDL (which is used to describe the entire data base) and host-language dependent subschema DDL's (which are used to describe the parts of data bases known to specific application programs). At the time, however, the committee felt that its most immediate purpose was the publication of a DDL specification as soon as possible, and that this was best accomplished by temporarily limiting its activities to clarification and only minor extensions of the schema DDL as specified in the April 1971 DBTG Report. With the publication of the CODASYL Data Description Language Journal of Development, June 1973 [2], this initial phase of the DDLC's activities was concluded. Since the publication of this initial Journal of Development (JOD), there has been great interest, activity, and development in the data base and data description technologies. This activity has been international in scope, and has been performed under the aegis of various institutions including computer societies, user groups, standards organizations, academic institutions, and governmental departments. The CODASYL DDLC has either informally, by the outside activities of individual members, or formally, by establishing relations with other groups and activities, continuously monitored these developments; and various changes have been made to the schema DDL language specifications to reflect the development of data base systems technology. It is the purpose of this paper to describe briefly the current status and activities of the CODASYL DDLC, the current status of the DDLC's language specifications, and future directions for DDLC's work.

Before presenting the basic material of this paper, however, two disclaimers and a warning must be stated. The first disclaimer is that the statements made in this paper are the responsibility of the author, not of the DDLC or CODASYL. The second disclaimer is that only those specifications contained in the June 1973 DDL JOD [2] are CODASYL-approved language specifications. Changes reported here as having been made by the DDLC are changes to the "working" JOD maintained by the DDLC for internal use, but are not yet "official". It is possible that some of the reported changes could be "undone" or otherwise altered prior to the approval and publication of the next official JOD. The warning is that an acquaintance with the June 1973 DDL JOD, or with the April 1971 DBTG Report [1], is necessary in order to fully understand the DDL changes which will be reported here.

2.0 Data Description Language Committee Structure

The CODASYL Data Description Language Committee (DDLC) is a standing committee under the CODASYL organization, and as such, is responsible for the specifications of the DDL in the same way that the Programming Language Committee (PLC) is responsible for the specifications of the COBOL language. The DDLC has, since its beginning, been a focal point for much of the data-base-related activity within CODASYL. Membership on the DDLC is institutional in nature; each member is usually represented by one or two persons continuously. The list of organizations which have been members of the DDLC since its beginning is shown in Appendix 1, while the list of current DDLC members is shown below:

Aberdeen University, Scotland
B. F. Goodrich Company
Cincom Systems, Inc.
Consolidated Analysis Centers, Inc.
Control Data Corporation
Computer Sciences Corporation
Defense Communications Agency
Department of the Navy
Digital Equipment Company
General Electric Company
Honeywell Information Systems, Inc.
IBM
International Computers, Ltd., U.K.
National Bureau of Standards
National Security Agency
Ohio State University
Philips-Electrologica, Netherlands
Scientific Control Systems, Ltd., U.K.
Southern Railway System
Sperry Univac Corporation
U.S. Air Force
U.S. Army
University of Florida

In addition to its member organizations, the DDLC maintains on its mailing list a number of other organizations which either are applying for DDLC membership, are designated observers of DDLC's activities, or are cooperating with the DDLC in its development activities. These organizations are listed below:

CODASYL Programming Language Committee
British Computer Society (BCS)
BCS Advanced Programming Group
Bell Telephone Laboratories (observer)
Boeing Computer Services (observer)
Statskonsult, Sweden
European Computer Manufacturers Association (ECMA)
ECMA TC-22 (Data Base Management Systems)
Information Processing Society of Japan (DBLWG)
Academy of Sciences of the U.S.S.R.
NCR (observer)
Software Sciences Limited (observer)

Since 1973, the DDLC has formed task groups and working groups to study and make recommendations in several particularly important areas.˙ In general, membership in the DDLC has not been a requirement for participation in these groups, nor has participation in these groups, in itself, conferred DDLC membership. These groups, the Subschema Task Group (SSTG), Data Base Administration Working Group (DBAWG), Working Group on Environment (WGE), and the Data Manipulation Task Group (DMTG), are briefly described in the following sections.

2.1 Subschema Task Group (SSTG)

The Subschema Task Group (SSTG) was created during the August, 1973 meeting in order to further develop the subschema facility for data bases. The idea for the task group was prompted by the consideration of several working papers within the DDLC which indicated that the subschema facilities which could be designed for a number of different host languages had numerous features in common. From this beginning, .the current program of work for the SSTG was developed; it is:

a.   To develop an approach to a common subschema framework for the most commonly used host languages (COBOL, FORTRAN, PL/1, ALGOL) and for the most commonly used data structures (networks, hierarchies, relations).
b.   To develop a functional description of differences which should be allowed between schema and subschemas, and of the mappings which should be required to support these differences.
c.   To develop language specifications for the subschema framework and for the schema to subschema mappings.
d.   Ultimately, to consider the incorporation of a subschema facility into those host language specifications the developers of which deem a data base facility a necessity.

Ray Seth, of American Can Company, was appointed Chairman and the first SSTG meeting was held in April, 1974. The SSTG has continued to meet regularly and has concentrated on the development work described in items a. through c. above specifically for network subschemas. The SSTG is now producing a report to the DDLC describing the results of these activities.

It should be noted that it is not the intent of the SSTG to replace the current COBOL subschema facility developed by the Programming Language Committee with its own subschema facility. The SSTG exists to develop the subschema facility in general. The language specifications to be produced by the SSTG are, as described above, for a schema to subschema mapping language (to the extent that this is appropriate), which does not currently exist, and for a subschema framework common to many host languages. These languages will almost certainly not be host-language dependent, and, thus, would have to be adapted for use with a particular host language by the developers of that language. It is certainly not unreasonable to expect that, if the SSTG were to develop enhanced. subschema facilities, the Programming Language Committee might incorporate them into its COBOL subschema facility. However, this would be a decision for the PLC.

2.2 Data Base Administration Working Group (DBAWG)

The Data Base Administration Working Group (DBAWG) was created to develop tools for the use of the data base administrator to control the efficient and reliable use of the data base. The primary motivation for the establishment of this working group was recognition of the fact that there were data base administrative functions which were recognized as important by the DDLC (and earlier by the DBTG), but for which language specifications were not provided. As a result, the following program of work was adopted for the DBAWG:

a. To examine the requirements for and objectives of the following data base administrative facilities:

Control of data base system performance

Mapping of data to storage

Data base reorganization and restructure

Backup and recovery

Collection and analysis of usage statistics

Control of data base procedures

Other data base utilities

b. To develop a functional description of these facilities.

c. On the basis of the functional descriptions, develop language specifications where appropriate.

The DDLC at its December, 1973 meeting decided to ask a working party of the British Computer Society (BCS) to become the nucleus of this task group. The working party accepted this offer, but wished to remain within the BCS; consequently, the resulting group is termed a Working Group (DBAWG) by the DDLC. The Chairman of the DBAWG is Mr. J. S. Knowles of Aberdeen University. Within the BCS the DBAWG is a working party of the Advanced Programming Specialist Group whose chairman is Professor Peter King of Birkbeck College, London. Before undertaking the DBAWG work, the working party existed to study CODASYL's data base specifications and has submitted proposals to the PLC as well as to the DDLC.

The DBAWG has continued to meet approximately once every two months in the U. K. and, in June, 1975, published a report [3] containing the following six chapters:

1. Introduction

2. Concepts

3. Data Storage Control

4. Integrity Control

5. Statistics

6. Restructuring and Reorganization

At the June, 1975 DDLC meeting in London, the DBAWG spent two days making a detailed presentation on the last four chapters. In subsequent DBAWG meetings a detailed plan of work was developed; it called for analysis of data base administration issues and drafting of working papers and proposals during the remainder of 1975 and for submitting specific proposals to the DDLC in July, 1976. The following items are scheduled to be presented to the DDLC by the DBAWG by July, 1976:

a. A working paper on DBMS architecture.

b. Proposals to remove the dependence of other DDL elements on tuning and resource allocation elements, and a proposal to remove tuning and resource allocation elements from the DDL (some DBAWG proposals on this subject have already been acted on by the DDLC).

c. A working paper or proposal on a low-level Data Strategy Description Language (DSDL), which would incorporate tuning and resource allocation statements.

At its June, 1975 meeting, the DDLC requested (in its review of the DBAWG report), the DBAWG to investigate a high-level DSDL in addition to the development of the low-level DSDL. The high-level DSDL would enable the specification of the tuning effects desired by the data administrator, but would not dictate the methods used by the DBMS to achieve the effects. As a rough example of the difference between "high-level" and "low-level" statements, a high-level tuning statement for a key item might be "OPTIMIZE FOR DIRECT ACCESS", while a low-level statement for the same key might specify the type of hash-coding or indexing to be used in performing the optimization. Of course, other types of optimization statements (including even higher level statements) may also be developed. The DBAWG has already done work on both types of tuning statements.

2.3 Working Group on Environment (WGE)

The Working Group on Environment (WGE) is an informal subgroup of the DDLC particularly concerned with the architectural environment in which the DDL is meant to operate. The WGE was specifically formed to consider questions raised by the architecture proposed by the ANSI/X3/SPARC Study Group on Data Base Management Systems [4], whose work was first described to the DDLC by Mr. Charles Bachman in October 1973. The WGE was created shortly thereafter. Since then, the WGE has produced a number of working papers primarily aimed at interpreting the intent of the current CODASYL schema/subschema architecture, the intent of various language components of the DDL within that architecture, and the architecture of the ANSI Study Group. To some extent, the DDLC's efforts in categorizing its language (described below) are the result of this activity. In addition, WGE members have followed the activities of the ANSI Study Group, informally exchanged working papers, and occasionally attended Study Group meetings. In October, 1975, the WGE sent a letter to the Study Group asking for clarification of certain points related to the Study Group's architecture and describing the WGE's views on assignment of various DDL constructs to various points in the ANSI architecture. Written response was received from Mr. Tom Steel, Chairman of the Study Group. More recently, Mr. Steel gave a presentation to the DDLC at their February, 1976 meeting describing the status and future plans of the Study Group. The DDLC anticipates further liaison with the ANSI Study Group, as the Study Group evaluates both the COBOL data base facility adopted by the PLC and the DDLC's own language specifications. With the establishment of this closer liaison between DDLC and the ANSI Study Group, the WGE has suspended its activities.

2.4 Data Manipulation Task Group (DMTG)

The Data Manipulation Task Group (DMTG) was created at the October, 1973 meeting to further develop data manipulatiion facilities. The suggested program of work for this task group, as defined in its charter, is as follows:
   a. To develop a functional description of a DML appropriate to hierarchic data structures.
   b. To develop a functional description of a DML appropriate to relational data structures.
   c. To develop a functional description of host language independent enhancements to the data manipulation functions included in the April 1971 Data Base Task Group Report. Some suggested types of enhancement to the data manipulation functions are:
   1. Addition of more complex record selection expressions;
   2. Addition of set level operations;
   3. More control over DBMS update of currency indicators;
   4. Selective OPEN statement;
   5. Generalized statements;
   6. More sophisticated locking mechanisms.

   d. Ultimately, to consider the incorporation of the data manipulation
       facilities into appropriate host language specifications.
So far, the DMTG has not had sufficient membership to begin its activity.
Work on some of the subjects listed above is, however, currently going on
outside CODASYL. In addition, the DDLC itself has taken up a number of
these subjects directly.   It was the intent of the DDLC that the DMTG
concentrate on functional capabilities; any   language   specifications
produced would be in the nature of a framework, which would be tailored to
specific host languages or non-procedural language interfaces.   Thus, the
role of the DMTG would be analogous to that of the SSTG in its specific
subject area. In additiion, another role of both the SSTG and DMTG was to
be feedback to the DDLC regarding the schema DDL and its ability to support
both advanced subschema and data manipulation facilities.

3.0 Changes to Language Specifications

Since the publication of the June 1973 DDL JOD, the DDLC has made a
substantial number of changes to its language specifications. While not
all of these changes are particularly significant (in the sense that they
involve major changes in functionality), some of them are significant
enough to be discussed in this report. These changes are the results of
two general types of DDLC activity:
   a. The analysis of the functionality and possible uses of the various
       DDL clauses in order to categorize them.
   b. Various suggested enhancements to specific parts of the DDL.

The more significant changes in the DDL are described briefly in the
following sections.

3.1 DDL Categorization

The schema DDL defined by the DDLC is viewed primarily as a tool to be
used in the design, creation, and further development or maintenance, of a
data base. In its development of the DDL, the DDLC has found that the
categorization (or classification) of the statements of the language,
according to a defined set of criteria, is a very useful technique.   In
this categorization, the language statements are examined for common
properties which may be used to assign them to the appropriate category.
Once these language statements with common properties have been placed in a
category, the common properties may be set aside in the interests of
studying the differences among the statements.
The DDLC has presently categorized the DDL in two ways, one for
presentation (grouping) in the JOD and one for analysis. In the first of
these categorization schemes, clauses of the schema DDL are classified,
listed, and presented in accordance with the data construct types which the
clauses are used to describe. Thus, clauses exist to describe records,
data items, sets, and the schema itself. This method of classifying
clauses is useful because it groups together all those clauses which
describe a single data construct, and it allows the examination of their
roles in describing that data construct. This method was used in grouping
the language specifications in the 1973 JOD, and continues to be used in
the present JOD.
The second of these categorization schemes, and the more important one
for the purpose of analyzing and refining the DDL, is based on the basic
function of the clause, as described in the language specifications.   The
basic function of a clause (or phrase of a clause) and its appropriate
category assignment is based on the answers to the following questions:

a. What kind of function does the declaration of language elements in the category being defined provide?
b. Is inclusion of language elements from this category required in each schema? If not, what does the absence of a declaration mean?
c. Must the specifications of language elements in this category necessarily depend on declarations in any other category; or may this be the case; or even, must this specifically not be the case?
d. What relation has the declaration of a language element from this category with a subschema; in particular, is redeclaration possible? If so, does it replace the schema declaration or add to it?
e. What impact will modification of the schema declaration of a language element from this category have on:
    1. Existing subschemas?
    2. Existing application programs?
    3. The contents and organization of the data base?

The DDLC considered that a meaningful categorization should accomplish the following:
a. Help a data administrator to use the language when designing, implementing, and maintaining a data base system.
b. Facilitate the use of the language specifications by other groups concerned with language design, particularly the design of subschemas and data manipulation languages.
c. Aid the DDLC's own understanding of the language and hence the rigor of its specifications.
d. Help implementors of data base software to understand the specifications of the DDL.

The following categories were distinguished by the DDLC: Schema, Structure, Validation, DML Interface, Access Control, Measurement, Tuning, Resource Allocation, and Administration. Some of the major categories will be described briefly in the following paragraphs.

The schema category consists of the language elements whose function is to declare characteristics of a schema considered as a collection of declarations. Thus, declarations in the schema category have no direct relation with the data contained in a data base, but only with its descriptor, i.e., the schema. For example, functions which belong to the schema category are the identification of a schema and the control over schema operations such as displaying a schema.

The structure category consists of the language elements whose function is to declare the types of data constructs that will be referenced in other schema declarations or in subschema declarations and--depending on the actual subschema involved--in data manipulation statements. These data construct types may also be referenced via other languages interfacing with the schema, such as storage mapping languages. For example, the structure category contains those language constructs used to define data items, records, sets, and set orders. The structure declarations of a schema declare the overall data base structure on which other, application oriented, structures may be mapped by means of a subschema mapping language. Modification of structure declarations in a schema has the following effect on existing subschemas and application programs:

a. If the change does not involve data referenced by a subschema, that subschema and the application programs working with it are not affected.
b. If the change does involve data referenced by a subschema, the mapping of the application-oriented structure on the schema structure

must also change; and:

i. if the latter change is possible, then the associated
    application programs are not affected.
ii. if the latter change is not possible, then the application-
    oriented structure itself has to change, which is likely to
    invalidate the logic of the associated application programs.

Modification of structure declarations--whenever existing data constructs
are involved--causes modification of the data contained in the data base.
Also, modification of structure declarations will always require a
modification in the organization of the data stored in the data bse.
Depending upon the implementation, such a modification may be realized, for
instance, by means of changing the mapping between the schema data
constructs and the stored data constructs, or by means of changing the
stored data constructs themselves, etc. Structure declarations take
precedence over declarations in the other categories except the schema
category, in the sense that declarations in the other categories and the
specifications for them will refer to the structure declarations of the
types of data constructs.

The validation category consists of the language elements whose function
is to declare rules that restrict the set of values that may be assigned
to, or the relationships that may exist between, occurrences of the various
types of data constructs that have been declared. For example, such
declarations may enforce that values of a data item type lie within a
certain range; or they may provide criteria for ensuring that a member
record is associated with the correct owner record. Validation
declarations are not required. If validation declarations are absent,
changes to values or relationships in the data base will not be restricted
except by the rules that are inherent to the types of data constructs
involved. Validation declarations cannot be overridden in a subschema;
however, by means of a subschema language, additional restrictions may be
declared. The effect of modifying validation declarations in a schema on
existing application programs is that certain DML functions that had been
executing successfully before schema modification may fail after schema
modification, or vice versa. In the former case, the application programs
may have to be modified in order to deal with the possible failure of those
DML functions. Modification of validation declarations may invalidate the
data contained in the data base if additional constraints on values or
relationships are introduced.

The access control category consists of the language elements whose
function is to declare rules that safeguard against unauthorized operations
upon occurrences of the various types of data constructs that have been
declared. For example, a clause that declares an access control lock for
the retrieval of certain data items belongs to the access control category.
Access control declarations are not required. The safeguards declared in a
schema cannot be bypassed by means of a subschema. However, by providing
proof that it is authorized itself, a subschema may enable an application
program to perform otherwise unauthorized data access operations. A
subschema language may also provide facilities for the declaration of
additional safeguards. The effect of changing access control declarations
in a schema upon existing subschemas and application programs is one of
success or failure. Modification of access control declarations causes no
modification of the data contained in the data base.

The tuning category consists of the language elements whose function is
to declare information for use by the DBMS to improve the performance of
application programs operating on the data base or to decrease the cost of
the storage of the data in the data base. Different DBMS´s may react quite

differently to such declarations. One DBMS might adjust the organization of the stored data in accordance with the declarations; while another DBMS might not react at all because it allows no options or because the declarations are overridden by information gathered by the system itself; etc . For example, tuning declarations may provide knowledge about how the data base is going to be used (e.g., the SEARCH KEY clause) or populated; or they may offer a choice between alternative techniques for representing the data construct occurrences (e.g., indexed versus non-indexed sets). Tuning declarations are optional; the absence of any declarations will cause the DBMS to assume suitable defaults. A subschema language may also provide tuning declarations; however, these would have effect only during the lifetime of run units using the subschema and only for the data referenced by the subschema. Changing tuning declarations in a schema may affect the economic feasibility of existing subschemas and application programs. Note that the logic and results of application programs are not directly affected, only their efficiency. Modification of tuning declarations causes no modification of the data contained in the data base. However, as pointed out above, modification of tuning declarations may well cause a reorganization of the data. Declarations in the structure and validation categories and the specifications for them should not refer to any declarations in the tuning category.

The resource allocation category consists of the language elements whose function is to name and control the assignment of occurrences to organizational units to be used by the DBMS in the allocation and management of its actual resources. For example, an area may be defined, and records assigned to it, as a convenient unit for mapping to a storage device of particular characteristics. Resource allocation declarations are optional; the absence of any declarations will cause the DBMS to assume suitable defaults. Resource allocation declarations are not part of subschema languages. Changing resource allocation declarations in a schema may affect the economic feasibility of existing subschemas and application programs. Note that the logic and results of application programs are not directly affected, only their efficiency, unless the programs contain DML functions which are dependent on allocation units. Modification of resource allocation declarations causes no modification of the contents of the data base. Declarations in the structure or validation categories and the specifications for them must not refer to any declarations in the resource allocation category.

It is fair to say that the categorization of its language by the DDLC has had a substantial effect on the DDLC´s activities. The categories have led to more thorough and precise discussions of the purpose of proposed language constructs and to useful re-evaluation of existing constructs. The increased insight into the nature of many of the language constructs provided by the categories has stimulated the following DDLC activities:

  a. The elimination of undesirable dependencies between constructs in different categories (e.g., between structural and tuning constructs).
  b. The reorganization of language constructs so as to reflect their intended category (e.g., the separation of constructs which are simultaneously validation and tuning into separate constructs).
  c. Proposals to move the "less-logical" language constructs (e.g., those for tuning and resource allocation) from the DDL to other languages.
  d. The clarification of the intended meaning of the language constructs.

It is expected that the end product of such activities will be a language which is more functional and easier to use and understand.

The categorization of the language constructs is explicitly stated in the

language specifications. Each category is defined in the concepts section
of the JOD in a manner similar to that given above. The definition
includes expected effects on subschemas and programs when the declaration
is changed and the intended interactions between constructs in different
categories. Further, in the language specifications themselves, each
category is briefly defined again, and a complete assignment of language
constructs to categories is provided.   This assignment is attached as
Appendix 2 for reference purposes.

3.2 Specific DDL Changes

In addition to, and to some extent because of, its activity in
categorizing the DDL, the DDLC has made a number of significant changes to
the DDL. These are grouped into general categories and described below.

3.2.1 Enhancements to Facilities for the Declaration of Value-Based Structures.

Three DDL enhancements fall into this general category, the IDENTIFIER
clause, the STRUCTURAL CONSTRAINT clause, and SELECTION BY STRUCTURAL
CONSTRAINT, which is a new option of the SELECTION clause.

The IDENTIFIER clause within the record declaration provides for the
declaration of user-specified unique identifiers for a record type. A
given unique identifier may consist of one data item within the record or
of some combination of data items within the record. The general format of
the IDENTIFIER clause is shown below:

IDENTIFIER IS {data-identifier-1} ...

More than one IDENTIFIER clause may be specified for the same record type.

The STRUCTURAL CONSTRAINT clause within the set member declaration
provides for the declaration that the set membership of a particular member
record type within the set is to be constrained to a set occurrence which
has owner data item values identical to the values of specified data items
in the member record. The general format of the STRUCTURAL CONSTRAINT
clause is shown below:

STRUCTURAL CONSTRAINT IS {data-identifier-1 EQUAL TO data-identifier-2}
...

where data-identifier-1... must be data items in the owner record type,
and data-identifier-2... must be data items in the member record type.

More than one STRUCTURAL CONSTRAINT clause may be specified for the same
member record type. Note that the combination of data items specified by
data-identifier-1... need not necessarily be an IDENTIFIER of that owner
record type, although they may be. The DBMS will prohibit the
participation of a record of the member record type as a member of a set of
the set type being constrained unless the constraint is satisfied by the
values of the identified data items in the owner and member records
involved.   This integrity check will be performed during any data
manipulation function that either creates a new member of any set of the
specified type or that changes the value of any of the data items specified
in the constraint. Such constraints may be applied to sets with MANUAL as
well as AUTOMATIC members.

The SELECTION BY STRUCTURAL CONSTRAINT option of the SELECTION clause
provides a simplified form of the SELECTION clause for use when a
structural constraint exists and the conditions for set selection are the
same as the structural constraint. This is often the case for value-based
structures. In this case, the owner data items specified in the STRUCTURAL
CONSTRAINT clause must be declared as an IDENTIFIER of the owner record.

The general format of this option is shown below (note that this is the third format of the SELECTION clause):
  SET SELECTION IS BY STRUCTURAL CONSTRAINT This option allows for the automatic construction of set occurrences which satisfy the structural constraint.
  Using these new facilities, the structural declarations for the "standard" part-supplier-order example (excluding set orders) would be as shown in Figure 1:

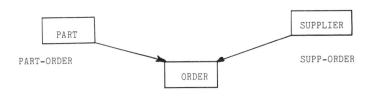

```
RECORD PART
  IDENTIFIER P#
  P#,NAME,COST
RECORD SUPPLIER
  IDENTIFIER S#
  S#,NAME,LOCATION
RECORD ORDER
  IDENTIFIER O#
  O#,S#,P#,DATE,QUANTITY
SET PART-ORDER
  OWNER PART
  MEMBER ORDER
  INSERTION AUTOMATIC RETENTION MANDATORY
  STRUCTURAL P# OF ORDER EQUAL P# OF PART
  SELECTION STRUCTURAL
SET SUPP-ORDER
  OWNER SUPPLIER
  MEMBER ORDER
  INSERTION AUTOMATIC RETENTION MANDATORY
  STRUCTURAL S# OF ORDER EQUAL S# OF SUPPLIER
  SELECTION STRUCTURAL
```
Figure 1

3.2.2 Removal of Dependence on Tuning Constructs

  Four basic changes to the DDL fall into this general category. These are the removal of the dependence of other clauses on the LOCATION MODE clause, the removal of the data base key construct and its associated constructs, the addition of a WITHIN ANY AREA option, and the removal of the TEMPORARY AREA facility.
  Two specific changes fall under the general heading of removal of dependence on LOCATION MODE. The first change is that the DUPLICATES ARE NOT ALLOWED phrase has been removed from the LOCATION MODE CALC option. This means that CALC no longer defines an identifier, but only a storage

option. If it is intended that the CALC-key also be a unique identifier, it must also be so-defined using the IDENTIFIER clause. The second change is that the SELECTION clause (Format 1) has been altered so as to allow set selection based on any IDENTIFIER. Thus, at the entry level of the SELECTION clause, there are now the following options: SELECTION by SYSTEM, APPLICATION, IDENTIFIER, and using the SELECTION clause defined for another member record.

The data base key facility was removed largely because of its mixed logical and physical connotations and because of the lack of any control mechanism over its use. With the removal of data base keys, the DIRECT option of the LOCATION MODE clause was also removed, as well as the DATA-BASE-KEY option at the entry level of the SELECTION clause. As a possible substitution for the logical aspects of the data base key facility, the DDLC is considering optional facilities for the declaration of "system-generated identifiers", i.e., facilities for specifying that one or more data items within a record are to have guaranteed unique values generated for them by the DBMS. Unlike data base keys, however, these items will have data-administrator-supplied names, will be part of the logical content of the records, and will (presumably) be accessible to application programs like any other data items. The physical aspects of the data base key facility, having to do with placement control within the data base, will probably be incorporated into other tuning or resource allocation statements, or into the DBAWG's proposed DSDL (see section 2.2).

The new WITHIN ANY AREA option allows application programs more freedom from the area construct. When WITHIN ANY AREA is specified, the DBMS performs area assignment, and run-units need not supply any information regarding areas to the DBMS. Such facilities reflect the DDLC's categorization of the WITHIN and AREA constructs as being concerned with resource allocation, rather than with logical structure.

The TEMPORARY AREA facility was removed because the intended facility could be better provided by alternative schema and subschema facilities.

3.2.3 Miscellaneous Changes to Existing Facilities

Under this general category are five specific changes: the addition of a FIXED set membership option, the addition of the POSTPONED RESULT data item, the addition of a BEFORE/AFTER CALL procedure facility, the deletion of the ENCODING/DECODING clause, and the addition of the ability to use the record type as a general sort control key and to define the "collating sequence" of the record types.

FIXED set membership is a set membership option similar to the MANDATORY and OPTIONAL set membership options. If a member record type is specified as a FIXED member, then once an occurrence of this record type becomes a member of any set occurrence of the defined set type, it must remain a member of that particular set occurrence until it is deleted from the data base. This is unlike the MANDATORY option, in that a MANDATORY member must remain a member of some occurrence of the defined set type, but it may be switched from one such set occurrence to another. The FIXED member may not be switched. The example shown in Figure 2 illustrates this difference for a personnel data base. There may be a rule that a PERSON must always be assigned to some DEPARTMENT. However, PERSON records may be reassigned to different occurrences of the DEPTPERS set to reflect personnel transfers. Thus, MANDATORY is the appropriate set membership option for the PERSON record type. However, JOB HISTORY records are unique to individuals, and should never be moved from one PERSON (and thus from one PERSHIST set) to another. Accordingly, FIXED is the appropriate set membership option for the JOB HISTORY record type. This provides the data administrator with a simple means of guarding against accidental or malicious misuse of the data base through set reassignment of JOB HISTORY records.

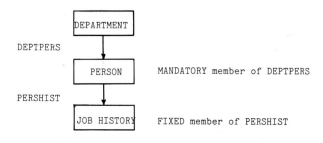

Figure 2

   POSTPONED RESULT data is a type of derived data similar to the ACTUAL and VIRTUAL RESULT data provided in the June 1973 JOD and in the DBTG Report. The motivation for this new type of derived item is as follows.   When the value of a RESULT data item is derived by means of a procedure which is at all lengthy, the data administrator will wish to make some attempt to minimize the number of times the procedure is invoked. If he declared the item as VIRTUAL, then the value would be recalculated every time the item is accessed, even if no change at all is made to the data from which it is derived. If, on the other hand, he made it an ACTUAL item, then it would be recalculated every time a change was made to any of the data from which it was derived, even if no access at all was made to the RESULT item itself.   The POSTPONED facility provides for an intermediate category of derived item whose value is stored in the data base, but whose recalculation is postponed until the time of the first access to it after a change is made to the data base which necessitates that recalculation.
   The BEFORE/AFTER CALL procedure facility allows the data administrator to more precisely control when a CALL procedure (formerly an ON procedure) is invoked relative to the time it is triggered by the invocation of a specific data manipulation (DM) function.   In the June 1973 JOD, the general format for the CALL data base procedure facility was:
   ON [ERROR DURING] ["stack" of DM functions] CALL data-base-procedure-1
The present general format is:

$$
\text{CALL procedure-name-1} \left\| \begin{array}{l} \text{BEFORE} \\ \text{ON ERROR DURING} \\ \text{AFTER} \end{array} \right\| [\text{"stack" of DM functions}]
$$

with the words BEFORE and AFTER having their obvious meanings.

   The ENCODING/DECODING clause was deleted from the DDL because, after an analysis of its possible uses, the DDLC felt that it should not appear in the schema. The DDLC felt that, if the clause was to be used for conversion between schema and subschema formats, it should be in the subschema, since different subschemas may require different formats and,

thus, perform different conversions. On the other hand, if the clause was
to be used for encryption or data compression, there would have to be a
rule requiring a corresponding DECODING clause for each ENCODING clause
(which did not then exist). In addition, more efficient data compression
was likely from procedures which processed complete records, or larger
units of data, than from procedures which processed single data items. The
DDLC also felt that the effect of ENCODING could be achieved by using CALL
BEFORE STORE and of DECODING by using CALL AFTER GET.

The ability to use the record type as a general sort control key, and to
define the "collating sequence" of the record types for this purpose,
involves changes to both the KEY and ORDER clauses of the DDL. In the
declaration of a sort control key using the KEY clause, each component of
the key (there may be several) may be declared using the syntax:

$$\begin{Bmatrix} \text{ASCENDING} \\ \text{DESCENDING} \end{Bmatrix} \begin{Bmatrix} \text{data-identifier-1} \\ \text{RECORD-TYPE} \end{Bmatrix}$$

Within the ORDER clause, the ORDER may then be defined as:

ORDER ... SORTED BY DEFINED KEYS RECORD-TYPE SEQUENCE IS {record-name-1}
...

The record-type sequence defines the "collating sequence" for the RECORD-
TYPE entries in the sort control keys defined using the KEY clause.

3.2.4. Name Change

The DDLC has changed the name of clauses concerned with the control of
access to specific constructs within the data base (and to the schema
itself) from PRIVACY clauses to ACCESS-CONTROL clauses.   This was done
primarily in recognition of the fact that the term "privacy" has come to
have a somewhat different meaning than that for which the clauses are often
used, particularly with the passage of the Privacy Act of 1974 in the
United States. "Privacy" is felt to be something which people have (or
ought to have, rather than something which computers or data processing
systems automatically provide. While clauses which control access to data
in a data base (e.g. DDLC´s ACCESS-CONTROL clauses) may be used to support
the concept of "privacy", they may also be used in other ways.
Accordingly, the DDLC felt that it might be misleading to continue to refer
to these clauses as PRIVACY clauses.

3.2.5. Other Changes Considered

In addition to having made the above-described changes to the DDL
specifications, the DDLC has considered in its discussions a number of
other issues which appear to be of "continuing interest". These issues are
often brought up in published papers or public comment concerning the DDL.
Some of these issues continue to be on the DDLC´s technical agenda.   Some
of the more "prominent" of these issues, along with the action taken by the
DDLC with respect to them, are described below:

a. Allow the same record type to be both owner and member in the same set
type. This facility, often referred to as the "recursive set" or
"unicycle", has been the subject of three proposals to the DDLC. In all
three cases, the proposals were referred back to their authors for further
work. The DDLC has, in general, been receptive to this idea. However, the
DDLC wants to ensure that, before the facility is added to the DDL, all
problems related to DML operations on such sets, and the integration of
such sets into the rest of the DDL, are solved. The latest proposal was
considered at the February 1976 meeting, and it was felt then that the
addition of the facility should proceed to some extent in parallel with

further development of the facility of cycles of set types, and that the
facility should be added in such a way that "recursive" sets have all the
facilities of present sets. A number of useful working papers have been
presented on various aspects of the problem, and it may be possible to
incorporate this facility before the next JOD publication.

b. Eliminate the repeating group within records. The repeating group
capability within records, provided by the OCCURS clause in the DDL, has
occasionally been denounced as a "storage" concept, having no place in the
DDL, and at least one proposal has been received for its removal. At the
time the proposal was considered, however, most members did not see the
repeating group as a storage concept, but rather one which facilitated
certain types of mappings to subschemas. For example, if all subschema
records are COBOL records with repeating groups, the schema to subschema
mapping of those records is obviously easier to define if the repeating
groups may be specified in the schema. It is also true that a facility for
controlling the number of member records in a set, corresp[onding to the
facility for controlling the number of occurrences of a repeating group in
a record, does not presently exist in the DDL, and thus removal of the
repeating group would be a removel of functionality from the DDL. Once
logical set population control facilities are available in the DDL, it may
be appropriate to consider the removal of repeating groups again.

c. Change the name of the CODASYL "set" construct to something else. It
has occasionally been argued that the term "set" used for the DDL's inter-
record relationship construct may be confused with the mathematical term
"set". Both are relevant in discussions of data base management, and it
is, therefore, argued that some change in terminology is needed. One such
proposal suggested "coset" as an alternative. This proposal was not
approved for a number of reasons, one of which was that "coset" is also a
mathematical term. However, the DDLC did not necessarily rule out a change
in terminology if a suitable alternative could be found.

4.0 Technical Objectives

During the coming year, the DDLC will be considering technical input from
three major internal sources: the DDLC itself, the DBAWG, and the SSTG.
The current DDLC agenda includes proposals or working papers on the major
subjects decribed in the following sections.

4.1 Improved Definitions of Data Manipulation Functions

The June 1973 DDL JOD and the present specifications contain definitions
of a set of "basic" data manipulation (DM) functions which are assumed to
be possible on structures defined using the DDL. Thus, for example, such
generic types of functions as FIND, INSERT, and STORE are defined, but
without specific syntax and without the implication that they necessarily
perform the same functions as implemented functions with the same names.
These DM functions are referred to in the specifications in describing the
effects of certain DDL declarations on operations on the data base, e.g.,
when derived data values are created, when certain validity checking is
performed, etc. Thus, the meaning of these functions must be properly
defined in order to properly define the DDL. In addition, these DM
functions provide a conceptual interface to the DBMS which may be used in
implementation. For example, implementors of a DBMS based upon the schema
DDL could choose a different set of basic DM functions based on their
individual implementation requirements. They would then map their own set

of DM functions onto that defined in the DDL specifications, and vice-
versa, in order to properly relate the specifications and the actual DM
functions implemented. Similarly, complex DML commands which might be
provided in host or query languages by the implementor could be defined by
resolving them into a sequence (or, possibly, multiple sequences which may
be executed in parallel) of basic DM functions.

The DDLC has found that the present set of DM function definitions is not
precise enough for its growing requirements, and as a result is engaged in
an effort to more precisely define them. In addition, the present set of
DM functions is defined such that the execution of any single DM function
must transform the data base from a state consistent with that data base's
schema into another such consistent state. However, the DDLC is also
considering the definition of what are termed "primitive" DM functions. A
primitive DM function is one which processes the same types of data
constructs as are processed by the basic DM functions defined now, but
which may, when executed, transform the data base from a state which is
consistent with its schema to one which is not, and vice-versa.

As an example, a "basic STORE" function applied to a record which is
declared as an AUTOMATIC member of a set will insert that record into the
appropriate set in addition to storing the record in the data base. A
corresponding "primitive" function might be a "create record" function
which stores a record in the data base without checking that the data
values contained comply with the provisions of the DDL's CHECK clause, and
without inserting the record into any set in which it is declared to be an
AUTOMATIC member.

The present DDL specifications do not contain the definitions of any
"primitive" DM functions. However, the DDLC recognizes that it may be
necessary to specify such primitive functions for future work, including
the more detailed specification of the data base procedure facility, the
incorporation of the DBAWG's work on lower level facilities, and the
incorporation of more complex types of structural validity-checking
facilities. Included in these primitive functions would have to be
functions which informed the DBMS when to suspend and when to reinitiate
validity checking on the structures created using the other primitive
functions.

4.2 Extensions to the Set Construct

As noted in section 3.2.5, the DDLC has considered a number of proposals on the most frequently discussed extension, the recursive set facility. Another extension which has been discussed in several working papers is to allow alternate owner record types for the same set type. For such a set type, the owner record of a particular set could be of several different types, but the restriction of only one owner record occurrence per set occurrence would still be enforced. The data structure diagram for such a set type might have the form:

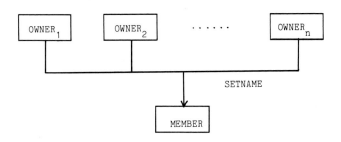

where OWNER1,..., OWNERn are alternate owners of the set type "SETNAME".

Figure 3

Other extensions have been mentioned, such as removing the restriction that a record occurrence can be a member of only one set occurrence of a given type at a time, or that a set may have only one owner record occurrence. However, no formal input has been received by the DDLC on these subjects.

4.3 Additional Tuning Statements

These include such statements as search keys at the record level for optimizing access to individual records irrespective of set relationships (i.e., so-called "out-of-the-blue" access) and declarations of probable populations of sets, areas, etc. Major questions with respect to such statements are whether they should be part of the schema DDL or included in another language (discussed below) and whether they should be "low level" or "high level" (see section 2.2).

4.4 Freer Syntax for Writing Schemas

The present schema DDL syntax is rather rigid, in that it insists, for example, that all declarations pertaining to a particular record type be grouped together with the record name specification and that set declarations follow record declarations. A number of proposals to allow a freer grouping of DDL constructs have been discussed by the DDLC, and are

on the current agenda. Such freer grouping would, for example, allow all
the ACCESS-CONTROL clauses to be grouped together, all the tuning and
resource allocation statements to be grouped together, etc. This should
assist the data administrator in that it allows him to write the schema in
whatever order he wishes.

4.5 Additional Consistency Declaration Facilities

An example of this type of declaration would be a facility for declaring
the logical population of a set, e.g., that a particular set type must have
exactly one member of each of the declared member record types. Some
proposals along these lines have already been discussed. The DDLC has
found, however, that the definition of more-primitive DM functions would
assist in the definition of such facilities.

4.6 Elimination of Undesirable Dependence on Tuning or Resource
     Allocation Elements

Steps in this direction have already been taken, as noted in section
3.2.2.   This process will continue, particularly in connection with the
activity described below concerning removal of tuning and resource
allocation elements from the DDL.

4.7 Elimination of Tuning and Resource Allocation Statements from the
     DDL

The DDLC has already received proposals and working papers concerned with
the removal to the DBAWG's DSDL (see section 2.2) of PRIOR PROCESSABLE and
LINKED TO OWNER declarations, SEARCH KEY and INDEX declarations (including
the new proposal for record-level search keys), and the LOCATION MODE
clause. Needless to say, the activity of removing dependence on tuning and
resource allocation statements is already underway, and is a necessary
preliminary to the total removal of such statements from the DDL. However,
some members of the DDLC question the difference between such statements
being a "separate language" and their being a different category within the
same language (as described in section 3.1), assuming that in either case
the undesirable dependencies are removed and the meaning of their being in
a different category is well-defined. During the DDLC's consideration of
the above proposals and working papers on specific statements, many members
felt that they would prefer to see what the "separate language" (DSDL)
would look like before removing these facilities from the DDL.
Accordingly, it is likely that some more definite decision will be made on
this subject at the July 1976 DDLC meeting, at which time the DBAWG will
present their ideas for the DSDL.

4.8 Other Objectives

As already noted, both the DBAWG and SSTG are expected to contribute
material to the DDLC agenda. An additional element of the technical input
will be proposals (as required) to resolve any differences determined to
exist between the DDL specifications and those of the COBOL data base
facility adopted by the CODASYL Programming Language Committee (PLC).
Other general topics of interest to the DDLC (some of which are explicitly
reflected in the DDLC's agenda or future plans) are:
  a. activation of the DMTG to investigate functional capabilities of
      enhanced data manipulation functions, e.g., support of Boolean
      operations and support of non-procedural languages.

b. improvement of the access control mechanism.
c. improvement in the data base procedure control mechanism.
d. consideration of improvements suggested by external (to DDLC) sources
    (e.g., through the liaison activities discussed below).

5.0 Liaison Activites

The DDLC currently maintains liaison with a number of groups which have
contributed (and still contribute) valuable input to the DDLC's technical
activities. This liaison activity is briefly described in the following
sections.

5.1 British Computer Society (BCS)

As described in section 2.2, the BCS has maintained a continuing interest
in CODASYL's work related to data bases for some time, one effect of which
was the establishment of the DBAWG, a joint group of BCS and DDLC.   In
addition, the DDLC also plans to establish some liaison with the BCS Data
Dictionary Systems Working Party.

5.2 European Computer Manufacturers Association (ECMA)

ECMA has submitted numerous proposals to the DDLC in the past, and the
DDLC continues to maintain a useful liaison with ECMA. Recently, ECMA
formed a new Technical Committee, TC-22 on Data Bases, and the DDLC has
established formal liaison with that group.

5.3. Information Processing Society of Japan (IPSJ)

The DDLC established formal liaison with the IPSJ's Data Base Language
Working Group last year after a period of informal communications. This
working group has already submitted a request for clarification of a
particular DDL-related issue which was acted upon by the DDLC; the request
proved useful in illustrating the existence of a problem to the DDLC.

5.4 ANSI/SPARC Study Group on Data Base Management Systems

As described in section 2.3, the DDLC has maintained informal liaison
with the Study Group's activities via the Working Group on Environment.
The DDLC anticipates that the Study Group's comments on the schema DDL will
prove to be valuable input to the DDLC's consideration of various changes
to the DDL, as well as on the placement of various language components
within a DBMS architecture.

5.5 International Federation for Information Processing (IFIP)

IFIP is really not a "liaison activity" of the DDLC in the same sense as
the preceding groups. However, it is listed here on the strength of recent
conferences on data-base-related subjects [5], [6], which contained papers
of direct relevance to the DDL. The latter conference had as its specific
aim "an in-depth technical evaluation of CODASYL DDL". In addition to the
normal objectives of a conference, one of the objectives of this specific
conference was the development of a set of specific recommendations to the
DDLC concerning possible modifications of its language specifications for
the DDL. Such a list of recommendations was produced, and more details of
this process may be found in the conference proceedings [6]. Volunteers
were solicited at the conference to produce specific proposals or working

papers to the DDLC for each item on the list. As a matter of interest, the list of recommendations prepared by the IFIP conference is presented in Appendix 3, along with a brief description of DDLC activity with respect to each item on the list. In some cases, DDLC consideration of the subject was a direct result of input generated from the volunteer at the IFIP conference. In other cases, DDLC consideration of the item was the result of input from a DDLC member, who may or may not have been affected by the IFIP conference results (many of·the ideas considered there have also been suggested elsewhere).

The DDLC engages in this liaison activity because it is interested in getting outside comments on its DDL specifications, in disseminating the products of its activities, and in finding out about related activities in progress elsewhere. To a great extent, the ability of DDLC to actively solicit outside comments, and to disseminate the results of its interim work, is limited by the voluntary nature of the CODASYL organization. However, each CODASYL-approved language specification contains an invitation to submit comments on those specifications to CODASYL. The DDLC takes that invitation seriously, and is prepared to take any reasonable action to cooperate with persons or organizations seriously interested in improving the DDL [7].

6.0 Publications

At the September 1976 meeting, the DDLC will again consider whether to publish a revised JOD. It is hoped that enough progress has been made in the technical work on the agenda to justify a new publication. While it is not expected that a publication in the near future would include any significant input from SSTG, such a publication would include input from DBAWG (perhaps a substantial amount). In addition to a revised JOD, it may be that the SSTG report to DDLC would be suitable for publication. If so, however, this would be published for "information only", as was the initial DBAWG report [3] to the DDLC.

Acknowledgements

I must express my thanks to the entire DDLC for their "involuntary" help in the preparation of this paper, not only because the accomplishments which I report here are accomplishments of the entire DDLC, but also because much of the wording and examples come from sections of the draft JOD, and from DDLC proposals and working papers on the associated material. I also express my thanks to Mr. Stan Wilson, of the Naval Research Laboratory, for his editorial comments.

References

1. CODASYL Data Base Task Group, April 1971 Report, available through the Association for Computing Machinery, New York.
2. CODASYL Data Description Language Journal of Development, June 1973, National Bureau of Standards Handbook 113, January 1974 (available from the U.S. Government Printing Office, SD Catalog No. C13.6/2:113).
3. Data Base Administration Working Group, June 1975 Report, available from the British Computer Society, 29 Portland Place, London W1N 4AP.
4. ANSI/X3/SPARC Study Group on Data Base Management Systems, "Interim Report", 8 February 1975, published in FDT (bulletin of ACM-SIGMOD), Vol. 7, No. 2, available through ACM, New York.
5. J.W. Klimbie and K.L. Koffeman (Eds), Data Base Management, North

Holland/American Elsevier, 1974 (Proceedings of the IFIP Working Conference on Data Base Management, Cargese, Corsica, France, 1-5 April, 1974).

6. B.C.M. Douque and G.M. Nijssen (Eds), Data Base Description, North-Holland/American Elsevier, 1975 (Proceedings of the IFIP TC-2 Special Working Conference, Wepion, Belgium, 13-17 January 1975, "An in-depth technical evaluation of CODASYL DDL").

7. Address CODASYL DDLC correspondence to:

Emile B. Broadwin   or   Frank A. Manola
Chairman, DDLC   Secretary, DDLC
Computer Sciences Corporation   Code 5403
650 N. Sepulveda Blvd.   Naval Research Laboratory
El Segundo, CA 90245   Washington, D.C. 20375

Appendix 1

Organizations which were at some time members of the DDLC:
Aberdeen University, Scotland
Bell Telephone Laboratories
B.F. Goodrich Co.
Blue Cross/Blue Shield
Boeing Computer Services, Inc.
Burroughs Corporation
Cincom Systems, Inc.
Control Data Corporation
Computer Sciences Corporation
Defense Communications Agency
Department of the Navy
Digital Equipment Corporation
Fireman's Fund American Insurance Co.
General Electric Co.
General Motors Corp.
Honeywell Information Systems, Inc.
IBM Corporation
International Computers Limited, England
Manufacturer's Hanover Trust Co.
The MITRE Corporation
National Bureau of Standards
National Security Agency
NCR Corporation
The Ohio State University
Philips-Electrologica B.V., The Netherlands
RCA Corporation
Scientific Control Systems Ltd., England
Southern Railway System
Sperry Univac Corporation
U.S. Air Force
U.S. Army
University of Florida
University of Michigan
Xerox Corporation

Appendix 2

DDL CATEGORIES
There are nine functional categories appropriate to the schema DDL. When

viewed as functional entities, each syntactic element of the schema falls
into one of the categories. The categories, their definitions, and the
schema elements that compose the categories are listed below. When a whole
clause is in a single category, it is designated by the name of the clause
followed by the word "clause", and syntactic elements subordinate to the
clause are not listed. When the entire clause is not in a single category,
then the clause name is listed followed by the subordinate elements that
fall in the same category. Thus, clause names appear more than once when
they have syntax and semantics for more than one functional category.

Schema
The schema category identifies a schema and declares its characteristics.
The syntactic elements of this category include:
  ACCESS-CONTROL clause (schema)
  CALL clause (schema)
  SCHEMA NAME clause

Structure
The structure category names the data structures that are described by
the schema. The syntactic elements of this category include:
  Data-name clause
  DYNAMIC clause; DYNAMIC
  KEY clause; ASCENDING, DESCENDING, RECORD-TYPE, DUPLICATES
  FIRST, LAST, SYSTEM-DEFAULT
  MEMBER clause
  OCCURS clause
  ORDER clause; FIRST, LAST, NEXT, PRIOR, SYSTEM-DEFAULT, SORTED,
      WITHIN RECORD-TYPE, DUPLICATES FIRST, LAST, SYSTEM-DEFAULT
  OWNER clause
  RECORD NAME clause
  SET NAME clause

Validation
The validation category declares rules that constrain the occurrences of
the data structures declared in the structure category. The syntactic
elements of this category include:
  CHECK clause
  DUPLICATES clause
  IDENTIFIER clause
  INSERTION clause
  KEY clause; DUPLICATES NOT, NULL IS NOT ALLOWED
  ORDER clause; DUPLICATES NOT
  PICTURE clause
  RESULT clause; RECORD, MEMBERS, ON, OF, USING
  SEARCH clause; DUPLICATES NOT
  SOURCE clause; OWNER
  STRUCTURAL clause
  TYPE clause

DML Interface
The DML interface category declares procedures which may be invoked by a
DML function and parameters to be supplied to these procedures. The
syntactic elements of this category include:
  KEY clause; RANGE
  SELECTION clause
  WITHIN clause; AREA-ID

Access Control
The access control category declares authorization mechanisms for access
to and change to the occurrences of the data structures declared in the
structure category. The syntactic elements of this category include:
  ACCESS-CONTROL clause (except schema)

Measurement
The declarations of the measurement category direct the DBMS   in
collecting data about data base use, population, etc. There are at present
no syntactic elements in this category.

Tuning
The tuning category declares guidelines for data base organization to
assist in tuning data base performance. The syntactic elements of this
category include:
  DYNAMIC clause: PRIOR PROCESSABLE
  LINKED clause
  LOCATION clause; CALC, USING, VIA, SYSTEM-DEFAULT
  ORDER clause; PERMANENT, TEMPORARY, INDEX NAME
  RESULT clause; ACTUAL, POSTPONED, VIRTUAL
  SEARCH clause; USING, CALC, INDEX NAME, PROCEDURE
  SOURCE clause; ACTUAL, VIRTUAL

Resource Allocation
The resource allocation category names organizational units appropriate
for managing system resources, and controls the assignment of occurrences
of the declared data structures to these units. The syntactic elements of
this category include:
  AREA NAME clause
  WITHIN clause

Administration
The administration category names and provides for the invocation of DBA
supplied procedures. The syntactic elements of this category include:
  CALL clause (except schema)

Appendix 3

IFIP Conference [6] Recommendations and DDLC Action:
  a. "Allow the same record type to be both owner and member in a given set
type"--proposals on this subject, including one from the IFIP volunteer,
have been considered by the DDLC, as discussed in section 3.2.5.
  b. "Eliminate repeating groups"--a proposal on this subject from the IFIP
volunteer was discussed and voted down, as discussed in section 3.2.5.
  c. "Allow specification of multiple identifiers in the record
declaration"--input from the IFIP volunteer and from within the DDLC was
received on this subject; this facility is now in the DDL (the IDENTIFIER
clause).
  d. "Introduce into the record declaration a SEARCH KEY clause for
optimization of access to record occurrences with designated item values"--
input was received from the IFIP volunteer, and a modified version of this
proposal is currently being debated, as discussed in section 4.3.
  e. "Provide an option in the DML for a record occurrence based only on
designated item values"--suggested DML syntax for this facility was
contained in the proposal received for item d. above; the DDLC in general
supports this idea--however, DML syntax is not within the jurisdiction of
the DDLC, but rather the PLC.

f. "Revise the SET SELECTION clause to accommodate the possibility that set selection might take place on identifiers other than that which is the CALC-key"--this facility is now in the DDL.

g. "Restrict the set to have only one member record type"--IFIP input was received on this subject; however, the proposal was voted down.

h. "Consolidate the SEARCH KEY and SORTED INDEX clauses within the set declaration"--no input has been received on this; however, it is likely that some consolidation will take place in connection with DBAWG´s proposal for a DSDL.

i. "Improve the record selection power in the SET SELECTION clause, including existential quantifiers"--no input received.

j. "Re-examine the facilities for item type declaration"--the DDLC has considered this an important area for some time; however, little work has been done on this subject.

k. "Allow cardinality constraints on set occurrences within the set declaration"--the DDLC has considered some proposals on this subject, as discussed in section 4.5.

l. "Consider extensions of the set attributes including VIRTUAL, PHANTOM, and an extended DYNAMIC set"--no IFIP input has been received on this subject; however, the DDLC has considered extensions to DYNAMIC sets, and has just completed discussion of a preliminary proposal on VIRTUAL sets.

m. "Base conceptual schema on units of information (e.g. binary relations)"-- no input has been received on this subject.

n. "Develop better integrity checks"--under development.

o. "Move various clauses to a ´storage structure language´"--this is currently under study, in connection with the DBAWG´s proposed DSDL.

p. "Rework SOURCE/RESULT clause to specify the execution sequence"--the POSTPONED RESULT facility may be considered work on this subject; preliminary input on more precise specification of SOURCE/RESULT timing has been received.

q. "Extend SOURCE/RESULT clause"--input from the IFIP volunteer was received on this subject, and some extensions (e.g. POSTPONED RESULT) were adopted as a result.

r. "Allow multi-level subschemas"--this facility was one of the initial ones considered by the WGE in its study of the CODASYL architecture, and is currently being developed by the SSTG.

s. "Make higher level operations available in the DML"--this is within the province of the DMTG in terms of the development of functional descriptions of such operations; however, the production of syntax specifically for the COBOL DML is within the province of the PLC.

t. "Provide for alternate owner of a set"--this subject is under study as discussed in section 4.2.

DISCUSSION

SWENSON: Your objectives seem to be somewhat in conflict. One advocated elimination of tuning and the other increased tuning features. If you´re going to include tuning features in the DDL, you should completely isolate them in that specification and make it quite clear which are tuning and which are not tuning features. Another objective should be a greater production of examples or even a primer on the usage of the DDL. In fact, CODASYL should not publish items without primers on how to use them. The DBTG report was very difficult because it was never clear how to use it or even that it was consistently usable.

MANOLA: The two objectives are not in conflict; rather, they are separated by defining the categories and eliminating dependencies between tuning items and other items in the DDL. We have attempted to encapsulate the tuning and resource allocation elements such that there is no more dependence on them than is necessary. Obviously a tuning item will reference some structure but the reverse should not be true. We can clearly add to that category, that is, define more and different types of tuning. Should we now go further and simply take tuning out of the DDL altogether and put it into a separate language? At the moment there is some question on the committee as to exactly what the trade-offs are. Some members feel that the separate language is the way to go, others feel that the same effect can be derived from complete encapsulation within the same language. As far as the primer is concerned, I would appreciate it if you would write the chairman insisting on that, because I've been insisting on it for four years and it hasn't done any good at all. The examples used in the justification for proposals should be collected together in one place, because those are educational items for the committee and they would serve also as educational items for the outside world. So far the committee has not been interested in that activity. It is unfortunate.

LOWENTHAL: It appears that the DDLC has been very responsive to objections that have been raised to the 1971 report. But one suggestion I have heard that has not been included relates to the ability of the data base designer to include multiple set member types within a given set type. Some people feel that the set type should represent a binding relationship between two record types, a single type of member and of owner. The DDLC seems to have gone in the other direction, by not only retaining multiple member types, but also opening up the possibility of alternate owner types. Can you explain the reasoning behind that approach.

MANOLA: In fact, we did consider a proposal to allow only one member type. It was rejected for the following reason. If the data administrator chooses to exercise that discipline over the design, he can do so. That is, he can restrict himself to declaring one member-record type, and if alternate owners were added, only one owner-record type. It is, at the moment, not clear to the DDLC, other than its convenience in mathematically describing the DDL, what such a restriction would gain the data administrator. If there were available some pragmatic advantage to requiring that set declarations be restricted in that way, possibly the committee would reconsider its decision.

GALLITANO: At one time, COBOL was a very useful language for solving business-oriented problems and as it developed it became more and more expanded, and today it is more a system than a language. There has been considerable comment in the last several years about the degree to which the language has grown and become complex and cumbersome, to the point where the average programmer now does not understand anything that can be described as a consistent, minimal, useful subset of the language. While the user of thee DDL may be slightly different from the COBOL programmer, he is ultimately going to be faced with the same problem. It would be a useful exercise to stand back and see what could be taken out before you put anything else in.

MANOLA: To some extent we're up against the developing technology that allows more and more things to be done. The general solution has been to

separate functions. The declaration of the logical structure is separated
from, say, optimization. One of the reasons we tried to encapsulate tuning
and resource allocation was to enable that to be done.

SENKO: We also tried categorization in DIAM. We have separate languages at
the various levels.   We differ from the DDLC work in two significant
places. We regarded both sets and repeating groups as access paths and
actually part of the tuning category. This has the advantage that the
language for accessing the repeating groups becomes the same as the
language for accessing sets. Have you considered, or looked at the
possibilities of, putting sets into a tuning category.

MANOLA: We haven't had a proposal to put sets into the tuning category.   I
really don't intend to get into the data model debate at this point. At
the moment we have a data model that has values, records, and sets.   I
think some members of the committee still feel that the set is more than
just an access path, it's the declaration of a relationship. We've had a
proposal on virtual sets, which is starting to consider the idea that some
sets are more permanent than others.   When you start that, you start
considering what the set really is. At the moment, the repeating group is,
as I've said, a convenience.

SENKO: But it does have mainly efficiency considerations.

MANOLA: It does, depending upon how you assume repeating groups declared in
the schema get mapped onto storage. The repeating groups declared in the
schema are not accessed by DML's, it's the subschema that's referenced by
DML's.   That's one of the reasons why we want the SSTG to further develop
the schema-to-subschema mapping capability, to enable some smoothing of
application-structure versus schema-declared-structure to take place during
that mapping.

STEEL: I sense from what you describe a shift to putting tuning `in one
place and other things in another place. I'm beginning to sense the kind
of distinction that the SPARC Report is trying to make between external and
internal schemas.   Would you agree that this is an accurate reflection of
what you're trying to do?

MANOLA: I think the members of the committee would consider it to be a
conceptual to internal distinction. However, I know we're going to have a
fight about that.

JARDINE: Firstly, I really do support the idea of getting the tuning or
internal aspects into some separately defined area. Whether the tuning
aspects remain part of the DDL or whether they become a separate language,
is not very relevant at this point in the development. If they are indeed
separate, distinct and non-interacting, then it is possible for an
implementor to decide whether he wants to implement them either as one
language or compiler or to separate them into two separate languages.   The
important thing is that they be cleanly separated so that the interactions
that would prevent eventual complete separation be removed. With regard to
that, there still seems to be a couple of things lingering around inside
the schema definition that appear to be tuning oriented. You spoke of the
question of the control of the number of member records in a set. That is
a storage problem, and is not an appropriate item for inclusion in the
definition of the structural relations among the data. My comment is
similar with regard to ordering. We should not continue to insist upon

maintaining a concept of order at the structural declaration of the logical
schema.   This is either, or both, an internal storage consideration for
purposes of efficiency, or an application view of the data. My third point
is one of clarification, and it has to do with the proposal for the
structural constraint. It´s unclear to me what problem this is intended to
solve. I wonder if you could make some comments on it.

MANOLA: While we could construct, using the Selection clause, structures
which in effect satisfied a value-based structural constraint, we couldn´t
necessarily guarantee ability to perform a validity check at some later
time when a DML statement tries to switch members around, or change a
derived data item which would cause such switching. In the set-selection
clause and some of the options, the values used in performing selection are
provided by the application program, and the application program might not
be around at that later time.   What we wanted is a declared validity
constraint, which was separated from the construct used to create the
structure, and also ensure that the structural constraint was based on
values in records, so that those values would be present at any arbitrary
time when the DBMS decided that it wanted to recheck that validity
constraint. I disagree with you that controlling the number of members in
a set is storage. If you´re talking about population, in terms of how do
you implement the set, or where do you put it, that is storage.   However,
declaring that you have only one member occurrence per owner occurrence is
the declaration of a one-to-one relationship and that to me is logical. As
far as ordering being tuning is concerned, I happen to agree with you but
the DDLC does not.

TAYLOR: Various relational systems have taken the approach that it is
convenient to embed the facilities of the relational query language in the
data declaration language. This gives you a good deal of flexibility, not
only with access control, but also with various kinds of triggered updates.
Could you tell me what is the attitude of the DDLC about putting some
higher level of data manipulation function into the DDL?

MANOLA: DDLC hasn´t really expressed an opinion on it. I think it should
be done, and I suggested so in several papers to the DDLC. I believe it´s
possible to define a high level language which uses sets as declarations of
relationships between objects, and which can be used in the way you
suggest, that is to do triggered updates, to declare constraints and to
generally substitute for data base procedures.   I think that´s a very
important step for the DDLC to take.

HARRIS: Could you clarify what you mean by primitive data manipulation
functions (as defined in the paper) and give us some idea of their use.

MANOLA: This is a purely arbitrary distinction that we´ve made.   At the
moment we have basic data manipulation functions. Given a data base
consistent with its schema before such an operation, the data base is in a
state consistent with its schema after the operation. For example, suppose
you perform a store function, the object of which is a record which is an
automatic member of a particular set. The ´store´ consists of the storage
of the record in the data base, and also the insertion of the record into
the set relationship, so that the automatic declaration is satisfied. By
primitive function, we mean one which performs exactly one distinct
operation.   A primitive function might be to store the record in the data
base. We would have a separate primitive for the connection with all the
automatic sets in which it happens to participate. References in some of

the DDL rules to data manipulation functions would be much easier to write if we had such a primitive level of data manipulation function. In addition, we would gain more thorough control over the output of a subschema-to-schema mapping from a source language operation to a sequence of basic data manipulation operations on the database. We feel if we start to investigate higher level languages, such as query languages or other types of data manipulation languages, we will need a more basic level so that we can have more flexible mappings from whatever the host language deems an appropriate operation to whatever is an appropriate operation on the database.

COHN: I'd appreciate your clarification on the dictionary work being done by the British Computer Society Working Group. Are they going to consider dictionary facilities for just the storage part or are they considering it for the schema and subschema as well?

MANOLA: The latter.

COHN: Second, I believe that, since DDLC owns the subschema as well as the schema, you're looking at the comments on override of the schema by the subschema that were made by the Study Group. Would you care to comment on that.

MANOLA: Yes, we are. I think most people in the DDLC agree that the subschema access control facilities should not override schema access control facilities. Certainly subschema validity constraints should not override schema validity constraints although they may add to them. One of the reasons for separating validity checking from the selection clause was to provide a validity constraint which could not be overridden by the subschema. But there are some reasons for having selection overridden by the subschema for the reason that selection should not be used as a validity constraint.

WINTER: SPARC has proposed a system architecture which would appear to be inconsistent with the current CODASYL DDL. I was wondering if, in the long run, you would expect that CODASYL, through a series of evolutionary steps, would develop a DDL which is consistent with this architecture? What long term plans do you have to address that problem, and how would a standard come about? How would CODASYL and SPARC work together so that the requirements were satisfied?

MANOLA: We don't think that we're all that far away from the SPARC architecture as some people would think. I note that there seems to be some difference of opinion in the Study Group about that. Nevertheless, it is our long term goal to progress in that direction. We think we're taking steps in that direction now, and are interested in whatever additional comments the Study Group comes up with. We do anticipate progress in the direction indicated by the Study Group. We certainly are interested in the best liaison we can get with the Study Group. We hope that while they're considering the DDL they talk to us and indicate the way that their discussions are going so that we can start considering those matters within DDLC. How long the evolution takes depends on the result of the Study Group's ideas on what language to use for the conceptual schema. I know that there is disagreement about that, and it depends on who wins. We think, through evolution, we will eventually get there as far as standardization is concerned. We're interested in standardization, but it's ANSI that makes the decisions about that. I don't know if an occasion would arise where ANSI might say: you have to do this in order for it to be a standard; and we say: no, we won´t do that.

STEEL: Speaking for the Study Group, we are attempting to co-operate with and co-ordinate with the DDLC to that extent we have invited members of the DDLC to meet with us this weekend, and we intend to continue this kind of co-operation and liaison.

ON CERTAIN SECURITY ISSUES
RELATING TO THE MANAGEMENT
OF DATA

Marvin Schaefer
System Devolopment Corporation
Santa Monica, California 91307

ABSTRACT
In this paper, the concept of controlled data sharing is examined in the
context   of   volatile   data   bases.   Particular   attention   is   paid   to
alternative data classification schemes, commercial and military, and their
implementational implications.

1. THE PROBLEM
There is great concern over the use to which very large data bases will
be put since they are so abundant. The public has demanded legislation in
the area of privacy that would enforce the correctness of records in such
data bases, as well as restrict the dissemination of those records to
authorized agencies.

Commercial firms and military organizations have had similar concerns for
a considerable period. Basically, it is agreed that sensitive data is to
be revealed only to authorized viewers and modified only by responsible,
authorized agents.*

Large data bases tend to contain information of varying sensitivity.
Much of the data may be of such low sensitivity as to be public record,
e.g., the sex of an individual, while other information may involve the
national security or the financial future of a corporation, e.g., the
amount a firm is bidding on a contract proposal.   Traditionally, the
security policy of the United States Department of Defense has required the
classification of a document to the levelof the most sensitive information
contained therein.   This policy can lead to serious overclassification of
documents, preventing the person with a legitimate need-to-know but a low
clearance from accessing the unclassified information contained in highly
classified documents. It is legendary that there exist large data bases in
the Pentagon that are classified at the Top Secret level, but of which only
3 percent of the data is legitimately classified at the Top Secret level.
The contents of these data bases are inaccessible to individuals who are
not cleared to the Top Secret level. Such clearances are granted only after
expensive investigations into the lives of the 'trusted' individuals who
will be examining parts of the data.

Thus, in the interest of protecting certain sensitive data from the view
of unauthorized individuals, the entire data base has been protected from
the view of all people unauthorized to view it in its entirety.

----

*This paper does not contain a discussion of the rights of individuals to
view and audit records related to themselves since this is a legislative
and judicial matter beyond the scope of the investigation.

1.1 TRADITIONAL PROTECTION MEASURES

Protection takes place in two ways. First, the following physical protection measures are taken. The computer is placed in a locked, guarded room. The computer operators are cleared so that they can be trusted. The computer room is lined with alternating layers of lead and copper foil so that electromagnetic radiations emanating from the computer cannot be monitored electronically. Communications with the computer either take place from within the room, the users being authenticated and identified by guards, or the users sit at special, "cleared" terminals and use encrypted communication lines and passwords as means of authenticating themselves to the data management system. Data is allowed in and out of the computer room only after specific procedural protocols are followed. Second, only data of one level of security is run on the computer at a time, so that only users with a need-to-know for all of the information on the machine can attempt to see any of the information stored on it: a "periods processing" environment is created in which a provision is made to protect against incidents of accidental disclosure of classified information in the event of machine or software malfunction.

1.2 LIMITATIONS OF THE TRADITIONAL PROTECTION MEASURES

Consider the possibility of a spy who has been unwittingly "granted" a clearance to view restricted information in such a periods processing environment. The following incident could happen in a commercial data processing environment: A corporation considers salary information to be sensitive, accordingly restricting access to salary data to a few individuals.

The timekeeping clerks are not granted access to salary information, but prepare tapes consisting of records that pair employees with the number of hours they worked during the week. These tapes are then brought into the "secure" computing environment, where a payroll program accesses the salary data base and prints pay checks. The spy, who wrote a portion of the payroll program, introduced code into the print routine such that a copy of the salary data base was written directly onto the computer facility´s billing tape, possibly in a form that looks just like normal entries on the billing tape. Such code is called a Trojan Horse. The data from the billing tape is later recovered by another program that operates in a less secure computing environment when computing bills are processed at the end of the month, restoring the billing tape to its original state afterward so that no record of the spying persists in the system.

The results of this incident are that sensitive corporate data is covertly stolen. The spy need not have been present at the time the theft took place. The stolen data is viewed long after the theft has transpired. No record of the theft remains after the fact. The stolen data is in machine readable form and can be sold to and analyzed by interested parties.

1.3 A POSSIBLE SOLUTION TO THE PROBLEM

Weissman [WEISS] and LaPadula and Bell [LAPAD] have proposed a way to circumvent the Trojan Horse attack. The device of monitoring the most sensitive level of data read during a run is used to generate the requirement that no file may be written during the run, unless that file is classified to at least this high level of security. In the Weissman ADEPT-50 model, this level is called the "high water mark;" no file can be written below the "high water mark" for the run without explicit intervention by the user. In the LaPadula and Bell approach, the *-property, called the star property, prohibits the writing of data below the high water mark, regardless of the desires of the user. The latter

solution prevents such disclosures of sensitive information. However, it
also   prohibits   the   legitimate declassification of "overclassified"
information.

1.4 OTHER PROBLEMS IN THE PERIODS PROCESSING ENVIRONMENT

Periods processing is an expensive way to operate a computer center.
After each classification level has been run, the machine environment must
be "sanitized" so that no machine-readable residue remains that can be
interpreted by the succeeding run. This sanitization process can take up
to one-half hour per run.

Programs running at a high level of classification cannot take advantae
of data modifications and updates that might affect the lesser classified
data they are processing. This can cause the rerunning of programs when
erroneous data is detected at a low level of sensitivity while it is being
processed by a program running at a high classification level in a
sanitized environment.

No direct provision is made for the true sharing of low-level data
contained in a file of high classification. The procedural safeguards and
the *- property make it almost impossible to permit the 97 per cent of
overclassified military information from ever becoming accessible to
individuals who have a legitimate need-to-know for the data.   Worse,
specialized personnel are required for even the most routine updates of
unclassified data within the data base since all people who deal with it
must have high clearances. These data bases tend to get out of date since
there are few such people.

2. SECURE MULTI-LEVEL, MULTI-USER OPERATING SYSTEMS

As an alternative to the periods processing environment, a number of
secure operating systems currently either are under design or
implementation, which should provide an environment in which a number of
user processes can coexist, each at its own level of classification. Each
of these secure operating systems [UCLA, MITRE, SRI, MIT, AFDSC, SDC/VMM]
is intended to provide for the controlled sharing of data classified at the
file level, subject to the constraints of some security policy.   These
systems are proposed to support general programming applications.

A number of secure multi-user, limited-use systems have been developed in
which the user communicates with the computer via the use of a high-level
transaction-oriented or abstract programming languages. Such systems may
restrict users to languages like APL or a data management system query
language. These systems all perform some form of user authentication.
Many of them require the use of passwords.

2.1 THE PRINCIPLES OF MULTI-LEVEL MULTI-USER SECURE SYSTEMS

Secure operating systems are based on the principle of the "reference
monitor" [ANDER], a body of software and hardware that mediates every
attempt of a subject, i.e., a user or a program acting on behalf of a user,
to access an object, i.e., data. The reference monitor must be:
  . always resident and always invoked on every path between a subject and
    an object,
  . tamper proof and uncorruptable, and
  . small enough to be formally proven correct in both design and
    implementation.
Subjects are awarded clearances, while objects are assigned
classifications.   The function of the reference monitor is to determine
whether or not the clearance of a subject is sufficient to permit him to
access data of a specific classification level.

The classification of an object may be as simple as a list of authorized subjects, or a password (in which case a subject has sufficient clearance to access the object, provided he knows or guesses the password), or it can be part of a hierarchy or partial order (such as the Unclassified, Confidential, Secret, Top Secret classifications of the military establishment), or it can solve a formula (such as a named individual operating from a specific terminal during certain hours of the day). Data classification is discussed further in Section 3.

Two other important principles employed in secure systems are that of Least Privilege and that of Least Common Mechanism. The first of these requires that no system component be granted more privilege than it absolutely requires in order to perform its function, while the second distributes security enforcement code and tables, such that no one system function has major responsibility for all forms of security enforcement. In this way, the likelihood is reduced that a system component can be duped or coerced into compromising security on behalf of an unauthorized penetrator.* The interested reader is referred to [SALTZ] for further information on the principles and technology of secure systems.

3. DATA BASE CLASSIFICATION SCHEMES

In this section, a number of schemes are discussed that can be used to classify data in order to establish a means of applying accurate classifications to the components of a data base so that data is not needlessly overclassified. But, while making data of low classification accessible to users who have low clearances, one does not wish to compromise the security of the more sensitive parts of the data base.

Accuracy of classification is required. Data classification is a specialized task that involves an understanding of the semantics of the data base. What is the classification of the number 1812? The answer depends on the meaning of 1812. If it is the date of birth of an individual, that is one thing; if it is the hour at which an attack is to take place, or the cruising speed of an aircraft, it could be the most sensitive portion of a data base.

In the following subsections, the possible means by which the components of a data base can be classified are discussed. A data base is considered to be built of a number of relations [CODD]. We use the terms "row," "record," and "tuple" interchangeably, as we also use "field," "column," and "attribute" when addressing the matrix representation of a relation.

In Section 4, the implementation considerations relative to these classification schemes are discussed. In addition, current implementation efforts relative to these schemes are mentioned.

----

*For example, if all of the passwords for obtaining access to objects are stored in a central table, all system security is violated if a penetrator can obtain access to the table. Compare this to the situation in which the access controls are distributed throughout the system, and the passwords are physically affixed to the objects. In the event a subject attempts to obtain access to an object, an access control function compares the password provided by the subject to the password of the object. The access control function has no record of the password until the attempt is made and retains no record afterwards. If the two passwords do not match, at worst only the one correct password for the restricted object has been uncovered. If the enforcement mechanism was correctly implemented, that password is not revealed to the subject. At worst, the subject obtains access to that one password and not to any other ones.

3.1 GLOBAL CLASSIFICATION BY RELATION

In this case, the entire relation is classified to the same level. If a subject can access the relation, he can access any row or field in the relation. There may be different controls attached to read access, write access, append access, et cetera. However, the entire relation is treated by global application of the classification convention.

This classification scheme can lead to data overclassification due to the lack of granularity of the classified items. In a sense, there is no difference between global classification by relation and global classification by data base, since any data base can be partitioned into a set of relations. Each relation is stored independently of each other relation, as a file. The file can be protected by a host secure operating system.

Sharing between users of different classifications can lead to data integrity problems and loss of information, particularly when the organization's security policy includes enforcement of the *-property. Two examples are:

. Synchronization of readers and writers: Suppose there are two relations, "Low" and "High," respectively, of low and high classifications. A subject capable of reading both "Low" and "High" cannot simultaneously have write access to "Low" because of the *-property. This is because he might deliberately transfer information from "High" into "Low," as could a Trojan Horse acting on his behalf. No action of this subject can be made observable to any subject who does not have read access to "High." Hence, the subject cannot signal his intent to read "Low" down to any other subject who intends to modify the contents of "Low," since a convention could be adopted by which sensitive information is signaled, albeit slowly, to unauthorized subjects. Hence, it is possible that the subject with access to "High" reads portions of "Low" that are being modified at the same time, hence are invlaid. The author has partially resolved this problem in [SCHA1].

. A data base transitive relationship is destroyed. Suppose "High" has fields Part#, Supplier#, and Low has fields Supplier#, Supplier-Address. "Low" and High" are transitively linked together by the field Supplier#. (See Figure 1.) It is not possible for a subject whose access is restricted to "Low" to determine the existence of the relation "High," much less whether or not there are any parts supplied by a given Supplier#. Nor, as explained above, can a current viewer of "high" signal to a low subject that the integrity of the data base will be damaged if a row is deleted from "Low." It becomes a possibility that there will be parts for whom the supplier is unknown. For example, in Figure 1, if a subject deletes the pair (200, San Jose) from relation "Low," the Supplier-Address for parts 15, 25, and 45 will be lost.

Part #	Supplier #	Supplier #	Supplier-Address
15	200	1100	Los Angeles
30	500	175	New York
25	200	200	San Jose
27	175	400	Montreal
45	200	500	Paris
		525	Pisa

Relation High   Relation Low
Classification High   Classification Low

Figure 1. Classification by Relation

3.2 GLOBAL CLASSIFICATION BY ROW

In this case, each row is assigned a classification at the time of its creation. A subject is either granted or not granted access to the entire row, and all of its field entries, as a strict function of its classification and his clearance. This classification scheme is subject to the same problems as the previous one. In addition, users may be able to make inferences about the contents of the data base if certain rows of the data base have volatile classification properties. Consider the following military security example.

A data base consists of rows that contain detailed flight plans and cargo information for aircraft. If an aircraft is carrying a nuclear cargo, the flight plan is considered to the Top Secret; otherwise, the flight plan is considered to Unclassified. The aircraft all have identification numbers, both in the data base and stenciled on the side of the fuselage. If aircraft #12 alternately carries peanut butter and nuclear warheads, the row for it is viewable by unclassified subjects only when the aircraft carries a cargo of peanut butter. It can be inferred that when the data base does not contain a viewable row for aircraft #12, at the Unclassified level, that it is either not flying or that it is carrying a classified cargo. A query directed to the air traffic controller, who is outside of the control of the DMS, will provide information about whether the aircraft is flying or not. In order to prevent this kind of inference, it might be necessary for the DMS to contain unclassified lies and a device that tells the truth to top secret subjects. Such devices are complicated and could lead to serious problems.

This classification scheme is not without value, however. It can certainly be used to maintain corporate data bases and hospital information in which records are unlikely to change classification in a volatile and compromising manner.

3.3 GLOBAL CLASSIFICATION BY FIELD

This classification scheme is similar to global classification by row. In this case, each field is assigned a classification at the time the data base is first conceived. It does not have the inferential anomalies, as did the global classification by row scheme described previously, since it is possible to grant to the subject a uniform partial view of each row. To illustrate the flexibility of the scheme, we consider a personnel data base in which salary information is considered sensitive. In particular, suppose that there are subjects authorized to view salaries up to $10,000, subjects authorized to view salaries up to $15,000, and subjects authorized to view salaries exceeding $15,000.

Accordingly, three fields are created: SALARY, SALARY1, and SALARY2, in increasing order of sensitivity (see Figure 2). The domain of SALARY is integers up to 10,000; that of SALARY1 is integers up to 15,000; and that of SALARY2 integers up to 100,000. The salary triples for employees earning, respectively, $8,200, $12,500, and $27,500 are (8200,~,~), (10000,12500,~) and (10000, 15000, 27500), where ~ represents "undefined." The view for the subject authorized only to see salaries up to $10,000 gives only the information that the first employee earns $8,200, and the other two earn no less than $10,000. He may infer that one of these other employees earns more than $10,000 due to his knowledge about the number of yachts owned by the individual, etc. However, he cannot infer the information directly from the data base.*

3.4 CLASSIFICATION BY DATA CONTENT
It is also possible to restrict access to data strictly as a function of individual data values. For example, in a personnel data base it may be policy that an employee can see but not modify his own current salary; a manager can see the salaries of the employees who report directly to him and earn less than he does, etc. Data-dependent access restrictions can be combined with data-independent classifications, so that certain fields or rows can be hidden from the view of unauthorized individuals purely on the basis of their global classification characteristics, while other data is hidden as a function of forbidden data relationships.

Field	Name	Dept.	Salary	Salary1	Salary2
Classi-fication	C1	1	2	C3	C4
	Jones	Toy	8200	~	~
	Smith	Candy	10000	~	~
	Thomas	Shoes	10000	12500	~
	White	Toy	10000	15000	27500

Figure 2. Classification by Field.
(C1 < C2 < C3 < C4).

3.5 CLASSIFICATION BY ACCESS TYPE
There are instances where specific data values, particulary when related to other specific data values, are of high sensitivity, but there are uncorrelated aggregations of such data which are of lower sensitivity. For example, a corporation might be willing to divulge the number of employees on its payroll earning between $10,000 and $12,000, but be unwilling to give their names. Or, a firm might be willing to publish the average salary for the corporation or for the toy department, yet be unwilling to give the average salary for department managers.
Such forms of access are often referred to as "statistical" access. Many data management systems permit various forms of statistical access to data

----

*The example of the aircraft and their cargoes is also amenable to this approach. We simply create an unclassified field for unclassified cargoes and a Top Secret field for nuclear cargoes, remembering to always require the aircraft carrying nuclear cargoes to carry some unclasified cargo as well. The telling of lies is still required in order to maintain deception, but the situation can be handled.

bases in which specific access is granted to only a few individuals. These include the systems of Fernandez and Stonebraker [FERNA, STONE] and the McAIMS system of Owens [OWEN1, OWEN2].

In general, statistical access is granted when the cardinality of the retrieved set is greater than a certain number. This minimum size restriction is imposed in order to reduce the probability of a penetrator successfully playing a game of 20 questions based on his outside knowledge of the data base. For example, in a census data base, there may be no objection to a query like: PRINT AVERAGE SALARY WHERE OCCUPATION = PHARMACIST AND EXPERIENCE < 5 since there is probably a large number of such people in the data base. On the other hand, there may only be a few individuals in the request: PRINT AVERAGE SALARY WHERE OCCUPATION = PHARMACIST AND EXPERIENCE < 5 AND CITY POPULATION < 10000 AND RELIGION = TAOIST AND BIRTHPLACE = PODUNK AND SEX = FEMALE.

The theory of statistical inference is well developed. The set of controls required to ensure security against more subtle forms of information divulgence could be quite complex. For example, a knowing interrogator could probably use indirection to establish the names of the employees on the payroll earning between $10,000 and $12,000. He might do this, for example, by establishing average salaries by occupational title, by department, and by years of experience. Then, he might ask for the names of all secretaries with two to four years of experience who work in the toy department. In order to foul the surveillance of any DMS routines, he could space out his queries by asking one question each Tuesday. He could also plan his attack with the assistance of collaborators in order to further obfuscate his traces.

Thus, while it is possible to grant statistical access to data bases, it must be taken into account that unscrupulous individuals may be able to derive restricted information from such controls by using completely legitimate means.

3.6 CLASSIFICATION BY GENERAL FORMULAE

The most general form of classification control is that discussed in the definitive paper by Lance Hoffman [HOFFM] on formularies. Formularies provide not only data-independent and data-dependent access controls, but they also provide for the restriction of queries to emanate from specific terminals, during limited time intervals, limiting the number of queries a subject can make in a time period, etc.

3.7 THE AGGREGATE PROPERTY

We conclude the discussion of data classification schemes by pointing out the problems posed by the data aggregation property. It is often stated as: the classification of a whole may be greater than the classification of its parts. Here, again, the possibilities of inference based on either partial views of a data base or on views of the data base augmented by knowledge obtained outside of the data base is discussed.

Hence, one may not know the exact number of personnel assigned to a military base, but he may be able to estimate it based on the monthly consumption of paper towels there. One can also deduce major changes in staffing if the average monthly consumption of paper towels takes a sudden change in either direction.

The above example is one of inference on a data base, since not all of the aggregated data reside in the same data base. In terms of data in one data base, we suggest the following examples:

. Suppose there is a catalog of radar units and a catalog of frequency tubes. Neither of these catalogs need be classified. However, the relationship between a specific radar unit and a specific frequency

tube could be of high sensitivity. Similarly, employee names and the
corporate salary range, hence individual numbers in that range, may be
unclassified, whilst the pairing of employee names with salaries would
be of higher security value.
The name, address, and phone number of one of a corporation's employees
may be of little value. But, the names, addresses, and phone numbers
of all employees, particularly if they all have a specific skill or
work on the same project, could be of high value to a competitor.
In the public arena, a large number of data bases currently exist that
are built on personal information about the citizenry. Each individual in
these data bases is uniquely identified by a Social Security number.
Organizations are beginning to pool these data bases, so that the set of
facts that can be derived about a person is immense.
The problems posed by the aggregate property are extremely complex.
There have been suggestions that some of thedifficulties can be resolved by
prohibiting concurrent access to two fields or relations, or by limiting
the number of queries a user is permitted to pose. But over what period of
time? The situation can be likened to permitting a user to have access to
yellow paint and blue paint, but not granting access to green paint. How
does one prohibit the user from mixing his own green paint from the yellow
and blue paint?

4. ISSUES REGARDING THE IMPLEMENTATION OF SECURE DATA MANAGEMENT SYSTEMS
In this section, the implementation of secure data management systems
that support the data classification schemes described in the previous
section is discussed. What has been done recently in both the military and
commercial security areas is described.
The selected approaches are motivated with implementational simplicity in
mind.   A system provides security only if it is implemented and designed
correctly. The data base and the data base structures have to be equally
protected.   For these reasons, we cannot overemphasize the requirement for
employing the principles of Least Principle and Least Common Mechanism in a
given system's design.
The concept of the Invisible Data Base [HINKE] is crucial to the
successful implementation of a secure data management system. This concept
requires that no user be given more information about the structure or
content of a data base than he is entitled to view. In the context, e.g.,
of a data base in which the fields are classified, the existence of
unviewable fields is to be hidden from users, just as stringently as their
contents. It is much harder for a penetrator to obtain access to
classified data if he does not know of its existence or of the name under
which it is stored.   ◂
Similarly, it is a good tactic to distribute classified information
according to its classification, rather than to store it all together as a
heterogeneous mixture of classifications.   For example, there   is
considerable risk in storing all of the system passwords in the same file,
since any user who breaches the protections of that file obtains the
passwords to all of the files in the system tout d'un coup.
4.1 IMPLEMENTATION OF CLASSIFICATION BY RELATION
Each relation can be stored as a file, which is protected to its level of
classification by the host operating system. This classification scheme
can be implemented on any operating system that has protection to the file
level.   As such, the best principles of Least Privilege and Least Common
Mechanism can be soundly applied, since the data management system need
contain no security enforcement code other than that provided by the host
system. This means that all of the actions of the data management system
will be monitored by the host operating system.   Precisely the same

security provided by the host system is provided by the data management
system.

4.2 IMPLEMENTATION OF CLASSIFICATION BY ROW

Like the previous classification scheme, this one can be implemented on
any secure operating system that offers protection at the file level. The
relations are now distributed over a set of files; hence, there is one file
for each possible row classification and each row is stored in the file of
the appropriate classification. When a subject logs onto the system, the
DMS determines the set of files containing the rows to which the subject
has read access. For each query made by the subject, the DMS searches the
appropriate files.*   This classification scheme has a higher search cost
than the previous one, as users will not generally know the classification
of all data they intend to have searched. But, the scheme does provide a
finer granularity of data classification than classification by relation.
Thus, it provides greater oportunity for the sharing of data between users
of different clearances.

4.3 IMPLEMENTATION OF GLOBAL CLASSIFICATION BY FIELD

The data management system is implemented on a host operating system that
provides for security at the file level. Each field is logically assigned
a file of the appropriate classification.   Several fields of the same
classification can co-reside in the same file if that is deemed desirable.
In this classification scheme, a DBDB can be built and distributed to
contain information about the structure of the relations that comprise the
data base, the identify of primary key fields, and their location within
the system file structure (see Figure 4). Such a secure data management
system was designed by Hinke and Schaefer of System Development Corporation
[HINKE] for a militarily secure MULTICS operating system.

It should be noted that all user requests are processed in the same way
by such a system. This is because the subject either has or does not have
a given form of access to each named field in his request. If the subject
names a field to which he does not have access, the DMS will be unable to
distinguish between the subject's referencing a nonexistent field and his
making a spelling error.   If the DMS derived the set of fields that the
user could name, the unauthorized name would not be in the DMS's central
tables, so his request would be rejected as a syntax error. If, on the
other hand, the subject managed to covertly place the unauthorized field
name in the DMS's central tables, the DMS would try to access the field on
the user's behalf, only to have the request blocked by the secure operating
system's always resident reference monitor.

Since the relation is stored by field, and since the file containing a
field will be accessible only if there is an active subject with access to
the field, there is a minor problem involving the preservation of alignment
between the columns.   This arises as a consequence of the *-property and
the use of Least Common Mechanism. The fields of lowest classification are
the most subject to use and to modification since the population of
subjects with low clearances is greater.   Presumably, subjects will be

----

*A data base can be built that uses the same mechanisms in order to serve
as a directory to the files in which the data base is stored. This data
base data base (DBDB) would have its own rows stored, according to the
classification of the rows of the data base in question (see Figure 3).
The data base data base approach permits the DMS to be implemented with
Least Privilege and Least Common Mechanism principles. As will be seen,
distributed DBDB's are used in several applications of this kind.

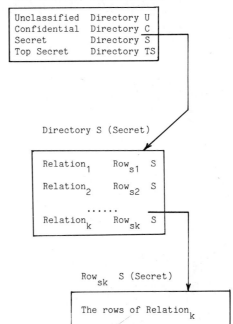

Row Directory (Unclassified)

Unclassified	Directory U
Confidential	Directory C
Secret	Directory S
Top Secret	Directory TS

Directory S (Secret)

This directory is
classified Secret.
Hence, no subject
may view its contents
unless he has a
Secret clearance.

Relation$_1$	Row$_{s1}$	S
Relation$_2$	Row$_{s2}$	S
......		
Relation$_k$	Row$_{sk}$	S

Row$_{sk}$ S (Secret)

The rows of Relation$_k$

that are classified Secret.

Figure 3. A Data Base Data Base Classification is Global by Row.

Secret field directory (Secret)

field name	parent relation	primary key?	file name
Emp#	Personnel.	Yes	P.E.
Name	Personnel.	No	P.N.
Supplier#	Parts & Suppliers	Yes	PS.S
Project#	Parts & Suppliers	Yes	PS.PR
Part#	Parts & Suppliers	Yes	PS.P#
Quantity on Hand	Parts & Suppliers	No	PS.QOH

Figure 4. Data Base Data Base Directory To Secret Fields

entering and deleting rows. Actually, these are partial rows since these
subjects are ignorant of the full set of fields comprising a row. In
Figure 5, it will be noted that the title of former employee 043 remains in
the data base, as do the salaries of employees 043 and 046; while title and
salary are missing for employee 195. In order for this to be done while
the integrity of the data base is preserved [HEATH], it must be possible
for every subject who can view any of the relation to view the relation's
primary key. If a value in a field of high classification is to be
deleted, the subject who deletes it cannot directly communicate the fact to
any user of lower clearance because of the *-property. Therefore, after a
period of time has passed, the data base will start to contain partial
rows.   In order that the rows can continue to be aligned, i.e., remain
meaningful to all users, it is required that each field value have
identifying information associated with it determining the row to which it
belongs. This cannot be achieved through the use of address pointers,* so
it must be achieved with logical pointers that uniquely determine the row

EMP# (Uncl)	EMP NAME (Uncl)	DEPT (Uncl)	TITLE (Confid.)	SALARY (Secret)
001	JONES	TOY	CLERK	8000
025	SMITH	TOY	MGR	15000
047	WRIGHT	CANDY	SALES	10000
125	FFINCH-RAVEN	ADMIN	PRESIDENT	75000
187	BLAGGARD	CANDY	SALES	9000
195	NEW-HYRE	ADMIN	~	~

(a) A Secret Subject's View of the Data Base.

EMP#	EMP NAME	DEPT	TITLE	SALARY
001	001; JONES	001; TOY	001; CLERK	001; 8000
025	025; SMITH	025; TOY	025; MGR	025; 15000
047	047; WRIGHT	047; CANDY	043; CLERK	043; 8500
125	125; FFINCH-RAVEN	125; ADMIN	047; SALES	046; 25000
187	187; BLAGGARD	187; CANDY	125; PRESIDENT	047; 10000
195	197; NEW-HYRE	195; ADMIN	187; SALES	125; 75000
				187; 9000

(b) The Data Base as it is Currently Represented After
Multi-Level Updates.

Figure 5. A Data Base With Global Classification by Field.

----

*Address pointers cannot be used to point to data of a different
classification. This is for the following reasons: To point to data of
higher sensitivity, one must obtain the address to which he is pointing,
and is then prevented by the *-property from writing the address in the
field of lower classification. In addition, by placing a pointer to
sensitive data in a less sensitive environment, one is implicitly
indicating the existence of classified data to unauthorized individuals.
If total alignment reliance is placed on the integrity of these pointers,
the situation is even worse, since unauthorized saboteurs can directly
destroy necessary information. On the other hand, one could point from
fields of high classification to fields of lower classification, but with

to which each field value belongs. Such a pointer is logically the equivalent of the primary key to the relation, i.e., it is either the primary key or a tuple-identifier, uniquely generated at the time a value is first stored in the key field for the row in question.

To our knowledge, there are no implementations of relational data management systems in which storage is organized by column rather than by row. It is interesting to note that the method of storage forced by the classification is not so bad as it first appears to be. This is because it is possible to arrange the storage organization of each column optimally with respect to the kinds of retrievals the field is anticipated to receive most often. That is, one field may be stored as a binary-tree, while another is stored as an inverted file, and so on. This freedom of storage organization is obtained as a direct consequence of the redundancy with which each field has been stored.

It should also be noted that the fields can each be stored on a separate computer, each field having its own access control mechanisms. As can be seen in [HINKE], the architecture is sufficiently general to support as distributed data management application.

The three classification schemes previously described are such that they can be implemented on any system that provides for the enforcement of security at the file level. As such, the systems do not require the implementation of additional security-related code. Since security-related code must be correct and consistent in order to provdide a correct implementation of the reference monitor concept, it is important to note that nothing in a data management system designed around one of these three global classification options requires certification. As will be seen, this is not the case in the systems designed to enforce the schema described below.

4.4 IMPLEMENTATION OF CLASSIFICATION BY DATA CONTENT

Data dependent classifications go beyond the normal purview of secure operating systems. Consequently, a data management system that enforces such classification conventions needs to provide all of the necessary enforcement code required to implement such a reference monitor. It is to be noted that this will require modification to the host operating system in order to provide full protection from tampering for the enforcement code, and possible modification in the event that it would be possible for a would-be penetrator to directly access the data without using the secure data management system. The DMS might also require its own means of identifying the user as additional protection from spoofing and impersonation.

Depending on other security requirements, it may be necessary to implement such a DMS on a limited-use operating system. This could be necessary if, e.g., there were no provisions in the existing operating systems to protect against penetration attempts written in assembly language that directly circumvent DMS security controls, or in higher-level languages that simulate terminals in order to barrage the system with computer-speed guesses at user passwords, or that permit utility programs to coexist with user DMS processes while containing Trojan Horses, as can happen in systems which do not enforce the *-property.

----

*(continued) futility. This is because a subject with authorization to modify the data at the lower level could delete tuple information at a time when there was no active process around to maintain the correctness of the higher classified pointer. One would be left with numerous "dangling" pointers and no data base integrity.

Assuming   a   sufficiently   flexible   operating   environment,   the
implementation of the required security controls can either take the form
of encoded algorithms, as in the formulary model of Hoffman [HOFFM], or it
can be achieved by simple modification of the subject´s queries. This
latter approach has been taken by Fernandez and Grey of IBM [FERNA] and by
Stonebraker and Wong of the University of California [STONE].

The latter approach is quite interesting.   For each authorized user,
there is established a set of logical predicates, each of which restricts
his view of the data base. Call these p1,p2,...,pn.   Then suppose the
subject   issues   a   query   Q.   The system changes the query into
Q & (p1 ¦ p2 ¦...¦ pn) such that only an authorized subset of what the user
would have retrieved is actually delivered to him.

For example, suppose Smith is only authorized to view salaries of
employees in the toy department and phone numbers of unmarried females in
the candy department. Then if Smith requests the salary of Jones, his
query   is   modified   to   the   form
PRINT SALARY WHERE NAME = JONES & (DEPT = TOY), while if Smith requests the
phone   number   of   Jones,   his   query   is   modified   to
PRINT PHONE# WHERE NAME = JONES & (SEX = F & MAR_STAT = UNMAR & DEPT = CANDY).

The query modification approach has some adverse effects on efficiency,
but it is conceptually simple and extremely adaptable to modification by an
authorized security officer.   In addition, the method is sufficiently
powerful to permit enforcement of the form of access control described in
the following section.

4.5 IMPLEMENTATION OF CLASSIFICATION BY ACCESS TAPE
The access controls are implemented in the front end of the data
management system.   They must be organized in concert with whatever other
access controls exist in the system so that it is impossible for user
processes to circumvent whatever protection is provided.

4.6 IMPLEMENTATION OF CLASSIFICATION BY GENERAL FORMULAE
Formularies are always implemented as procedures. Some of the formulary
controls must be invoked prior to accessing the data base, others
afterward, some both before and after.

There are many arguments against the use of formularies.   These revolve
around   questions of the correctness of the implementation of each
formulary, as well as the logical consistency of the class of formularies
that apply to a given subject. These concerns are not without their merit.
As has been indicated earlier, if there are logical flaws in the security
enforcement mechanisms, the security of the system remains in effect only
until such time as the flaws are discovered. Each time a new formulary is
introduced, it is granted a set of privileges with respect to the accessing
of data. It is necessary to prove the correctness and consistency of the
entire enforcement mechanism each time it is modified by the inclusion or
modification of any one formulary. The required logical analysis is costly,
cumbersome, and invites errors.

Proofs of system correctness are not yet within the state-of-the-art for
systems of any major size, although automated tools are currently being
developed to generate proofs of correctness for sufficiently small bodies
of code [SCHOR]. However, mechanical audits are required in order to ensure
the correctness of the proofs themselves. Surely, the proof of correctness
of a body of code must involve at least as many lines of text as which is
being proved. But, that means that the proof is on an order of difficulty
comparable to that of the body of code and, hence, at least as likely to
contain errors as the code itself. The likelihood of error in a 1000 line
program is extremely high.   So also is the likelihood of error in its

proof. Therefore, mechanical proof checking, if not proof generation, is required.

We have mentioned the subject of formularies in order to provide a broad-based approach to data base classification schemes. Business firms and military organizations are not yet prepared to handle formularies, but the time is coming when we will be capable of dealing with them in a mathematically satisfying manner.

5. CONCLUSIONS

Several meaningful ways in which the data in a shared data base can be classified have been discussed in this paper. The classification schemes are intended to provide protection for sensitive data while permitting the less sensitive contents of the data base to be shared by a body of less trusted users.

It is found that as the granularity of the unit of data to which classification is applied grows smaller, the degree of permitted sharing becomes greater. But as the degree of sharing increases, so also grows the complexity of the implemented control mechanisms. With increases in complexity comes the increased likelihood that the control mechanisms are implemented with logical errors--flaws that could lead to compromise of the protection of the data base itself.

Classification schemes in which the classification is globally applied to entities across the data base, i.e., the data base, relations, rows or fields, can be implemented atop existing secure operating systems, using the principles of Least Common Mechanism and Least Privilege. As such, only the protection provided by the host system can be enforced over the data base. But the data management system need contain no security-relevant code, and the correctness of its implementation need not be proved in order for one to have confidence in its enforcement of security policy.

Data dependent classification schemes depend upon the reference monitor enforcement code being specially produced for the data management system, regardless of what is present in the host system. The protection offered by such systems is fully dependent on the correctness of the implementation. Thus, although the degree of sharing permitted by such a system is greater and the degree of over-classification occurring from such a system is potentially lower than in the data independent schemes, the chances of error and penetration by unauthorized subjects is also significantly increased.

There remain numerous problems, particularly with respect to developing an understanding of the aggregate property, statistical inference, the control of concurrent accesses by subjects operating at different clearance levels, and the maintenance of integrity in data bases.

These problems are not insurmountable. As the need for data security grows, so also will our understanding of the uses and abuses of classification schema and implementation strategies. Certainly, limited use systems and periods processing systems (especially dedicated implementations on minicomputers) will propagate. But since there is a need for multi-level sharing of large data bases, there will be major implementations of data management systems of the kind we have discussed.

6. ACKNOWLEDGEMENTS

The author would like to acknowledge the helpful suggestions made by his colleagues T. H. Hinke and W. M. Shasberger during the editing of this paper.

BIBLIOGRAPHY
[AFDSC] "Security design analysis report for Air Force Data Services

            Center," Honeywell Information Systems, Inc., October 1973
            (draft)
[ANDER]   Anderson, J.P., "Computer security technology planning study."
            Electronic Systems Division (MCIT), AFSC, Bedford, Mass., ESD-
            TR-73- 51, October 1972.
[CODD]   Codd, E.F., "A relational model of data for large shared data
            bases," CACM (13, 6), June 1970, pp. 377-387.
[FERNA]   Fernandez, E.B., et al., "An authorization model for a shared
            data base," ACM SIGMOD Proceedings, May 1975, pp. 23-31.
[HEATH]   Heath, I.J., "Unacceptable file operations in a relational data
            base," Proc. 1971 ACM-SIGFIDET workshop on data description,
            access, and control, 1972.
[HINKE]   Hinke, T.H., and Marvin Schaefer, "Secure data management
            system: final report," RADC report TR-75-266, November 1975.
[HOFFM]   Hoffman, Lance, "The formulary model for access control and
            privacy," Stanford Linear Accelerator Center Report #117, May
            1970.
[LAPAD]   LaPadula, L.J. and D.E. Bell, "Secure computer systems: a mathe-
            matical model," ESD-TR-73-278, Vol. II, MITRE Corp., November
            1973.
[MIT]   Schroeder, M.D., "Engineering a security kernel for MULTICS,"
            ACM Operating Systems Review, Vol. 9, No. 5, November 1975, pp.
            25-32.
[MITRE]   Schiller, W.L., "The design and specifications of a security
            kernel for the PDP-11/45," MITRE Corp. MTR-2934, Bedford, Mass.,
            May 1975.
[OWEN1]   Owens, R., "Primary access control in large scale time-shared
            decision systems," Project MAC Report TR-89, MIT, Cambridge,
            Mass., July 1971.
[OWEN2]   Owens, R., "Evaluation of access authorization characteristics
            of derive time-shared decision systems," Project MAC Report
            TR-89, MIT, Cambridge, Mass., July 1971.
[OWEN2]   Owens, R., "Evaluation of access authorization characteristics
            of derived data sets," Proc. 1971 SIGFIDET workshop on data
            description, access and control, San Diego, California, November
            1971.
[SCHA1]   Schaefer, Marvin, "Quasi-synchronization of readers and writers
            in a secure multi-level environment," SDC TM-5407/003/00,
            September 1974.
[SALTZ]   Saltzer, J.H., Schroeder, M.D. "The Protection of Information
            in Computer Systems", Proc. IEEE V.63.n.9. (Sept. 1975) pp.
            1278-1308.
Schorre, D.V., "A program verifier with assertions in terms of abstract
            data," MRI International Symposium XXIV on computer software
            engineering, 1976.
[SDC/VMM] Weissman Clark, "Secure computer operation with virtual machine
            partitioning", SDC SP-3790, September 1974
[SRI]   Neumann, P.G., et al, "A provably secure operating system,"
            Stanford Research Institute, Menlo Park, California, SRI Project
            2581, June 1975.
[STONE]   Stonebraker, M., and E. Wong, "Access control in a relational
            data base management system by query modification," Univ. of
            Calif. memorandum No. ERL-M438, May 1974.
[UCLA]   Walton, E.J., "The UCLA security kernel," MS Thesis, UCLA, Los
            Angeles, 1975.
[WEISS]   Weissman, Clark, "Security controls in the ADEPT-50 time-sharing
            system," Proceedings FJCC, 1969, pp. 119-134.

DISCUSSION

LOWENTHAL: Even if you had a perfectly secure data base management system, it's only as strong as the operating system. I've been looking at the notion of a back end computer, that is, the idea of putting the data base management system into a small autonomous computer. Does that appear to solve the problem?

SCHAEFER: It does, very nicely. I didn't go into it because of time and technicality. We at SDC tried designing a multi-level multi-user secure data management system and settled on the idea of global classification by field, as the one we would attack. We stored each of the fields in its own separate segment in the MULTICS environment. You end up storing all fields of the same classification in the same segment, along with some other information like primary keys so that the data can be kept with some amount of integrity. This results in different user processes getting different views which are extracted from each of the fields they can view as a transitive closure. We found that that problem was no different from the problem of running with a distributed data management system in which you've decided not to distribute portions of the data base, but rather just the fields of the data base, so that each field could effectively be on its own computer. In fact, it's a little bit worse than that because the computers have funny protocols for communicating with each other due to the *- property which prohibits Trojan horses. Now each of those computers, which conceptually has a field of data in it, can be encrypted, using an NBS algorithm or something like that, and now you've got security that's as good as the management of the encryption keys and as good as the encryption algorithm itself.

LOWENTHAL: If you do have a back end computer such that a user can only access it through the DML, what would be the advantage of having multiple back ends, one for each field? What would be the disadvantage of having all the fields controlled by the same back end?

SCHAEFER: You mean the access to the back end is controlled itself. That is O.K.

STEEL: One should consider the cost of providing the security, and it should be the minimum of the value of losing the information to the owner and the value of the information to the prospective penetrator. Would you agree with that as a general principle?

SCHAEFER: Yes, I would. I didn't even allude to what kinds of costs we're talking about here. Those people who have been involved in formal proofs of correctness are aware of what I was getting at when I said that reference monitors had to be proven correct. We are talking lots of money, and features like password control might be very good if people stopped using passwords that anyone can guess, or that are long enough, because it takes a lot of time to get the password. Certain communication paths that are 20 bits per minute, or 1 bit per hour are considered too much by the military when national security is at stake. But, who cares if someone steals 38 discs out of a database, as long as the 38 discs aren't the right ones. It's always a hard question. There's a very high cost in producing a secure system because of the reliability, the correctness, the integrity issues that have to be addressed, and people are going to make compromises, especially since there are no garden variety completely secure systems lying around now to build with.

STEEL: I have seen estimates in literature that it may add as much as 30% to the cost of a system to make it essentially impenetrable. Does that sound like the right order of mangnitude to you?

SCHAEFER: I don´t know who the optimist was who said that. I think he´s off by at least a factor of two, right now. However, it depends on who is doing the penetration.

TAYLOR: With regard to your closing comments about access control, using query modification, at least one reason for using a view mechanism as opposed to dynamic query modification, is that by using a view mechanism at view definition time, you have some hope of making an optimization plan for the materialization of tuples from the relation and then storing that optimization plan in the library. Thus, when a particular query comes along, you don´t have to do a lot of work in terms of an optimization plan, and it may help the potential efficiency problems with sort of data-dependent authorization schemes that they both offer.

SCHAEFER: That´s true if you really have a clever system. In the design we made, we tried to get a clever system in that we´re certainly providing a vertical strip view of a database with global classification by field. However, it´s a view, and it´s known for each user, and one needs a great deal of redundancy in order to maintain integrity in a database environment where some fields are being modified all the time because they are unclassified, and other fields are rarely modified, because no one has enough authority, statistically, to update a top secret field. Since there´s no common mechanism in the system, if there´s no one there to look at a top secret field, then there´s nothing in the system that´s looking at it either. How do you then optimize anything? This can be done by having these fields stored in such a way that each tuple element is identified by tuple as well as its other attributes. You can do anything you want to the structuring of that field and still be able to identify the elements in it by role of the relation. That means that you can organize that particular field any way you want. You can also do statistical analyses of how people are accessing data in that particular view you´re enforcing, and optimize each field for the kind of access that it normally receives, be it query, be it update, or be it a combination. That is one way of using views to optimize performance for specific users. It´s a very special case, but I think it´s true that as long as the views are reasonably stable and as long as the union of the views is reasonably rectangular, then it is possible to optimize performance for users with that particular view. It is the saving grace of views as an enforcement mechanism. If there´s great flexibility in modifying the views, I´m afraid that you can end up with the general case, which is data scattered all over the universe. In that case I don´t know what you do with it.

GRIMES: How do you ensure that all accesses to data are made through the security monitor?

SCHAEFER: That is not an easy question to answer in days, much less in minutes. In effect, you have to have something which can trap every security-relevant instruction on the machine. Now, such a mechanism is often called a security kernel, and it´s built in such a way that it exploits the fact that on certain machines the security-relevant instructions are a proper subset of the privileged instructions. One puts

data in areas of homogeneous classification, for example, segments. I
don't care if it's a page, segment, word, whatever, it has a security
attribute. If the hardware is friendly enough, then the first time someone
tries to access the data, a protection interruption will take place, and
the reference monitor now has a way of figuring out whether to give access
or not.

GRIMES: Your assumption is that you can allocate that secure data together.

SCHAEFER: That's not always the case. If that's not the case, you can't use
just hardware. You have to use hardware at a very big level of granularity
and then call software, which interpretively decides whether or not to
allow the data to be viewed by the user. There's also the possibility of a
limited use system. If the only language people can use is the query
language, or the communication language of the DML, then you've eliminated
many ways that people penetrate systems, e.g. by writing assembly language
programs. If the only way of getting in is through a high level language,
you've already cut the costs considerably, probably by an order of
magnitude, or so.

GRIMES: Is the assumption that everything below that is proved?

SCHAEFER: No, if the only way you can get in is through the higher level
language, then, to start with, things down below that have nothing to do
with accessing the data are totally irrelevant, because there is no way for
them to be called from above. If, after the system has been designed, and
shown to be correct, someone comes in and modifies anything, including a
sort routine, then all bets are off, because he might plant a Trojan horse
or a trap door. However, if you have a system that has been working
reliably for some period of time, the probability that someone had thought
of putting code in that would attack what you haven't yet designed is
fairly low. It's called a second order attack, and so you might be able to
trust the code that does everything except actually access data, as being
correct and secure and safe. Now you examine the code that accesses data,
and see if it has anything clever, like looking for Jones' name when it
comes to modifying chequing account balances. If you don't see those
things, you might trust it, put in the front-end filter that mediates the
request by access type, and you've got yourself a fairly secure operating
system.

GRIMES: You think that would satisfy the Department of Defense or similar
users?

SCHAEFER: I don't think we know of very much at all that will completely
satisfy the DOD, because their needs are quite specific. They have
extremely exacting standards, they're not willing to tolerate a bit per
hour leakages in certain cases, and its easy to get more than a bit per
hour. That customer has really expensive data, and he really wants to
protect it. There are other places like life insurance companies that
can't afford to spend very much for protecting their data, but they're
going to have to worry about privacy laws pretty soon, and I really don't
know what they're going to do. In that situation, the security value of
the data is not the value of the data to a competitor, but the value of the
law suit when they give the wrong information out. One law suit could be
more expensive than the cost of implementing a system.

STEEL: I know what we're going to do...we're going to spend money!

MAIRET: People are spending a lot of time and money building data dictionary-directory systems and working very hard to define all the data, how it is stored, in what format it's stored, in what representation, etc. They're using this to control the data base management system as well as using it as a productivity aid. However, we also want to secure the data, and these seem to be conflicting objectives. If someone can get into the data set but does not know what the data are, or what format or doesn't have a template, its just a string of bits. But if you give him a template, plus the names of everything, plus textural definitions of what it means......

SCHAEFER: You've now given him the greatest common mechanism he could have desired: a complete guideline to reading the data. Figure 3 in my paper shows how such information can be proected. There is a master directory that lists the names of the files in which information from classified rows is stored. Taking, for example, the directory of secret rows, we find here a file which the reference monitor is protecting as a secret file. That's the first step. Now the protection mechanism protects itself. In that file, the names of the rows and the relations they belong to by classification are all secret. There's no information about whether top secret rows exist. From that directory, one locates the rows in that relation which are secret. That's the data, which is also protected at the secret level. Thus, we've distributed a directory. If there were four security levels for the installation, there'd be at least four directories. You put information about secret information only in a place that's itself secret. In terms of the schema that you're trying to visualize in this format, it means that there is an efficiency cost of putting everying back together when someone logs on and wants to use the database. Effectively, you must reconstruct the schema by starting at the bottom and reading the least privileged information about the information, and then the information about the information at the next higher level, and so on, until everything is together. This provides a representation of what the user can see, and no more.

STEEL: One of the basic principles of cryptanalysis is that while there are very-simple-to-design, theoretically unbreakable, codes, in practice, that's not the case because people have to use them, and people make mistakes. Would you care to comment on that kind of problem in this environment.

SCHAEFER: Some problems have been removed by new things like the NBS algorithm for encryption in chip form. It's supposed to be a very good algorithm which all but a few people think is reasonably hard to break. It's cheap, and it takes a long time to break unless you've got a lot of computers working in parallel on the problem. If you get enough chips going, you can break any code by dividing up potential keys into mutually exclusive classes. That doesn't solve the harder problem of managing the keys. A database can't be very safe if it's all kept in one place, because if you get everyone's key, you know where it goes, and you've got everything if you can break into it. No one has yet solved that problem, to my knowledge.

HARRIS: My position is that the data base management system should be able to maintain the integrity of the data base. In your example of deletion of supplier address, you seem to imply that another user process would have to delete the supplier name or any other attributes that are left. Either that function could be done automatically by the data base management system or the first user shouldn't have been able to locate it, in which case the data should have been reclassified.

SCHAEFER: The second answer was the correct one for that problem. We don't want to have the data management system working on all of the data base all of the time, in real time.

HARRIS: Why not?

SCHAEFER: If someone can exploit or subvert the mechanisms that are looking at higher information than people are looking at, they can get access to classified data.

HARRIS: You're suggesting that the database management system itself might have a Trojan horse.

SCHAEFER: The advantage of building a secure data management system on top of a secure operating system, is that you don't have to prove anything about the data management system code. I tried to indicate that proving the correctness of code is very very hard, and very very expensive. If you change anything anywhere, it must be reproved.   So, if you can use an operating system which is secure, then the entire data management system can be written by a competing company and you can rest assured that no one is going to get unauthorized information. If the data management system provides the security, there can be Trojan horses all over the place.   The only way you can be sure there are no Trojan horses is by proving the whole thing. I haven't looked at DMS's in a while, so I don't know how many hundreds of thousands of lines of code we're talking about, but the state of the art of program verification right now is closer to a hundred lines of code.

HARRIS: If you're assuming you can prove that the operating system is secure, why can't you do the same thing for the data base management system?

SCHAEFER: The operating system is effectively partitioned into two disjoint sets - security enforcement code, and the rest of it. The security enforcement code can be very small. Some existing security kernels are as few as 2000 lines of high level language code, such as some the Mitre Corporation has written. In the case of one of them, for the PDP 11/45, a team of Ph.D's in mathematics sat down for an unbelievable three man years, and hand proved the specification of the code, using formal mathematical techniques.   No one has penetrated that system to date, although there are still some doubts about the implementation, since the code itself has not been proved. Operating systems are not two to five thousand lines of code long, but the security-relevant portion of it was very small.   Since that was primitive to everything that ran in the operating system, it was next to the bare hardware of the 11/45, and there was nothing else to depend on. There were no known Trojan horses in the hardware, and they're not changing the micro-code or the machine model that they're working on, so there's reason to believe that they might have a secure system. Let's look at the data management system. It is vulnerable to a changed operating system. I don't care if there's a Trojan horse - what if there's a mistake? If you were counting on that particular routine being implemented correctly because your security mechanism depends upon it, the whole thing just went out the window. You don't need a Trojan horse, it can just be dumb.   It's the same with respect to any other routine in an operating system. The easiest case is, in fact, building on a secure operating system. You can get a secure opearting system by strengthening usage of your system to a very high level language; not allowing anyone else to ever touch your machine, by locking it up; and by using techniques like query modification at a low level right next to the data, rather than at a high level.

SEVCIK: In your presentation on relational aspects, I got the impression that there might be some distinct advantages in having the external view very similar to the internal represenation. This provides the flexibility of doing reference monitoring at a low level. In the more ideal situation, where we have many users with many external views, it seems like there are two discouraging alternatives. Either you have to repeat the query modification for each external view, which is a lot of redundancy, or else you must force everything down to the internal level where it looks very different depending on which external view it came from. Could you comment on how those two relate, or which is preferable?

SCHAEFER: Query modification scares the living daylights out of me, and the reason is what happens if the items that get handed on to the query are not self consistent, but in fact are self contradictory. I have a feeling that in order to put my faith in query modification, I must have something that executes or examines the query modification, that is, predicates to make sure that they're self consistent. With 'P and not P', I can get anything. If the constraints are strict enough, I'm not sure that I can tell that I don't have 'P and not P'.

SEVCIK: How vast is the advantage of dealing with only three security levels?

SCHAEFER: We're dealing with 2 to the 18th power. The United States Government has a complicated system of classification, and we certainly didn't store 2 to the 18 things in our paper design. As in all things, while they've got that many possibilities, they can't count that high either. I, as a pure mathematician, started looking at it from the point of view of definition, and I ended up with something which was a subset of the set of cartesian products of the domains. I worked out a whole algebra for it before someone showed me a paper by Ted Codd, so it turned out that the relational view fit naturally into what we needed for security. I'd not thought about any other view for the reason that I just end up translating everything into relational terms anyway.

JARDINE: You've talked about the problem of the contamination of the security mechanism which could result in the exposure of the data. There is the other possibility, of course, that a paranoid security kernel can result in my not being able to get at my own data. There is a distinct possibility that the more secure we make the system, the higher is the probability of the paranoid kernel keeping me out of my own data, which clearly implies that there be somebody who can bypass the security mechanism at some level to recover from such conditions. That person is bribable. Would you care to comment on paranoid systems?

SCHAEFER: There is a person called a chief security officer who is supposed to have the omniscience and omnipotence of God, plus a little bit more, since God has been known to change His mind on occasion too. He's [the security officer] bribable, and I don't know what good he does if he exists, other than for handing out authorizations for passwords to people in the first place. If you really do what I showed for this paranoid system, and distribute everything out in Hilbert space, then how is the security officer going to know where to look either? On the other hand it doesn't take a very paranoid or very secure system before you get into that kind of context. Some people at SDC managed to make several sucessful penetrations of VM 370 a few years ago when it was thought to be secure. The results of that study are published in a current IBM Systems Journal. That system was supposed to be secure, but it was penetrable. Some of the penetrators managed to lose files while they were doing it, which as far as we know are still living on a disc some place! If the system really does a good job, not even the chief security officer will really be of much help, and bribable or not, you're just stuck with it. On the other hand, what you say is extremely important and not laughable. The anomaly in terms of integrity loss that I showed before was because no one thought about the implication of classifying one relation low and the other one high. You can get yourself in the same bind by classifying things at levels that you don't know about, or don't understand. I feel that the Chief Security Officer really has to have the holy attributes I gave him a minute ago, and therefore should be a computer program that prints out, after some great deal of analysis, all the implications or a subset of the implications which are interesting.

MANOLA: The rigidity of the Defense Department security requirements tends to be overemphasized. The Department of Defense, it seems, operates on a very narrow railroad track. On the one hand you have Congress, which can apparently get to anything it wants, on the other extreme, you have operational users. The people in the middle, the DOD bureaucrats, including us, are constrained very rigidly by these requirements. The operational users have a secret password which they can use to bypass the security mechanism at any time. It's called operational necessity - that's when the Admiral says to the seaman, "Break down that door!" That's a very useful analogy to carry into the commercial security world.

SCHAEFER: I have to say Bravo! to that. I am scared to death of encryption for the reason that we've stated already. If anything goes wrong with management of the keys, no one is ever going to find out what's in any of the databases and I don't trust data management systems well enough to believe that they're going to be able to manage a database of keys at this point in time.

ROBERTS: It seems to me you've demonstrated conclusively, that the state of the art is such that we can't afford, certainly in a commercial sense, to even approach the kind of security that someone might say we ought to have. Possibly before we launch into spending these enormous amounts of money we ought to take precisely the opposite path, and assert that the best defense in this kind of situation make data freely available. Then you develop your strategy on the basis that another person already knows it or can learn it at a trivial cost.

SCHAEFER: I don't think you want to make it all completely available because of the privacy laws that Congress has enacted. You just can't put out people's criminal records. I'm not sure that you can even print records of people's driving habits too widely, and certainly you can't print medical records very widely without a lawsuit. One can only hope that some agency will fund the development of public domain secure systems which, like the NBS algorithm, are available to anyone who wants them, and which have known security properties. Remember that a good secure system is one whose code can be published openly, so that people can get to us it,

the major cost having been paid by government research or by whichever
other agency is going to be brave enough and munificent enough to pay for
it.

ABOVE THE CONCEPTUAL LEVEL:
SOCIAL AND ORGANIZATIONAL VIEWS OF DATABASE MANAGEMENT SYSTEMS

Howard Lee Morgan
Departmant of Decision Sciences
The Wharton School
University of Pennsylvania
Philadelphia, PA 19174

Introduction

I received the invitation to speak at this meeting about three weeks ago. During that time, I have been immersed in teaching, along with some colleagues, a course on very large databases, whatever they are, and have been focussing on the various levels we use in describing views of databases. Therefore, when deciding on how to best present some of my views on the social and organizational problems associated with the creation and use of databases, my technological bias won, and may show through in the rest of this talk.

When we talk of levels of a database, we are really speaking of a continuum from the bits, as they reside on a storage device, to the overall view of the database which might be taken by society. However, there has evolved over the years a classification scheme which has proven useful in focussing our attention on major problems related to the implementation of database management systems. What I shall try to do is to describe the various levels, and show that by viewing the organizational and social problems as related to levels of database "views," the implications for designers and implementers of DBMS become clear.

The "lowest" level view of a database is the physical level. This is typically the view that the machine hardware itself, and to some extent the operating system, has of the data. Historically, this was the only view of data available to users for the first twenty or so years of computing. Then, the concept of "logical" views of data appeared. These were views which the programmer wished to have of the data. The basic concept behind a "logical" view was that the aggregate amount of data which the program wished to deal with at any one time did not have to map one to one with the aggregate unit the machine wished to deal with. A simple example is the concept of "blocking," where a physical level aggregate, called a block, may contain many logical level aggregates, often called logical records.

In more recent years, the concept of data/program independence has gained much support. This concept argues for keeping the programs as ignorant as possible about the actual physical structure of the data, and permits references only through the use of a "logical level" description of the data. During the development of database management systems to support this data independence, the notion of another, higher level description, the "conceptual" level has been formed.

The conceptual level, or "conceptual schema" as it is called in the ANSI/SPARC report [1], serves as a connection between the logical description desired by some program (or "external" schema) and the physical level description (or "internal" schema). It is anticipated that the database administrator will embody his or her knowledge of the organization's data in this conceptual schema, and that systems for

automatically translating between conceptual and external, and conceptual
and internal schemas will be developed.
    Understanding of the existence of these levels has given rise to
generalized systems software to aid in processing them, and in translating
from one level to another. Thus, early IOCS's were an aid in handling
physical structures, early DBMS's helped with logical structures, and
proposals such as the ANSI/SPARC report [1], should help deal with the
conceptual level.
    To this same end, I propose that we recognize organizational and social
levels of data, so that more and better tools can be brought to bear on
major organizational and social problems found in organizations using DBMS.

Organizational Implications

    It is instructive to see how DBMS are perceived by managers in real
organizations. A recent survey of 64 companies, undertaken as a class
project[4], asked managers what they felt was the most important problem
area in their information system. The results are summarized in Figure 1.
It is clear that DBMS can help solve some of the problems in getting
accurate information.
    Right now, most DBMS are geared to supporting programmers and system
analysts and designers. It is easy to lose sight of the fact that it is
the management of the organization which the information system must serve.
This management has always had a "schema" for viewing the organizational
database. I contend that this "organizational" level view of the database
is not yet supported by DBMS, even in the ANSI/SPARC proposals, and I feel
that it should be.

Figure 1. Major Problem Area in DP

Major problem area	Cost of Data	Data Accuracy
Have DBMS	75%	25%
Do not have DBMS	25%	75%

    DBMS which work at the logical or conceptual levels tend to reinforce the
"rational" or formal systems of communications within an organization.
They argue for nonredundancy of data, and for formal controls on entry,
modification, and access to data. These systems have even given rise to
the new job of database administrator. But, as Berg [3] pointed out in the
last one of these conferences tihree years ago, there are also the
"natural" or informal systems within organizations. In fact, as one goes
up the organizational hierarchy, more and more of the communications
between the manager and the database occurs through these channels.
    It is also true that at higher managerial levels, a more holistic view is
taken of the data, i.e., more aggregation is desired, and correlation of
widely spread data. This aggregate level should be recognized as the
organizational level of data. We are going to need DBMS with the ability
to provide, as basic functions, this type of high level aggregation.
    In addition, we must recognize that current DBMS and online systems
technology can actually generate some fears which work against the
organizations "natural" systems. This occurs because these systems now
permit a high level manager to easily monitor very detailed, low level
transactions. This fear of "big brother" is very real.
    This also relates to the question of how organizational control and
authority is spread in an organization. An essential element in a

description of an organization is the amount of centralization and/or decentralization in each of its units. With the existence of distributed processing technology and distributed databases, high level management has the ability to materially affect the centralization/decentralization balance. In some sense, this is information which should be reflected in an organizational level schema for the organization's database.

Such an organizational schema might permit a high level manager to decide "decentralize division x as a profit center, and report only aggregate financial information to our central system as long as they remain within 10% of target costs," and to have this enforced including access controls by the DBMS.

There may be other benefits provided by trying to accurately define and support an organizational level of data. Bachman [2], speaking to this group three years ago, discussed the possibility that there are perhaps a dozen fundamental organizational data structures, e.g., a banking structure, a manufacturing one, insurance, etc. If we understood the organizational level, we might begin to build generalized systems that would support entire industry groupings.

Impact of Office Automation

Another area in which the present levels of data views seem inadequate is that of supporting less structured views of data, such as those seen in office automation applications. In a typical report generator, there is a medium amount of formatting ability if one is to present a large number of items from the database. Thus, tables, long listings, etc. are supported

In office automation applications, such as word processing, one often wants only a single item from the database, but a lot of ability to do formatting, or to aggregate. Thus, I may wish to write a memo and include the current year's budget for some division - which can only be obtained by a large amount of aggregation of typical data elements. Yet it is this level of data that is usually needed in the organization schema.

Social Implications

It is not just high-level managers who are being shortchanged by our current technological view of databases. Society is taking a less naive view of the large, complex and interconnected databases which the technology is going towards. What few database designers have yet recognized is that the societal view of data is quite different than the classical views. Society may wish to examine how and by whom data was entered, updated, and used, without being concerned at all about the actual value of the data item. Society is more likely to require the transaction history that produced a value, and with verifying the authority and validity of these transactions, than with the data itself.

This has already beocme apparent in the logging requirements of the US Federal Privacy Act of 1975. Here again, is a clear area in which DBMS that understand the existence of this level could support the level. For example, a privacy definition language or schema might contain information about how long traces of each item needed to be kept, what aggregates could and could not be released simultaneously, etc.

Also at the societal level are problems associated with the meaning and accountability for data. The multinational firms bring up these problems. The data item "shipping date" may seem to have only one meaning, but a large company found that many different dates were reported in different countries as "shipping date". In one country, the date was the one at which the product was sent to the loading dock. In another, it was the date the product actually left the gates of the plant. In a third country, where the manager wanted to understate sales for a particular year, it was set to one or two days prior to the expected time of arrival at a customer site.

The accountability problem is also one where society's demands and regulations may impact the technology. Who, for example, "owns" the data of a European company which is using GE MARK-III time sharing service. The bits are physically located in the US, but the company need not even do business with any US company. Does the US government have subpoena power over this data?

Finally, societies throughout the world are recognizing the harm that can come from misuse of data -- especially with computerized DBMS. By recognizing the views of data which society wishes to take, we can design DBMS that support enforcement of restrictions aimed at preventing "data pollution," while still permitting the "lower" organizational and conceptual levels of data to exist and flourish.

Conclusions

We as technologists must become much more sensitive to the needs of higher levels of organizations with respect to data. We must also understand society's fears of and right to control the use of data. By recognizing the types of activities of these levels, and supporting them explicitly with new types off DBMS tools, we contribute both to organizational success and to a stronger society.

I have not discussed the costs of providing support for these two "higher level" views of databases. This is because of my feeling that, whatever they are, they will eventually have to be borne since the demands of top management and governments are becoming ever stronger. Therefore, the sooner the database community recognizes the problem, the sooner we can come up with efficient solutions.

References

1. ANSI/SPARC Report. FDT, February 1976. Available from ACM.
2. Bachman, Charles, Informal comments made during the 1973 SHARE Working Conference on Database Management Systems.
3. Berg, Ivar, "Information, Management and the Status Quo: Some Organizational and Social Implications of Data Base Management Systems." in Jardine, D.(ed.), Data Base Management Systems, North-Holland, 1974.
4. Gach, Donald, "A Survey on the use of security features in DBMS," unpublished report, Dept.of Decision Sciences, 1976.

DISCUSSION

KIRSHENBAUM: In fact, at Equitable, the database administrator is an officer of the Society and reports to within one level of the Chief Data

Processing Officer, who in turn reports to within one level of the Chief
Executive Officer.   About what you are calling the organizational level,
there have been people who have postulated that there is a three level
schema concept for data.   There is a three level schema concept for
process, one of whose levels is organizational at the process level, so
that you can in fact have what we'll call logical processes, logical
processes that were organizational structures, or physical processes that
were organizational structurees and logical processes which were in fact
'the way it ought to be', with some level of processes in between. I don't
see it as a higher level, just another orthogonal level of descriptions of
the real world.

MORGAN: I think I will disagree somewhat. There may be process levels, and
I probably would agree that there might be such things, but I think there
are such higher level, more aggregated, more abstract data levels as well,
where we're talking not about the individual items but about chains of
instances.

MOERKE: There are both hierarchical processes and hierarchical data and
they're interconnected, but they're not necessarily even level by level as
you go up and down. You must, in order to communicate with top management,
communicate in some mechanism that they can cope with. There isn't
anything particularly unique about management that's any different than
most of the rest of us with the possible exception of mathematicians. The
only thing that might be characteristic of top management is that instead
of not understanding but being ashamed to say something about it, they're
more likely to throw you out. In order to validate a business system in
terms of meeting organizational objectives, one has to communicate what in
fact that business system is doing. You don't communicate that in terms of
transmittals or data base elements. You don't draw pretty diagrams with
10,000 data elements on them all interconnected and say, here it is.   You
aggregate both data and processes, because managers don't look at the data
by itself, they look at the processes and the data together. This is the
answer to solving the problem, and our experiences in doing this are very
good. Our experiences in trying anything else to accomplish the same
objectives have been generally mediocre.

STEEL: A couple of weeks ago I was at a meeting in Bloomington, Illinois,
and the evening speaker was the Chief Executive Officer of State Farm
Insurance. His topic was how top management views data processing. One of
the points he made was that he wants human staff between him and the output
of the date processing system. He wants humans to do the refining and the
aggregating at the highest level.   That sounds like it runs a little
counter to some of the things you were suggesting.   Would you care to
comment?

MORGAN: This is a particularly long running argument in the literature of
management, science or law, etc. that is, who mediates between the very top
management and the data base. Is it a staff person or can we ever hope to
have the console on the President's desk? I think that as people get less
and less afraid and as the tools provided to them get more and more
powerful, we can, in fact, not necessarily require that human staff do the
aggregation. On the other hand, we shouldn't underestimate the ways that
top management uses the computer that we don't realize. For example,
somebody told the story that they did a survey in General Motors of the
reports that were being provided to management and found this manager who
was getting a two hundred page report delivered once a week.   The

consultant said 'I've been here three months and you have never looked at that report and we're going to delete you from the list'. He said 'You better not. I don't ever look at it but my staff knows I get it. They don't know that I don't look at it and therefore they look at it. If I don't get it, they won't look at it'. There is this question of how people use process, but I think that, in fact, there is hope for the next generation or the next two generations from now of managers that have been trained in the business schools and out in the universities and out in the trainee levels of businesses. For example, look what happened to Xerox where a lone manager someplace in Canada decided to use APL to do his next month's budgeting instead of doing it by hand the way the rest of the company people did it, and in two years the whole company was using APL to do it. Clearly you don't want the chief executive to get hooked on a computer and sit there spending all his day on it, because the major function of management is communication of top management, of going to a meeting like this and telling the people back at the shop what you heard that someone else is doing. That's a large part of the time of a manager, and therefore they won't spend all of it on the machine.

COLLINS: One unusually interesting thing I think you said is that the DBA would be used by top management to help them understand the data. Is that based on this survey or on some other perception?

MORGAN: No, I what I said was that the DBA was not being used by top management to make policy on the data, it was being used to administer the data. I don't think that I said that the DBA's were being used to help them understand the data. I don't think that's the case, in fact.

KIRSHENBAUM: I've noticed that the lower management, the supervisory level of our company, tends to get a fear because of data base systems, a fear of accountability without authority. For example, at one point we had a policy holder index in tub files as far as the eye could see, with 38 people on roller skates pulling things out. We automated this into a big database management system, on line, and eight people did it. That didn't bother the manager because it happened he got a two grade promotion out of the deal. What bothered the manager was the following: Before the change people would yell at him when he didn't get the policies processed in time, and in fact he felt they were justified in yelling at him because either he had improperly budgeted for his staff and didn't have the resources available, or wasn't properly managing those resources. Now they still yell at him, in addition to yelling at the data processing department, and he no longer has control. If the online system goes down or the data base system is some way not available to him, he can't do his job. There is nothing he can do about it, and yet he is made to feel responsible for getting that job done. We've given him a fairly high level of availability. It hasn't been too bad, but it's a nagging fear in the pit of his stomach that this is going to hinder his movement in the organization.

MORGAN: Well, there's an answer to that, and the answer is, in a sense, the cost. The Bank of America has decided that when they go online they will provide a higher level of responsibility to keep the number of yells and amount of screaming lower. That's a managerial choice in terms of allocating budget to do things in a different way. For that manager to think he doesn't have control is wrong. He does have control. It may be very costly, but that manager still has control over what's happening. He doesn't have control over the computer going down, but he, or presumably someone like him, authorized that system design. [inaudible comment]

Well, in that case, if he doesn't have the control or the responsibility,
then somebody's in there roaring and yelling at him and he should, in fact,
tell them 'You are wrong to yell at me'. Probably he has control, in that
he can go back to top management and say 'this is the wrong system design,
this is too crucial to our operation. If we put it on more computers it'll
cost us another $50,000 a year but the reliability will go up by a factor
of N.'

JARDINE: I think Pogo expressed it some years ago when he said 'we have
seen the enemy and he is us'. It seems to me that the problem, as the
general society perceives data bases, is not with the data base or with the
technology, but clearly the fact that people use information in an
inappropriate way. I'm not afraid of people collecting information about
me. I know very well that anybody who really wants to try and spend the
money can find everything out about me and I won't even know that they've
done it. A private detective can do that probably in a few days, and it
doesn't bother me. I don't care whether people know that I've been sick or
whether my bank account if $40 overdrawn, or that I've been in prison for
the past five years. That's irrelevant. The problem is that the rest of
society uses that in a prejudiced way, and what we're arguing about is not
the effect of the data base, but the nasty conclusions and decisions that
society, which is all of us, comes to as a result of getting that
information. I'm wondering whether the privacy laws are not counter to a
longer-range strategic objective. What would happen, indeed, if the data
processing industry had enough guts to say the privacy laws are not
implementable, and we're not going to implement them. That's different
than saying that each person should be able to get at the information about
himself and correct it. The dissemination of that information which has
become suddenly explosive as a result of the technology would, it seems to
me, result in a profound change in society. It would suddenly be faced
with the problem of having to deal with a whole bunch of situations that
had been swept under the rug before.

MORGAN: I think what you're really bringing up is the phenomenon that Joe
Weizenbaum deals with very well in his book "Computers and Human Reason"
which is that a lot of what computers have done is to keep us from
changing. They have rather helped us to go along with business the way
we've done it before, only faster and better when the rest of society
around us has been changing. We haven't changed our structures and
because we didn't need to since we have these computers to do it. That
ties exactly to what you're saying. We haven't changed the way we use this
data. I don't think that the corollary is that the privacy legislation is
unimplementable, or that we should place that challenge to society in that
way. I think it's useful and important to point out to society, that where
the problem lies is in the use of the data. What computer technology can
do is limit the amount of random dissemination of data, more easily than we
think, although at some more cost, perhaps, than we want to make explicit.
But your basic point is correct. It's not the technology that's bad; it's
the way people use the end result of it. Knowing how nuclear fission works
may be used to both ends, similarly with data bases. It's still to our
responsibility to provide five back-up systems when we build a reactor just
in case some of that nuclear material tries to escape. In the same sense we
can provide a couple of back-up systems on the data base just in case some
of that material tries to escape in ways inwhich it shouldn't.

KIRSHENBAUM: I caught one connotation in your paper that I don't know that
you wanted to give, and I'd like to redefine it and see if you agree with

me. You seem to imply in the paper that distributed data was synonymous
with distributed authority over that data. You were saying that a means to
give a manager control over that data, and thereby his organization, was to
distribute it. In today's technology that may be true. In fact there are
two completely disparate problems in the sense that you can have a database
in a central site where parts of the data is distributed in terms of
authority, and you can have data that is distributed in sites where they do
not have any ability to do anything that a central authority mechanism
doesn't allow them to do. It's really two separate issues: authority over
data means power organizationally. Is my analysis correct, or do you
disagree with it?

MORGAN: I guess your analysis is correct. What I was thinking about is
some recent discussions with Soviet officials. They just had a delegation
going through the U.S. to study data base management systems. The thing
they were most worried about was how do we handle distributed data bases,
because to them it means decentralized processing in authority feeding to a
centralized system since their economy is all centralized in terms of its
planning. Their authority over the data and their authority over its
processing in the sense of this manager of yours who doesn't have the
authority over the processing, is something that they want to distribute.
For example, they want auto plants in different areas to have their own
computers with their own data bases which are, from a central point of
view, all part of the central base, accessible in that way. It is true
that you can implement a distributed system in both ways. I'm worried
about the fact that we don't really support very well the type of
integration of data that they're talking about and a number of companies in
the U.S. are talking about.

TURNER: It's generally considered that the distribution of authority in
organizations is one of the primary organizational issues that computers
affect. How do you see data base systems affecting the distribution of
authority in organizations in the future?

MORGAN: I think what they do is give us more flexibility in distributing it
than they have before. There are some options that now exist that we
didn't have before, but I don't see that it's fundamentally changing
anything. I think we've been through several cycles and we'll go through
several more of decentralization, centralization, and so on, and they
depend on the distribution of costs of the day among computers,
communications, storage, back up, etc. I think that what may change it is
the legislation question. If we get very strong privacy legislation, that
may force the companies to centralize more of the data because they feel
they have better control over it if it is centralized. By centralizing
that, the authority over that data is very likely to be maintained in that
central group.

TURNER: I guess my question goes to a deeper issue of the distribution of
authority, not just over data, but really the way that decisioons are made
in organizations. For instance, the trend toward centralization in the
'50's and to certain data. Companies were getting larger, there were
conglomerates, and one put P & L responsibilities at lower levels, the idea
being that people closer to the decision would be better able to make an
informed decision. Now, we've removed the constsraint, by having the
information more readily available at different points, so that there may
very well be a general trend back toward centralization, or at least a
tendency for the individual management styles not to be constrained by the

absence of information.

MORGAN: That, I think, is exactly the case as what Berg pointed out here three years ago. The data base management system helps the formal system, and the formal system to a large extent pushes toward centralization. It pushes toward centralization of general corporate authority and the data base management systems help that tend. You don't need the informal channel. You don't need to call three levels down in the organization. Just call in the data base management system to find out that number. Therefore, I can make that decision at a higher level, and I can also make it faster, because I can make twelve of them at the same time by using the same mathematical model. Personnel satisfaction may go down, however, and therefore good managers have to let people do some things themselves. Even if this may not optimize the immediate corporate dollar profit, it may optimize the long run corporate profit, because if they're happy they'll be more productive.

TURNER: Do you see us beginning to get a level of our informal systems within our data bases? In the case of the decentralized situation, in order to somewhat filter the information that's available at the centralized location, we might have to put some mechanisms into our decentralized systems. In other words, there could be a tendency to have several levels within our data base systems, one that directly supports operations and one that, in the process of aggregation, more approximates the informal activities we see today.

MORGAN: It sounds like two sets of books. What happens is that you're going to have to keep that other set out of the computers if you're going to keep it out of the hands of top managers. If you look at Italian companies, for example, you find amazing things happening in terms of what's on the books and what's not on the books, and they have problems when they're being audited; not just the bribery stuff that's been going around lately, but just things to keep out of the tax collector's hands. I think that's going to have to be done, and it's being done now by going around the computer - doing it off the computer - and you won't see two sets of books on the computer. You brought up another point which is the informal systems, and this is not directly data base management. One of the biggest pieces of office automation, in terms of this impact, has been the informal communication systems; the mail and message switching systems that get set up. The ARPANET is a prime example, where the people involved send a tremendous amount of mail, messages and informal chit-chat around. The same thing has happened at some big New York banks that have put in this type of internal computer mail system. Those create a new informal channel where you have some interesting implications with the types of data bases you build. I send a memo out which says automatic return receipt; that is to say as soon as Turner looks at it I get a message sent back saying Turner has seen it. I then call you and you say I didn't get that, the mail must be slow today, and I say no, I got this notification, John, you saw it at 12:07. So the technology is driving us in funny ways in terms of the informal channels. As we automate them we may tend to formalize them and cause more problems than we solve.

[Editor's Note:
The following responses to the papers and discussions at the conference
were provided by those vendors of Data Management systems who attended the
conference.]

CINCOM SYSTEMS INC.

SEWALL:
   On behalf of Cincom Systems, I would like to express our gratitude for
inviting us to attend this conference. As a vendor it is always
interesting, informative and, at times, frustrating to hear the opinions
and   ideas   of data processing professionals intimately involved in
developing data base standards. The past three days have certainly greatly
reinforced our concept of the role of data base in the computer industry.
   It is important to establish our position as a vendor of data base
management systems. It is Cincom's philosophy to make the same, and I
emphasize the same, data base management system available to all users of
computer hardware.   A commitment such as this requires us to provide data
management tools, not only to the entire IBM base, but to all other
manufacturers of hardware - both maxi and mini. It is essential that the
data base standards developed by ANSI/SPARC be available to the entire
spectrum of hardware. Standards developed for the large user should also
satisfy the requirements of that extensive army of smaller users.
   Cincom is determined to maintain a delicate and intelligent blend between
the large user requirements and those of the smaller user. This is
particularly relevant when we consider the use of distributive systems.
There is a relationship here between the large and small users. The large
user today may well be intimately involved with smaller computers when a
distributed system is to be implemented. We must not overlook the
requirements of a data base distributed across multiple CPU's and we must
evaluate the SPARC report within the framework of this distribution.
   The papers presented and the questions that they have elicited have
provided much thought-provoking material. I would like to comment on some
of this material and define our position.
   It was interesting to note the comments of several of the attendees who
indicated that perhaps the implementation of Data Base Standards is
premature at this point in time.   Why is this?   Is it technological
advance?   Is it changing Data Base requirements? Is it changing business
needs? Does our ability to pose questions outstrip our ability to provide
answers? Is the complexity of data base beyond simplistic standardization?
   Of all the discussions of the past few days, the paper on External Schema
produced the most controversial view points. It would seem that conceptual
schema and external schema can be related to man and the development of
tools to satisfy man's needs.
   Man's most primitive needs were readily satisfied by the invention of a
simplistic tool.   Were not man's subseqeunt needs tempered by the
availability of such a tool? Is this not the case with conceptual and
external schema? A simplistic conceptual schema may well be satisfied by a
simplistic external schema.   That simplistic external schema may well
influence subsequent conceptual schemas.
   Cincom's philosophy has been to provide a tool that can adopt to complex

conceptual schema, but can also, at the same time, satisfy simplistic needs. We must take care when we develop our standards to recognize both simplistic and complex requirements and ensure that our schema, be it conceptual or external, fully meets these needs.

The idea of a conceptual schema demands a more definitive and clarifying definition. Personal view points give depth, breadth, and substance to new concepts. However, if we are to use the conceptual schema as an effective interface to the System of Management within an organization and as a management tool it must be more concrete in nature.

The desirability of new, better tools for the Data Base Administrator to build data bases and maintain data bases has been pointed out as a continually growing need. In the future, tools will be required for the Enterprise Administrator to assist in determing what business decisions or what business areas data bases can be constructed to solve business problems.

Tools would be available to determine what decisions and what levels within the organization's system of managmement can be affected by changes in the Data Base structure.

The small user who has a part time DBA function has a greater requirement for these type business tools than the user who can dedicate full time personnel to this function. Both needs are great. The concept and the potential of DBA tools has been expanded by the SPARC recommendations. By dividing three areas of DBA activities into Enterprise, Applications Administration, and Data Base Administration, new requirements have been generated for more comprehensive tools in each area. Perhaps the development of good software tools in each one of these three areas will make the entire process much less complex than it is at this point in time.

The concept of a data base being a reality insensitive to change has always been a key data base consideration. Discussions have indicated here that the level of data independence required by constant business changes and multiple system interactions will continue to be a very high prioritized need for all Data Base Management Systems. Our experience in Data Base, Data Communications and mini computer endeavors leads us to the conclusion that end user interfaces to data bases, whether they can be centralized or distributed, will become more and more critical than they are now.

The question was raised whether or not any one has had any experience with Query Languages in a network environment. Cincom has been experimenting with a Query Language which operates with a network structure. The Query is a simple set of non-technical procudures that allows for ad hoc retrieval without any prior knowledge of the physical data structure or the data element names on the part of the user. The only requirement on the user's part is that the individual know the generic name of the information that he is interested in. The results of our experimentation has been that a Query capability for the casual user is quite feasible in a network structure.

In conclusion, it has become evident from the discussions of the past days, that the complexity of producing standards for data base that satisfy all criteria is a demanding task. It is a challenge to all of us, be we users, or be we vendors. Clearly, much progress has been made since our involvement in the 1973 meeting as evidenced by the latest ANSI/SPARC report. Cincom is determined to remain involved in the activities of the committee. We would like to reiterate the point we made earlier. We must not allow ourselves to myopic in our view of data base systems. The smaller user must be recognized as well as the larger user. Cincom is committed to both the large user and the small user.

COMPUTER CORPORATION OF AMERICA

WINTER:
  CCA is a computer science research and development company, which
emphasizes database technology and database products. Presently we market
and support Model 204, an advnced database management product, and are
engaged in the development of a large-scale data utility called the
datacomputer. Both of these systems will be affected by, and have needs
which should be considered by, groups working on the standards area.
  Model 204 operates on the middle to large IBM 360 and 370 systems and has
special strength in its handling of large online databases, its clear and
easily grasped data model, its versatile user language and its ability to
handle change and growth in databases and application systems. It is a
successful product primarily because of technical innovations - because it
has been able to offer some users capabilities they were unable to find in
any other product.
  Our experience with Model 204 has impressed upon us the importance of
operating in a climate in which innovation is encouraged by the industry
and the market. It is certainly vital that standards efforts avoid
solutions which will increase the difficulty of making better technology
available to users.
  The data computer is a large scale computer installation dedicated to the
function of offering database services to other computers. Conceptually,
it is a database system in a separate box: a database machine. Further, it
implements a particular concept of the database machine: it is designed for
the network environment, for databases in the trillion bit range, and for
the service of processes executing on other systems rather than for the
direct service of human users at terminals. Each of these design goals
sets the datacomputer apart somewhat from conventional database systems,
and may have implications for the appropriateness of any standards
proposal.
  The development of the datacomputer is funded by ARPA and that sytem is
currently servicing the ARPANET.
  Before I address the specific requirements of these two systems, I will
make some general comments on the work presented here by the SPARC study
group. I think the work is very promising; I think that by approaching the
database standards problem thoughtfully, and modelling database management
systems very comprehensively, the SPARC study group has opened the door to
some beneficial development for the industry. We need a standard which
permits a variety of implementations of the database system, without
compromising the integrity of the user interface; SPARC has outlined an
approach in which this could be achieved.
  SPARC has also directly addressed anothe vital need: evolution. They
have provided for evolution of applications, evolution of languages,
evolution of database internal structure, evolution of the technology
itself. It appears that any of these elements can change in a fundamental
way in a SPARC system, without great impact on running applications,
perhaps with no impact. This is essential to the future of our industry;
it means that users can afford to make very substantial investmentss in
application systems designed around database systems. Such application
systems can be planned without fear of forced obsolescence through the
evolution of database or storage technology; in fact, one can anticipate
the steady enhancement of the database system underneath the application,
with little or no disruption to the application itself. Such change is
achieved now; CCA and other vendors continually enhance their product in a
compatible fashion, but the entire process from design of the software
through cutover in the user's installation is slow, limited in scope and

expensive. In the architecture presented in the SPARC interim report, we have provision for coordinated use of multiple versions of virtually everything from schemas to application programs to the data itself. Mr. Mairet has discussed the importance of this in phasing into production a new version of an appmlication system, while continuing to run an existing version. My comments here apply to the evolution of the database system itself. It is this type of evolution which can enable the industry to thrive and the standard to remain vital over an extended period of time.

I share the general concern expressed in this conference about the conceptual schema, and doubt that a design for it in the next two or three years can solve all the problems that the study group wants to solve in a conceptual schema. However, I feel it is important to avoid placing too much emphasis on the unsolved problems of the conceptual schema. In order to gain the full benefits of the SPARC approach, it is necessary to model the semantics of the database at a very fundamental level in the conceptual schema. Only by doing that will we be able to present significantly different database semantics to different users of the database. However, it is not necessary to go so far in order to develop an exciting, meaningful, timely and enduring standard. Any standard incorporating most of the concepts in the interim report, particularly one with a properly separated three-level schema, will be an enormous step forward. There seems to be some considerable danger to me in moving too slowly, in spending too much time grappling with problems which are too difficult. Some of the more profound goals for the conceptual schema seem too distant, and I worry about the SPARC effort progressing too slowly toward a solution. Thus my recommendation is to consider more modest approaches to the conceptual schema, in the interest of insuring that we will obtain some standard of the general form described in the interim report.

I would now like to return to the subject of CCA's database efforts and their interaction with the SPARC work.

In the datacomputer system, the interfaces which are most significant for standardization differ from those typically considered in regard to conventional systems. For example, the DML of concern in the datacomputer environment is comprised of the message transmitted from the host computers to the datacomputer, typically across a network. This language has been defined and implemented in the datacomputer and is called datalanguage. Datalanguage requests have quite a different structure from the extensions to COBOL proposed as a standard DML by CODASYL. One can imagine DML statements in a COBOL program being translated into datalanguage requests and then transmitted to the datacomputer. With a well designed standard at each of these levels, such a translation should be not only feasible but quite efficient. I cannot tell from the SPARC interim report whether the interface corresponding to datalanguage has been identified by SPARC. If not, it clearly needs attention, as the datacomputer represents a whole class of products for which a standard interface is most desirable.

In addition to a language specification at this interface, there is need for a protocol specification; however, this is a problem for which we may not yet be capable of selecting a good industry-wide solution.

There are several more problems unique to database machines in the general network environment which the study group should examine. CCA and other developers of database machines will surely have more to say on the matter.

In regard to Model 204, I am aware of no special technical needs which a system based on the interim report would fail to meet. Our most important input in relation to Model 204 is that we would like to see SPARC push ahead and complete its work, and the sooner it does so, the better. SPARC appears to offer us the opportunity to market advanced and truly unique products like Model 204, while still supporting a standard. That is, they have structured the interfaces in such a fashion that a class of standard products, offering standard facilities at the user interfaces, can differ significantly in implementation. While this is true to some extent in the case of CODASYL, it appears to be true to a greater degree with SPARC. Some reasons are that more interfaces are formalized, more semantics are modelled, and semantic properties are more obviously separated from less fundamental properties in the database.

I have three suggestions for additional issues for the SPARC study group to consider.

The first is to pay attentionn to how users are to transfer existing applications to a SPARC-based system. What do the various administrators (enterprise, application, database) need to do? What interfaces are involved?

What technical problems exist in migration from existing systems? Is there a way for users to develop systems so that they will later migrate with a minimum of fuss? Can vendors direct their development to minimize the eventual gap? We would certainly try, but our job is obviously easier with some help from those developing the standard. Finally, what is the actual process by which the data itself is transferred. Is it written in a canonical form, then loaded? These questions merely scratch the surface of an issue that will assume great practical importance when a standard exists. It appears that sufficient lead time exists to be ready with a solution.

The second suggestion is to examine the problem of implementators deviating from the standard in order to satisfy legitimate needs. Two obvious deviations should be examined: extension and subsets. Most implementations of a standard involve both. Implementators will surely want to define their own options in addition to the standard for virtually every interface (e.g. If I implement COBOL for model 204, I want a way to say that a field is an inverted file access key). And they will certainly want to leave out or defer other options. Each selective extension and exclusion is essential and yet is a real problem to the user wanting transportable application systems. I know of no answers, but perhaps a group of knowledgeable people could provide us a basis for the development of a methodology in this area.

Third, I suggest that SPARC develop and publish some kind of program for the completion of its objectives, tied to a loose time frame if feasible. As an observer of the process whose interests are very much affected by standards development, I would like to know what the steps of standards development are.

Who has to agree to a standard, and what are the significant intermediate stages of the process? What are some scenarios for a successful effort? How exactly does this work get interfaced to other standards efforts? While I am sure there is a great deal of uncertainty, and no one can say just what will happen, I would like very much to have some basis for speculating on the outcome of these processes which will so greatly affect us all.

Thank you for your attention.

DISCUSSION

STEEL: Speaking for the study group, I wonder if you could elaborate a little bit on your point about non-standard extensions? It's not clear to me what that means in the context of the SPARC architecture.

WINTER: The chief problem is that it is unrealistic to expect everyone to

implement a system which is no more and no less than the standard.   Surely
this is the case for most COBOL implementations today. This poses a
problem to the user. How does the user understand the implications of using
a facility which is more or less than the standard. Sometimes when using
less than the standard, one is forced to solutions which reimplement part
of the standard system. In a DBMS, this may sacrifice data independence,
if its not done properly.

My thought was really only that this is an area which has not been
analyzed systematically and may be worthy of your attention. You may be
able to come up with techniques or guidelines for dealing with the problem.
Further, you may be able to provide standard hooks for the extension (e.g.
for implementor defined terms).

COLLINS: You mentioned the datacomputer approach to the problem of data
sharing. I'm asking, in the light of the conceptual schema, which
apparently would also be one of the factors helping us to bridge the gap
between application views or cuts, the sharing of databases by
applications. Are there any new insights when you take this separate
computer out, with respect to data sharing, that could be applied to the
conceptual schema?

WINTER: The data computer system has not been designed with the SPARC
framework in mind. The one pre-dates the other. It is in many ways
conceptually no different from any other data base system. Most of the
differences which have arisen to date, I think, are implementation
differences arising from the fact that there are data representations of
more than one machine involved. In many cases where you expect to be
interacting with the person, you are interacting with the process, in the
case of the data computer. In general, that system is designed to
interface to processes. But the data definitions typically originate in
programs on other machines and are transmitted to the data computer. In
regard to the conceptual schema I don't know of any special considerations.
The data is still all in one place, not distributed.

COLLINS: That's communicational transmission of format and protocol and so
on, would amount to a general protocol for the external schemas in your
data computer?

WINTER: What I was suggesting about interfaces was that there needs to be
some formal protocol and also some set of commands and data formats for the
interface. The architecture we have in mind now is a house language program
executing on a house machine calling some system on that machine, perhaps
part of the operating system or extension to it, and this program uses
standard DML and what have you, but it's the stuff we've already been
talking about. This system has to take whatever commands it has, format
them into some kind of message, transmit that to the data computer, and the
data computer has to transmit replies, so data and commands are passed back
and forth, and error messages, and a whole lot of other things. And the
point is that that interface between that system and the host and the data
computer is an interface which is not very important, whereas it's an
interface which previously people have thought in terms of being internal
to the DBMS. You'd like the data computer, or this sytem, to present the
same interface to all systems. And in fact, that's exactly what we did, we
designed a language and a protocol for that purpose. There's only one data
computer in the ARPANET and that so it's sort of an ad hoc standard, but
one would like the industry standards to address this problem and I saw Jon
Turner nod so I guess that one of those interfaces on the picture is in

fact the interface that I was talking about. Apparently the interface is already identified in the SPARC architecture and it's just a question of evenutally standardizing. Thank you.

CONTROL DATA CORPORATION

ROBERTSON:
I would like, first of all, to take the opportunity to thank SHARE for the opportunity to attend the conference and participate in the discussions. It has been very valuable for me and for CDC.

My remarks today will be divided essentially into two parts: First, I will talk about specific reactions that I and, as much as possible, Control Data has to the discussions here at the conference. Second, I will spend a small amount of time on where CDC is and where it's going in the area of data base management.

I have attempted to pick out the topics that have been discussed here at the conference that appear to be the hottest issues -- the ones that have provoked the most audience reaction and questions, and those most discussed at coffee breaks. These issues are:

ANSI/SPARC/DBMS Architecture Data Models Standardization

Our response to the ANSI/SPARC architecture is somewhat mixed, but essentially favorable. It is positive in the sense that it represents excellent work by the Study Group who, at a very appropriate time, took the opportunity to step back from what had been done already to look at the DBMS situation from scratch and to come up with what I feel is indeed a better architecture or a better model for data base management systems. On the other hand, Control Data, and I am sure a number of users, feel somewhat frustrated over the prospect for no immediate DBMS standards. CDC has been involved, along with a lot of other people, in an attempt to get to the point where we can produce industry standards for data base management. It is frustrating to get to the point where we are now, after ten years of hard work, only to be told, maybe we ought to take another look at this! I think that SPARC is essentially saying that while we have a good deal of work that has been done and we can adapt from there, there is still a lot more to do.

There are also some potential problem areas with the architecture. One of the problem areas, the one that seems to have been the most confusing and interesting to people here at the conference, is the conceptual schema. I think that the conceptual schema will be a very tough concept to nail down. There will be a lot of work necessary to define just exactly what it is. What sort of language is it? For whom is it intended? Is it two schemas or one? Finally, when it is finally resolved, it will be a difficult one for software implementors to implement. I think you have to expect that it will probably be one of the later things that's available on commercial DBMS's.

The second potential problem area is that the architecture itself is complicated and extensive. We had some initial reaction the first day to the effect that, 'why do we have to have so many interfaces?' 'Why does it appear to be that we are complicating things?' And it is a potential problem. It is from the standpoint of a software implementor, one who has attempted to look at the Data Base Task Group Report for implementation. And the ANSI/SPARC architecture has the potential of being more complicated than the DBTG Report. We ought to be pushing for simplicity, for an initial subset which is easier to both understand and implement.

Finally, the architecture leaves open the question of which data model.

This is not necessarily undesirable, but I do feel that there is still a good deal of work yet to be done before we get to a complete standard that addresses all of the reasonable data models that might be possible, and I think the effect will be to postpone the eventual standard.

The second conference issue that I'd like to spend a little time on is data models. Control Data is not pushing any one particular data model, but we do have some reactions to the subject. It was mentioned in the presentation on data models that the approaches are converging. CDC agrees with that. I know that what Control Data is doing, and we've had a chance to get started a little later than some of the other systems that are already available, is a combination of some of the better aspects of some different data models.

It was also mentioned that there may be multiple data models available on data base management systems in the future. I'm not so sure that is going to be true. If it is done, it will be a considerable job for implementors to provide such a capability. In addition, I think there are some other possible problems in terms of performance and in terms of size. Multiple data models may not even be able to co-exist very well within the same software. So, it may eventually happen, but I don't think it will happen right away.

Another possible problem is the effect emerging standards could have in suppressing some models. For example, if the network model were standardized first, this could have the potential of suppressing the other models by putting too much emphasis on the network model.

Finally, I wanted to say that there is a lot more work to be done in the area of data models. Some of the models ae much better defined than others. For instance, there are still a lot of unanswered questions about the relational model in terms of exactly what features an implementor should provide.

The final topic from the conference I would like to address is the topic of standardization. I would like to make it clear that the first item on the slide has nothing to do with Gene Lowenthal's end-user interface shown yesterday. What it is intended to show is that from the outside the situation with regard to standardization looks confused, and that the ANSI/SPARC Study Group and CODASYL must move closer together. It appears that ANSI/SPARC is telling CODASYL that their work on data base management was all right, but did not address the entire problem. In point of fact, about 80% of the interfaces to standardize have been ignored. ANSI/SPARC and CODASYL should make it clear to the outside world that the two groups are not in conflict and indeed they are working together, as they are this weekend. There is an awful lot of work to be done. Developing standards is a very difficult and time-consuming task in a volunteer organization and I think the two groups need to work together to get the job done.

ANSI/SPARC's specific recommendations on which interfaces to standardize first could cause some problems. The question must be asked: is it the right subset? Does the subset represent an implementable system? What will be the effect on Federal Government requirements, data models offered, and vendor development? Maybe these questions have already been addressed, but it appears there are some potential trouble spots with ANSI/SPARC's recommendations.

Finally, I would like to mention that standards are important. That seems pretty obvious, certainly from the user's standpoint. But it is also important to users from the standpoint that when a standard is available, vendors will place added emphasis on data base management development. It will provide a needed focus for the converging of development as well as a shot in the arm for data base management development budgets.

Now I would like to talk about what we are doing at CDC and what we have planned for the future. To us, DBMS is very important and we are placing a lot of emphasis on data base management development. CDC does have a data base management system which it has developed, named DMS-170. Some of the key aspects of DMS-170, in relation to the topics of this conference are described below. First, it is evolutionary and simple to use in terms of the simplicity and elegance of the DML and its processing of conventional files. Second, the DDL is based on the CODASYL specifications. Third, the data model is based on the relational data model, however, it has been expanded to allow networks to be defined. It is relational in the sense that records are joined, or linked, via matching fields within the records. These relationships are defined, however, in advance via the DDL and may be to any number of levels, or can join any number of record types. Physical access is provided by file inversion; the data base itself can be normalized, but does not have to be. Finally, the DML is not navigational. Records are not processed one-at-a-time along paths or relationships. Instead, related records are processed as projections or as if they comrpised a virtual file. This allows a simplified DML based on the straightforward syntax of the host language.

Of course, DMS-170 has many other important features, but I have only mentioned those that are specifically related to the topics of discussion here.

What is the future of data base management at CDC? In the near term we will be participating in, helping to shape, and moving towards emerging standards as much as we can. But primarily we will be concentrating on improving our existing system, without making any great changes in direction. We will be doing those things that enhance the salability of DMS-170, such as improve reliability, performance, and features. In the long term, Control Data will be looking at such areas as distributed data bases (because we are heavily involved in computer networks), hardware advances in the area of mass storage and of accessing techniques, and we will be moving towards a DBMS standard when an acceptable one finally is adopted.

DISCUSSION

STEEL: In your third from the last slide, if I remember correctly, you made some points about the ANSI approach causing problems. I really wish you'd elaborate on that. I could also make a remark about using the mathematical sign for equivalence between CODASYL and ANSI/SPARC.

ROBERTSON: That really wasn't intended. It means only that the two groups should get closer together. As for your first question, I'm not saying that the ANSI/SPARC aarchitecture is going to cause problems; I'm talking about tthe specific items that were recommended for standardization. What I'm trying to say is, and you may have examined this question already, that you should look at your recmmendations in terms of what effect they are going to have on vendors and implementors. They will be looking at what's adopted first as a standard, and it will have an effect on what they produce. It might possibly put too much weight in the area that gets standardized first, such as, for example, the network data model.

NELSON: If you pick those areas that are easiest for the Study Group to identify and to describe and to write SPARC 90's on, that could result in specifying exactly the wrong prospective standards as ANSI efforts. From the point of view of implementor development efforts, and we're seeing this already. There is a DML being considered now for standardization and the committee, X3J4, is being urged (by whoever it is that urges these people) to take immediate action, in the face of a DDL effort which is still admittedly developmental. From the standpoint of a developer looking at data base management systems and trying to build to a standard, I would find that disconcerting.

ROBERTSON: Let me just make one comment. That is exactly what I had in mind. One example that comes to mind is if, indeed, the conceptual schema takes a long time to get well enough defined to standardize, what is it going to mean to have an internal schema and an external schema defined, standardized, and having implementors trying to implement those two, without the conceptual schema being defined? It is supposed to be the traffic cop over both.

STEEL: Admittedly we are a long way from agreement on the part of anybody as to what a conceptual schema ought to look like--what it's form ought to be and so on. The point that the Study Group has tried to make is that the conceptual schema has to be general enough so that it can subsume any of the external schemas that people want to write -- any of the data models. Our recommendations are that work ought to go ahead now on a conceptual schema development effort. There's no notion of 'let's go off and standardize on it' because we don't even know what it is yet. However, if that work is done correctly, and I for one believe that there are directions that research is going to take that make this possible, one can take existing proposals for some of the other interfaces like the external schema interface, interface 4, and the DML interface, interface 7, develop standards, subject to certain criteria and constraints. That's the thrust of the recommendations for change to the DML that the Study Group made, to make it consistent with the overall framework. Given that, you can develop standards in those areas prior to having available a standard conceptual schema. When the conceptual schema notion is sufficiently developed for a standard, it can slide in on top and will be consistent with what's already been done. That's the objective.

NELSON: If it's so tough to build multiple data models into one DBMS, how come Control Data did it?

ROBERTSON: I was referring to the data model we have as a single data model, but it's a combination of some of the features of the important data models. What I identified as being tough, was to have three separate, individual data models in one system.

NELSON: This wasn't a system that suddenly became relational in its later life?

ROBERTSON: It's true that we were originally looking at COSASYL and we changed our emphasis somewhat.

NELSON: You're claiming it's still one data model.

ROBERTSON: Yes.

INTERNATIONAL BUSINESS MACHINES CORPORATION

COHN:
    First of all, my thanks to SHARE for the opportunity to participate in

this conference. This has been an excellent arena for interchange among users, vendors, and the academic and research communities.

Secondly, my congratulations to SHARE for the selection of timely, important, and provocative subject matter; for the local arrangements and facilities; and for the expert handling of the conference. You have planned and executed well, Gentlemen, and, again, I congratulate you.

IBM's position on the ANSI/SPARC interim report is one of general agreement with the principles, concepts, and requirements stated in that report. We have worked with the committee since its inception, and we plan to continue to work with it. We feel that the architectural concepts and requirements are consistent with IBM's interaction with SHARE and GUIDE over the past decade, and we're happy to see that this has been so generally accepted in the national and international communities.

I'd like to discuss what it means when I say IBM agrees with a requirement or an architecture. In a technical sense it reflects our involvement with standards activities, research, and user groups and the belief that the stated architecture or requirement is both feasible and within the state of the art for future products. It does not mean that IBM has committed itself to a product that satisfies either the architecture or the requirement. It also does not mean that IBM is committed to implement an ANSI standard, regardless of which way IBM may have voted on the standard.

Product decisions are based largely on business opportunity and financial justification. The existence of a standard may affect the business analysis. However, many other factors must be considered in this analysis and you would .be wrong to assume that the adoption of a standard would lead to an IBM product commitment.

Now, I think that it should be made clear at this point that while we agree with the concepts and requirements, we feel that standardization of any existing specification is, at best, premature. It has , been demonstrated at this and other conferences and by a lot of input from our customers, that we must retain a climate in which the requirements and technology surrounding DB/DC systems, including the migration of current users, and solutions to a whole host of problems that have been stated and restated, can be more fully understood.

On the subject of three-level architecture, IBM has supported this approach throughout its work with SHARE/GUIDE and in the ANSI Study Group. We give great consideration to these efforts in considering enhancements to our DB/DC and dictionary product line and in planning long range design and technology.

Again, regarding the subject of the report, we agree that one of the points that needs to be expanded in the report is the subject of distributed data base. On a similar note, we feel that business processes and flow should be expanded and made more explicit in the context of the conceptual schema.

Moving to another topic, I think it appropriate to offer a commendation to the DDLC for its work over the past few years. The Committee has had an open mind in accepting criticism and contructive input. In chartering sub task-groups, it has recognized the validity of hierarchical and relational structures. It has demonstrated positive action in architectural clean-up and categorization. We hope that their constructive attitude becomes contagious and infects their sister committee, the PLC We applaud the suggestion, made at this conference, that some attention be given to subsetting CODASYL specifications and that consideration be afforded the human factors related to learning and using the DDL.

With regard to data structures, or models, I can only repeat the statement made by IBM at the 1973 conference, that we recognize the

relational and network structures as valid requirements for future data
base management systems. I should like to point out, however, that while
we recognize the requirements for network structures, you should not infer
that this recognition should be interpreted in the DBTG context. We repeat
another statement made in 1973, and repeated several times since then, that
we are not now, nor do we have any plans for, implementing the DBTG
specifications.

On the subject of multiple data structures, we share the concern that the
present pragmatics may not provide an adequate performance base for volume
production use of a data base management system that supports multiple
structural views--at least at this time.

A major area alluded to by the report, specifically addressed during this
week, and heard about often in the halls of SHARE and GUIDE meetings is
data administration. IBM recognizes the critical need for improvement in
thee   tools   and   methodology of data administration, such as data
independence, definition languages, data dictionary   directory,   data
security, privacy of information, auditability, and data base planning,
design, and simulation aids. We feel that the interaction of those
concerned in these areas should be encouraged.

On one of the sub-topics of data administration, security, we note and
endorse a user-vendor challenge to define the appropriate levels and
trade-offs to be made in cost and performance versus function.   In
addition, we suggest that SHARE continue its work on privacy and on
understanding the cost and technical implications of proposed legislation.

IBM considers the query function to be an integral part of an overall
DB/DC and dictionary product line. Our activities in this area are best
characterized by the enhancements considered for current products using,
for example, the GUIDE user language document as a source for requirements
and by multiple activities in research, including SEQUEL, Rendezvous, Query
by Example, and human factor studies. We note the concern raised at this
conference that it is not clear what a product strategy in this area should
be and which class or classes of users should such products be addressed
to. We don´t believe that a product that would serve every class of user
is within today´s state of the art. SHARE should look at this area to
consider, in its interaction with IBM, just what the priorities of classes
should be.

Again, thanks very much.

DISCUSSION

BRODIE: You mentioned the internal development on query languages, several
that you are working on. Would you care to comment on how many years it
might be before you have one in the market place?

COHN: The internal developments that I mentioned were in the Research area.
I have no comment as to if or when any of those activities might lead to a
product.

Many of the technical papers for these activities are in the public
domain, and are worth reading by those interested in the subject. This
week has certainly shown that along with the interesting activities in
query, there is the specific problem of identifying and clarifying future
business opportunities and providing an appropriate product.

In the meantime IBM continues to consider enhancements to its current
product along with the consideration of other alternatives.

STEEL: The chairman said not to be unnecessarily provocative, so I will try
to do this unprovocatively. If you will recall at the last annual meeting,

the SHARE Working Conference on Database Management Systems, there was an
IBMer who made an observation that the speed of light was ten feet per
nanosecond. That's a factor of ten, of course, over what it really is.   If
IBM can change the speed of light, SHARE can change the length of the year.

SECREST: One of Standard of Indiana's concerns in the movement towards the
integration of data and applications is our inability to deal with the data
independence and shared data problems that currently confront us. I don't
know if it's just unique to large-scale customers or not, but the level of
data independence provided by your current product in 1976, is in my
opinion, no better than the level of data independence provided by your
product in 1968. The level of one's ability to develop applications and
share data across multiple CPU's in 1976 is no greater today in 1976, than
it was in 1968 with the initial issue of the product.   I know that the
Cincom representative and the Computer Corporation of America
representative dealt with data independence and shared data as being viable
concepts in terms of the evolution of applications implemented under DBDC.
And I am here to ask -- one could interpret of course that lack of
functional support for these two concepts in IBM's current product line was
--- one could interpret the lack of functional support that the requirement
is not valid, or what is IBM's position on data independence and shared
data?

COHN: We definitely support and recognize the requirement for shared data
and data independence. There has been a lot of action in our product line
over eight years that was not specifically directed towards shared data and
data independence but I don't think it is appropriate at this conference to
review IBM's product activity over eight years. We definitely agree with
the concepts and recognize the requirements for data independence and
shared data; beyond that I cannot make a statement. As you know, it's been
an accepted requirement from GUIDE for some time.

SECREST: I'm groping for a rational explanation of the lead time for the
inclusion of these concepts in the products. Is it a business case --
strictly a business case?

COHN: No. I think one would have to look at the entire history of DB/DC
and IBM to answer that. In 1968 there were several products, and over the
course of the last eight years there has been a consolidation and
improvement of the IBM product line in the DB/DC area. In 1971 we came out
with the first statement of direction, that future development was going to
concentrate on IMS/CICS and GIS. Since then, there has been more product
consolidation and considerable effort to increase the reliability and
performance of those products, to have them support the devices announced
in that time frame, to migrate them to the virtual systems environment, to
marry them with VSAM and VTAM and a lot of alphabet soup which is strictly
IBMese. But the products have had to do a lot of things, in that time
frame and the business judgment had to be made as to whether to do these
things at the expense of data independence or do data independence at the
expense of the overall strategy of the company in terms of virtual systems.
I think you know what the results of that decision were. I think it had to
be the correct decision, but looking at it strictly from a data base point
of view, I agree with you, increased data independence and data sharing is
still lacking.

SOFTWARE AG

JODEIT:

I want to briefly characterize our product because I think it is not as well known, in the general familiarity of this audience, as IMS or the CODASYL DBTG. ADABAS supports multiple interrelated files in a data base, provides Boolean multi-key access to the records in the files, allows for completely variable record content in the files, permits the user to view subschemas which are defined or bound at execution time, incorporates complete facilities for logging, recovery, physical integrity of the data base, security, etc., and includes all utilities needed for maintenance, both of data base content and definition, as well as for data protection.

I would like to relate our system to the three-level ANSI/SPARC work that has been discussed here. We didn't plan our system this way, but I think it's very interesting to relate what we have and have been using for several years to the architecture that is proposed and is becoming accepted and I think extremely sound. The ADABAS data model is very like the completely general network model that Professor Tsichritzis described in this meeting. This I would identify as the conceptual model with which we do our design and documentation of data bases. The mapping from this conceptual schema to the internal schema is not something that we have ever very formally isolated; it is done by a human being. It is very nearly a one-to-one mapping with the imposition at that point of some information about how the data will be stored, access paths, etc. so it's a little more than one-to-one, a little more than what the user has to see when he is thinking in terms of the conceptual schema. On the other side, the mapping from the conceptual schema into the external schemas, we do follow the pattern that's been laid out here.

For ad hoc query we have a query language capability that can be used on-line or in batch and we have a report generating facility; in the use of these, it is in effect the conceptual schema that the user employs, that is a one-to-one mapping again. In the case of application programs, it is again very closely a one-to-one mapping from the conceptual schema, and we have recently introduced some software into that stream that allows the application coder to see hierarchic subschemas and utilize those in his code.

An important question, I think, to people in this audience, is "What does software ag think of standardization and will ADABAS go with a standard?" We have rather staunchly resisted going to the DBTG definitions for a data model and DML because we thought we had something that was more comprehensive in a number of very important respects. But I'm quite certain that, as far away as a standard seems to be and as many things as can happen between here and there, when and if one is adopted, it will become one of our external views. I see no problem in doing that. I don't know that we will be convinced that we should, in a basic sense, depart from what it is that we use now, in terms of the data model that we enjoy and are extremely enthusiastic about. Our enthusiasm for the way that we view data is a very pragmatic one. It's extremely effective and efficient from the point of view of our user community, in terms of simplicity. The documentation on ADABAS is roughly two or three inches thick. The training in ADABAS takes only three days. It's a very simple tool to use. The user may view his data in terms of hierarchies, or networks, or very much in the relational sense; so we feel we have a model that accommodates and encompasses all of those that have been touted by others. Extremely important is that we allow a great deal of flexibility in the evolution of the data base. We are able to add entity types to our model, attributes of those entities, relationships between entities without any reloading or

reorganization of the data base and without impact on existing application
systems.   This buys a lot in the development of systems around this tool.
We completely separate the logical and physical models so that the user may
have materialized for him any number of logical views of the physical data
stored in the ADABAS data base.   All of these things make ADABAS an
extremely efficient tool.

   In view of the discussions at this conference, which I have found very
interesting, what are the directions that software ag will take with
ADABAS? I'd like to identify some of our thinking and anticipated
directions.   It has always been our goal to improve the operational
efficiency, the performance of the system, and we will continue to do so in
future releases.   Some of the interfaces in the ANSI/SPARC architecture, I
think, are very good ones which we and other vendors have glossed over in
the past, and I think we will make some of these explicit.   For instance,
we most definitely wish to introduce data dictionary capabilities, probably
in a framework very much aligned with the ANSI/SPARC architecture.   We want
to introduce software tools where humans are performing intellectual
processes now.   We will introduce aids, perhaps interactive aids, to assist
humans in the processes of documentation, definition, tuning and so on.   We
will provide more external schema capabilities for end users so that they
will be able to interact with the data base in more simplistic languages.
We will improve the data independence in the system, although it is
relatively very good at this point, but we do know things that will easily
follow in these lines.   For instance, we do not now name the relationships
between files, and were we to do this, and be able to span relations,
entities, relations again and so on in a higher level language, the data
independence features of our product would be improved considerably.   In
terms of the architecture and the implementation of ADABAS there are a
number of areas that we are looking at now and with which we do plan to be
involved in the marketplace: distributed data bases, backend data base
controllers, dedicated data base processors, and implementations on mini
computers.

SPERRY UNIVAC

HARRIS:
   In this reponse, I will summarize some of the issues of the conference
and in order to put a different perspective on those issues I will compare
them with issues which were addressed at the 1973 SHARE Conference on Data
Base Management.   In particular, I will be referencing the response given
by the Sperry Univac representative at that time, Mr. Hartley.
   I have compiled a list of issues which were raised at this conference.
They include:
   - First and most obvious is the three-level schema concept of the SPARC
     Study Group Report.   Let's refine that to indicate that data
     independence is the significant theme, because that is the main thrust
     behind the three level schema concept.
   - The need for many views of the data base, and for many interfaces to
     the database.   This need was also expressed in the form of discussions
     on end user facilities.
   - The need for security features.
   - The need for a generalized data base dictionary and directory.
   - The need for a solution of the problem of distributed data bases.
   - The need for integrity features.
   - The need for better tools to aid the data base administrator.

- The need for tools to aid in reorganizing and restructuring the data base.
- The concern which was raised about the cost of all these features.
  - The issue of standardization.

Now an interesting feature about this list is that it is very much the same as the list which was compiled by Mr. Hartley in his response to the SHARE conference of 1973. This does not mean that no progress has been made in the industry, however. Sperry Univac has made major advances in many of these areas.

Specifically, Sperry Univac has developed two types of end user facilities. The first is a query system designed for the knowledgeable user, consisting of a query facility, an update facility, and a report writing capability. For the non-data processing user, or what we have termed casual user at this conference, Sperry Univac has delivered an interactive report processing system which presents a relational interface to the user.

In addition to end user interfaces, we have produced COBOL and Fortran Data Manipulation Language interfaces and are currently developing a PL/1 DML. Sperry Univac has developed a comprehensive set of integrity features which support multiple concurrent access to the data base, including implicit and explicit locking facilities, deadlock detection, rollback and recovery utilities. We have developed extensive utility features to aid the Data Base Administrator in monitoring and maintaining the data base and we are currently implementing reorganization and restructuring utilities. My point is that data base management systems are evolving and they seem to evolving in the directions indicated by both of the SHARE conferences on data base management.

The industry is also making significant progress in the standards area. The SPARC Study Group report has provided a very valuable contribution with the three level schema approach, with its emphasis on data independence and on allowing many user views of the database. Sperry Univac is in basic agreement with this framework.

As part of this conference we have heard from members of the SPARC Study Group, the End User Facility Task Group, and the DDLC. And I think we have seen the convergence of ideas on fundamental issues. This emphasizes to me the importance and value of the standards activities. Sperry Univac does participate actively on these committees and others and wants to encourage others to support these committees which are providing direction for future standardization of data base management systems.

In conclusion, I would like to thank the SHARE committee for giving me the opportunity to participate in this conference. It has been a very valuable and informative experience. Thank you.

FORMALIZATION OF CONCEPTUAL SCHEMAS

T.B. Steel, Jr.
Equitable Life Assurance Society
New York, N.Y., U.S.A.

Elsewhere [Steel 1975] I have argued that the only acceptable choice of formalism for symbolizing a conceptual schema, in the sense of the ANSI/X3/SPARC/DBMS Interim Report [SPARC 1975], is that of modern symbolic logic. The argument is based upon assumption of the validity of Church's Thesis [Kleene 1952] which, broadly stated, asserts that any mechanical procedure for symbol manipulation (including computation) can be carried out by some specific Turing Machine [Boolos and Jeffrey 1974]. From this Thesis and the demonstrated equivalence of various formulations of the phrase "mechanically recognizable" [Quine 1961, p. 292] coupled with the reality that conceptual schemas used with data base management systems implemented in digital hardware necessarily describe discrete, limited models of the real world, it follows that formal logic is the most general scheme contemplable. From this it is deducible that anything expressible to a digital machine at all is necessarily expressible in formal logic.

Are there alternatives? Clearly the answer to this question is "yes". At the time of this writing no detailed examples have been published, despite some informal claims that the "schema" of the CODASYL DBTG Report [CODASYL 1975] is such an example. Nevertheless such partial efforts could be amplified to meet the criteria for conceptual schemas in various ways. It is my contention, based on the argument of the preceding paragraph, that any such formulation is definable in a suitably chosen logical formalism. Further, since the properties and problems of strict formal logic have been the subject of detailed investigation for almost a century, it seems unwise to make departures that gain nothing of substance and have the potential for unanticipated difficulty.

The existence of psychological barriers against formal logic and many of its subdisciplines is a point of significance andmust be analyzed and countered if the program I am contemplating is to be effectively realized. However, for the purposes of this paper I will assume away such difficulties. Here it is my intent to sketch an outline for the development of a suitable linguistic vehicle for the construction of conceptual schemas. What follows is not, of course, a full prescription for a conceptual schema language; that would be too much to expect at this stage of the research. What is intended is an illustration of the direction such developments could follow.

The objective of a conceptual schema is to make an appropriate repetoire of statements, claimed to be true, about entities to be included in a particular universe of discourse, enabling one to describe the enterprise of interest. In this context a statement is a declarative sentence and being true means provable from supplied asioms. Further, it is the case, necessarily, that the system is interpreted as it is intended as a model of reality (model in the engineering sense, not in the logician's sense where reality is a model of the system). Any conceptual schema is a selected subset of the provable statements (theorems). The system is not categorical so that there are many possible states of reality that will satisfy any given conceptual schema and, therefore, many possible states of the data base.

The philosophical approach taken is traditional and follows the logistical viewpoint [Whitehead and Russell 1950, Quine 1961] in that it is assumed that the well formed linguistic expressins have meaning and, thus, the theory has semantic content. That is to say the conceptual schema really described some abstraction of the "real world" and the concept of "truth" is applicable. Because of the objective of a conceptual schema, following the formalist program [Hilbert·1905] of pure symbol manipulation seems sterile. It can be argued that the intuitionists [Brouwer 1908] are on the right track so far as digital machinery is concerned with the emphasis on the finite. Perhaps so, but in the present context the dangers of introducing paradox through the limited use of realized infinities seems minimal, and the simplicity of formulation outweights the dangers. If conceptual schemas fall for this reason so will most of modern mathematics and we will all have more to worry about in that instance than conceptual schema difficulties. When all the world's application programmers learn to write error-free code one-hundred percent of the time it may be reasonable to worry about the possibility of contradiction at the extreme edge of conceptual schema formulation.

For this formulation I freely use an arbitrary alphabet, ignoring the problem of limited character sets in digital computers. Indeed, I would recommend that all research in this area follow the same lead. The clarity and conciseness that comes from this approach is desirable at the present stage of developments. Subsequent reduction to a limited, standard character set is an essentially mechanical exercise and future hardware developments may make it unnecessary. For the same reason Polish prefix notation is not employed. The conventional infix notation with grouping by brackets is much easier to read and understand. Suitable parsers already exist to cope with this problem.

In what follows much of the terminology of [SPARC 1975] relative to conceptual schemas is ignored. The reader will search in vain for conceptual "fields", "groups", "plexes" and the like. It is my contention that these terms designate unnecessary distinctions of questionable utility and considerable confusion. They could be arbitrarily reintroduced if one wishes to do so.

The working ontology for a particular conceptual schema will clearly depend upon the "reality" it is modelling. However, for all conceptual schemas two general categories of entities, the objects of the discourse, can be identified: individuals and classes. Individuals are the primitive, unanalyzed entities that establish the specific subject matter of the discourse. They may designate atoms, stars, people or machine tools; indeed whatever objects in the real world it is desired to have the conceptual schema describe. Classes are aggregations of individuals and other classes. Here I continue the traditional distinction between "classes", arbitrary collections, and "sets", classes that can themselves be members of other classes. This distinction, introduced [Zermelo 1908] to protect logic from paradox, is not one of major significance in what follows.

A conceptual schema is, then, a list of true statements about the entities of interest to the enterprise. If the list is sufficiently "complete" then the enterprise is sufficiently defined for the operation of the data base management system. A precise definition of "complete" in this sense is not possible at the present time but an intuitive notion is sufficient for the present purposes.

In order to make statements, true or otherwise, about entities it is necessary to have a language. We need names for entities, predicates (verbs) to assert things about the entities and connectives to permit

construction of compound statements. To avoid the complications attendant
to attempts to name non-existent objects, it turns out to be appropriate to
introduce variables (pronouns) first, then predicates that characterize
definitive properties of entities and express names of entities as
abbreviations for (or definitions in terms of) contextually defined
descriptions. The import of this observation will become clear in the
sequel.

Before proceeding it is necessary to remark that, while all that follows
is based on conventional two-valued logic, the logic of "true" and "false",
this is not an absolute requirement. There have been suggestions [Belnap
1975] that a four-valued logic, perhaps interpreted as "true", "false",
"undefined" and "missing", might be more appropriate to data processing.
As a first step, however, it seems prudent to proceed along conventional
lines.

In a brief account of this character it is not possible to do more than
state the preliminaries on the assumption that the reader is either already
familiar with the developments or is prepared to study ancillary works in
order to fill in the gap.   Let me claim at this point that nothing
extraordinary is being introduced; essentially all the preliminary
development is reported in literature available prior to 1930.

What is intended here is the description of a language, L, in which
conceptual schemas may be written.   In general, L will be richer than
required for any particular class of conceptual schemas, a point those
concerned with applicability should keep in mind. Certain concepts in L,
however, will necessarily be universal. It is to these concepts I now
turn.

Basic to L is an interpreted first order predicate calculus.   In any
particular use of L there will be a specific, finite set of predicates and
the entities of interest (universe of discourse) will be definitely
circumscribed.

To discuss L generally, however, it is necessary to think of a universe
with arbitrary individuals and arbitrary classes of individuals and other
classes, subject only to those constraints on class construction
necessitated by the need for consistency.

Putting aside for the moment the question of what entities are allowed,
the concept of _variable_ is introduced. A variable is an expression in L
which representes an arbitrary entity in the universe of discourse.
Variables play the role of pronouns in L.

In order to say anything about entities it is necessary to have
predicates, which play the role of verbs. As noted above, in any specific
use of L there will be a definite, finite set of predicates. To discuss L
generally it is necessary to have a denumerable infinity of predicates of
each type. Predicates differ in type depending on the number of entities
about which they say something.   Thus there are singulary predicates,
binary predicates, ternary predicates and so on.

For the sake of convenience, zero-ary predicates are allowed, although
there are only two of them possible (true and false) until modal operators
are intoduced.

It is not possible to define _atomic_ _formulae_. Any expression consisting
of an n-ary predicate, followed by n variables is an atomic formula.
Formulae generally will be defined recursively with atomic formulae as the
starting point of the recursion.

One way of constructing new formulae from old formulae is by use of the
connectives of the propositional calculus. The first connective introduced
is the _denial_ (not). The second connective introduced is the _conditional_
(if...then...).   Both the denial and the conditional are _truth-functional_
connectives in the sense that the truth value of the result is dependent

solely on the truth value of the components.

Another way of constructing new formulae from old formulae is by use of quantifiers. A single quantifier, the universal quantifier, (for all) suffices for the present purpose, interpreted in the usual way as being true whenever the following formula is true for every entity in the universe of discourse and false if there is even a single entity for which the formula is false.

All of the primitive notions required for the first order predicate calculus have now been introduced.

Formulae with free variable are fragmentary observations about the universe of discourse, exactly as are sentences with dangling pronouns. Formulae without free variables, on the other hand, are definite assertions about the universe of discourse that are either true or false. Such formulae are statements.

While the set of statements in primitive notation permits assertion of a greatdeal about the universe of discourse with an extreme economy of concepts, it is hardly economical expression as even the simplest statements become inordinately lengthy. There are two ways to proceed.

First, one may imagine the full primitive notation as always present and introduce abbreviations for frequently used forms to economize on the length of actually displayed expressions. If the objective is to study the expounded theory, this is the normal course chosen [Whitehead and Russell 1950]. Alternatively, and far less frequently, one may explicitly introduce new notation by statements incorporating the new notation that have the status of axioms. By following a complex to describe but intuitively clear set of rules (essentially the same rules that must be followed to keep abbreviations straight) it will always be possible to eliminate all new notation from any assertion and reduce it to a logically equivalent primitive statement. As thelanguage L is intended to be used rather than studied, the latter course appears best.

Thus far a mechanism for making (primitive) statements about the universe of discourse has been described. While this mechanism is incomplete for the purposes intended - conceptual schema description - it is a sufficient fragment to pursue unencumbered by further primitive concepts for the moment. The next step is to establish a further mechanism that permits sorting out the true statements about the universe of discourse. A convenient and conventional mechanism is the axiomatic method.

As is well known, in any system adequate to express integer arithmetic (and certainly conceptual schemas require at least that capability) it is not possible to construct an axiomatization that is complete (exhausting all true statements) and also consistent (excluding all false statements) [Godel 1931].

For present purposes consistency is far more important than completeness and what follows will be guided by that consideration. The incompleteness will not be troublesome.

Axioms are statements asserted to be theorems (theorems being those statements provable in the system and intended to be a subset of the true statements). Rules of inference are procedures whereby new theorems are generated from previously established theorems. If one employs axiom schemata, metalinguistic assertions that all statements of a certain form are theorems, it is possible to limit the requirements of a theory to a single rule of inference [von Neumann 1927]. This rule is the rule of detachment or modus ponens; viz:

  If A and (if A then B) are theorems, B is a theorem.

As noted above, two kinds of axioms are employed; those which are essential and characterize the properties of the primitive notions and those which are eliminable and serve only to characterize defined notation.

A suitable set of axioms for the propositional calculus in terms of the connectives of denial and conditional are [Prior 1955, p. 302]: the transitivity of the conditional, the principle of reductio ad absurdem and an assertion that a false premiss allows any conclusion. From these axioms and the rule of inference it is possible to deduce all the theorems of the propositional calculus, stated in terms of denial and condtional. By supplementing these axioms with some definitions (further axioms in this formulation) all of the propositional calculus in conventional form is obtainable.

Given the propositional calculus as a base, the next step is to exhibit the axioms characterizing the universal quantifier.

The first three axioms noted above establish the content of Quine's [1961] *100, while the axioms for the universal quantifier are essentially Quine's [1961] *101-*103. The rule of inference is Quine's [1961] *104. The first axiom of quantification asserts that universal quantification is distributable through the conditional. The second is the principle of vacuous quantification and the third is the essential principle of variable substitution.

An extremely useful additional quantifier, the existential quantifier (there exists) is defined as usual. At the moment no other quantifiers are required.

With the mechanism at hand, all of the first order predicate calculus is available but the predicates themselves remain uninterpreted. The key to approaching useful application of this mechanism as a language for describing conceptual schemas is the selection of suitable interpretations for the necessary predicates and devising axioms characterizing their properties. The nature of the predicates chosen will, in general, vary from situation to situation. Certain specific predicates, however, appear to have general application; in particular the binary predicates of identity and membership. Attention will now be directed to these specific predicates.

The predicate of identity generates atomic formulae of the form $x = y$, read as 'x is identical with (equals) y'.

Adequate characterization of the predicate of identity requires, in principle, a denumerable set of axiom schemata; n such for each n-ary predicate. In a specific application this reduces to a finite set of axiom schemata determined by the specific set of predicates chosen, asserting the principle of substitutivity of identity in atomic formulae.

With the availability of the predicate of identity it is possible to considerably enrich the vocabulary of L. So far only pronouns (variables), verbs (predicates), demonstrative adjectives (quantifiers) and conjunctions (connectives) have been available. Through the device of descriptions, nouns become a part of L. Rather than introduce the notion of noun as a primitive, the device of contextual definition is used. This has two advantages. First, it minimizes the required primitives but, more important, it resolves a thorny issue; how to name and discuss questionable or non-existent entities. Thus, instead of introducing, de novo, some form like 'God' and generating metaphysical argument over whether this primitive names something or not, a predicate 'God' and the corresponding atomic formula 'Godx' are selected. 'Godx' says that x has the attributes of Godhood, whatever they may be. If, now, in terms of already defined concepts the notion of the (unique) object x having the property God can be defined, then debate reduces to the logical argument where only the truth value of a claim that there exists an entity with the property 'God' is under debate.

One can develop a great deal of logic and methodology with nothing more than the mechanism at hand. With nothing else, however, it would remain a sterile exercise in any applied situation for all of the above is valid independent of the actual entities in the universe of discourse. In fact it applies to an empty universe. Additional specific predicates are required. As noted above, one such specific predicate is that of membership.

The predicate of <u>membership</u> generates atomic formulae of the form x e y (Please read ´e´ as epsilon and blame ASCII), and is read, in general, as ´x is a member of the class y´.

A question arises, however, in the event y is not a class, not the kind of thing that has members. The obvious solution, regarding any such situation as simply false, has the unfortunate consequence of forbidding the existence of an empty class which is far too useful a device to discard lightly. The simplest solution is to read ´xey´ in such case as the same as x=y. This has the curious but harmless effect of making it the case that every individual (non-class) is identical with the construct usually identified with the unit class (class whose sole member is) of that individual.

After some reflection this kind of interaction between identity and membership should not be surprising. It is a consequence of the reason for the ubiquity of identity and membership in this development, independent of the specific subject matter. Together these two predicates capture the major meaning of the verb ´to be´, which is, of course, linguistically central. It is hard to imagine any model of any significant part of the real world without these concepts.

Note that ´x=y´ can be read as ´x <u>is</u> (the same as) y´, and ´xey´ can be read as ´x <u>is</u> (a) y´.

An initial and critical step in developing the theory of the predicate of membership (set theory) is to note an axiom schemata that even more closely ties membership with identity. This is the axiom of extensionality: It asserts that a class is determined by its members (i.e., by extension).

Next it is necessary to introduce an axiom schemata that provides generally for the existence of classes. It is the axiom of comprehension, which restricts class membership to those entities that can belong to classes, but otherwise allows free generation of classes. This is required as arbitrary construction of classes is known to cause paradox [Russell 1903].

The remaining axioms of membership are solely concerned with admitting a maximum number of classes as themselves available for membership in further classes as is possible without producing inconsistency. For the purposes of conceptual schema description only the finite ones are essential, obviously, but an axiom of infinity is necessary to admit real numbers which are certainly a convenience if not an imperative.

Before any further general axioms are introduced much can be demonstrated with definitions. First, given the axiom of comprehension it becomes sensible to talk about class abstraction, defining the notion of the class of all x (which can be members of a class) with the property P.

The basic elementary definitions of the algebra of classes follow easily: (union), (intersection), (complement), (universal class), (empty class), (subset), (unit class), (unordered pair).

The universal class is denoted by ´U´, the empty set by ´O´, and sets are denoted in part by enclosing the denotation of its members in curly brackets, e.g. {x,y} is the set whose members are x and y.

So far the structures have been simple. Using a device due to Wiener [1912], order can be introduced by the following definition of <u>ordered pair</u>: ⟨x,y⟩={{x},{x,y}}.

Two ordered pairs are identical, assuming their components can be members of classes, if and only if the elements of each pair are identical <u>and in</u>

the same order. The notion of ordered pair can trivially be extended to the notion of ordered n-tuple.

Given the concept of ordered pair, the notion of a relation as a set of ordered pairs is straightforward.

A relation so defined is very simple but has certain limitations from the point of view of those who model the world in terms of relations. From the definition it is clear that the components of a relation are arbitrary so long as they can belong to classes. Thus, the concept as defined is the ultimate in un-normalized relations. The simplicity of this definition suggests some questions about the need for normalization at the conceptual level.

The domain of a relation is the set of all entities to which the relation is borne, the converse domain of a relation is the set of all entities that bear the relation to something, and the converse of a relation is that relation with domain and converse domain reversed. The rest of relational algebra can be built up with the concepts already introduced; concepts such as the Cartesian product, relative product, ancestral and various properties of relations such as reflexivity, symmetry, transitivity and completeness. Completeness is the property that for any two elements in the domains of the relation, say x and y, either $\langle x,y \rangle$ or $\langle y,x \rangle$ is a member of the relation. If a relation is reflexive, symmetric and transitive it is an equivalence relation.

It is now possible to define the notion of "order" systematically. A relation that is reflexive, antisymmetric and transitive is a partial ordering, and if it is also complete it is a linear ordering, the kind of sequential ordering so common in data processing.

It should be clear that structures of arbitrary complexity can be constructed through elaboration of the concepts discussed. It should be equally clear that use of the phrase "ordered set", common in data processing parlance, is somewhat sloppy. One should speak about ordering relations and their domains. Since different ordering relations can have the same domains, it is careless to speak about "the order of a set".

A function is a relation where every member of the converse domain bears the relation to only one entity. Thus, a function here is what is known in elementary mathematics as a "single valued function".

Functional abstraction can be accomplished using the familiar lambda notation.

Another useful definition is that of a correspondence, i.e., a one-one function.

By defining the successor of an entity, x, as the (set) union of x and {x}, denoted ´Scx´, it is now possible to define ordinal numbers:

1 = Sc0,
2 = Sc1, etc.

The 0 (zero) is the empty set, 1 is {0}, 2 is {0,1}.

The ordinal numbers are the members of the smallest class with the properties that the successor of every member is a member and every member of a member is a member. If there are infinite sets at all, and they will be permitted in this axiomatization, the set of ordinal numbers is an infinite class. The significance of ordinal numbers is that they permit counting in sequence. The empty set is an ordinal number and, if one considers the "natural" ordering relation for ordinal numbers it is the "first" ordinal number. This explains the choice of ´0´ as notation for the empty set. Zero is identical with the empty set, as noted.

Ordinal numbers are of two kinds; those that successors of others and those that are not (0 is an exception). The latter kind are called "limit ordinals". The finite ordinals or natural numbers are those ordinal numbers containing no limit ordinals and we can denote the class of all natural numbers by ´Nn´.

The natural numbers are, thus, 0,1,2,... as expected. It is also worth noting that the natural number n = {0, 1,..., n-1} and has exactly n members. This leads to the method of constructing the cardinal numbers. It will turn out that in the finite case cardinal and ordinal numbers are the same but they diverge - in the sense that not all ordinals are cardinals - in the infinite case. First it is necessary to define the notion of class similarity; that members of two classes can be put into one-to-one correspondence.

Cardinal numbers are ordinal numbers that are not similar to any of their members. All natural numbers are cardinal numbers, Nn is a cardinal number, but ScNn is not. The cardinality function can be defined as the relation (which turns out to be a function) of cardinal numbers to sets similar to that cardinal number.

The notation Kx yields the number of elements of x.

The developments now permit a transition from formal logic to traditional mathematics. Once the existence axioms of set theory are established it is possible to prove as theorems Peano´s postulates for natural numbers.

From Peano´s postulates it is well known that all the derivable properties of natural numbers can be obtained, that rational, real and complex numbers can be defined in terms of natural numbers and mathematical analysis can be built on this basis. The remainder of this essay will assume this done by one of the classic methods; e.g., [Landau 1930].

To conclude the exposition of set theory and the derivation of mathematics it remains only to state the remaining axioms. The controversial axiom of choice is omitted as unnecessary to these developments.

The first five axioms simply assert that if certain entities are members of the universe, then so are others. Thus, if x and y belong to U, so do {x,y} and the union of x and y. If x belongs to U and y is a subset of x, then y belongs to U, as does the class of all subsets of x (the power set of x). Finally, if F is a function whose converse domain (its arguments) belongs to U, then so does its domain (its values). The axiom of grounding, which says, in effect, that if one keeps looking at members of members of members..., eventually you hit bottom at either the empty set or an individual. It guarantees, among other things, that any relation can be normalized. The axiom of infinity, guarantees the existence of an infinite set. As it is the only axiom guaranteeing any set existence, if it is omitted it is necessary to add some existence axiom; e.g., ´OeU´.

Thus far in the development individuals have appeared only as a class of essentially degenerate items, having no significance except that of being distinguishable, one from another. On the basis of the axioms already introduced and the specific predicates explicated, there is no guarantee that any individuals exist. The entire development is consistent with an ontology that admits the empty set and the various classes compounded out of that set. As has been sketched, this is sufficient for mathematics. It is not sufficient, in general, for conceptual schemas.

Without predicates more pertinent to individuals per se and axioms to govern them, further progress would be sterile. To a large extent progress in conceptual schema development will be dependent on successful identification of such predicates and axioms.

Work has already been done in a number of directions that is applicable. Among the individuals that are of general importance in almost any data processing context are strings of characters from a defined alphabet. This is what data is! Conceptual schemas will, in general, be about objects in the real world, not their representations, but a large part of data processing involves treating artificial objects such as part numbers and the like.

There are a variety of ways to introduce an alphabet [Hermes 1938, Tarski 1936]. The procedure adopted here is derived from [Tarski 1936] as explicated by [Corcoran, Frank and Maloney 1974]. The objects (individuals) included in the now expanded universe of discourse are the finite (linear) expressions from a specified alphabet of N characters (signs). The size of the alphabet is not significant in what follows; only that it is specific in a given instance. If more than one alphabet is desired, the axioms and definitions can be replicated mutatis mutandis. Among the expressions is the degenerate or empty expression.

Two predicates are needed to provide the necessary discourse for string theory. A single predicate (the protosyntactical primitive of [Quine 1961]) can probably be reinterpreted to serve, but complexities ensue form the desire to retain the empty expression. The two chosen predicates are ´A´ and ´C´, interpreted loosely, respectively, as ´lexicographically precedes´ and ´concatenation´.

The axioms of string theory described below are probably not all necessary in the sense that it is likely that some can be proven from the others and the previously considered axioms, but because of the extended interpretation of ´A´ and ´C´ to have meaning, even trivial meaning, when the variables of the associated atomic formulae are not expressions, this remains open at the moment.

The first axiom asserts that there are exactly N distinct signs. Names for each of the N signs can be defined in terms of the predicate ´A´. Thus the first sign is the one that is lexicographically preceeded by nothing and, then, each additional sign is defined in terms of its predecessor. An axiom is needed to assert that each object defined this way is a sign.

The next two axioms assert that the empty expression is an expression and not a sign. An axiom is required asserting that signs are expressions, and another axiom asserting that the concatenation of two expressions is an expression.

These first five axioms are the counterparts for string theory of the first five for set theory, asserting what things are expressions. The remaining axioms delineate the properties of ´A´ and ´C´, especially with respect to the empty expression.

Four axioms explicate the properties of the empty expression, another (Tarski´s axiom) characterizes the conditions under which "different" concatenations yield the same string, and finally there is the axiom of string induction.

As a brief illustration of the value of string theory in conceptual schema formulation, consider an alphabet where the interpretations of the first ten signs are, respectively, the decimal digits ´0´ - ´9´.

One can, through a simple sequence of definitions arrive at a definition of a class of expressions, each member of which is a string of digits of length 9 and this class can be interpreted as the class of Social Security Numbers. (The definition could be modified by some complicated conditions to exclude those 9 digit sequences which are inadmissible as Social Security Numbers.) The obvious fact that one might also have 9 digit part numbers illustrates that more mechanisms must be introduced. The meaningful entities will be the functions that map Social Security Numbers onto individuals and parts onto part numbers. Since the arguments (counter domain) or values (domain) will be different, the distinction between people and part numbers will be made.

To proceed further with introduction of predicates other than by informal example is beyond the scope of this paper. A point of principle is necesary at this point. The predicates so far introduced are axiomatized with the intent of being categorical. That is there is intended to be only one acceptable interpretation in the real world. (Strictly speaking, this has not quite been done, as the consistency of both the continuum hypothesis and its denial attests, but in the finite case there is no problem.) For subsequent predicates and the individuals they encompass, this will, in general, not be the objective. One wishes to axiomatize only to the extent necessary to constrain conditions to those allowable in the enterprise.

Much can be done with the logical apparatus introduced so far but certain other mechanisms may well be fruitful. One of these is the introduction of tense logic. Among the suggested approaches are Petri nets [Petri 1975] and examination of the literature indicates that this approach should be pursued in depth [Petri 1975a]. Among the alternatives are tense logics with linear time [Prior 1966, Bull 1968].

This matter will not be pursued in any depth. The following operators (analogous to the connnectives of the propositional calculus in that they produce formulae from formulae) are basic: GP, HP interpreted respectively as ´it will always be the case that P´, and ´it has always been the case that P´.

A set of ten axioms governing G and H can be given. One formulation results in a time which is linear and rational. Some changes in the axioms will make time either integral or real.

The material presented above is just a sketch (getting sketchier as developments proceeded) of an approach to conceptual schema development. It should be kept clearly in mind that much of the detail of the formalism need be neither explicit nor necessarily even understood by the constructers of. conceptual schemas (enterprise administrators) in practice. A not quite accurate analogy is that this formulation is to the typical particular conceptual schema as the formal definition of a programming language is to a program written in that language. The definitions correspond to MACRO instructions and suitably chosen MACRO´s can eliminate the requirement for knowledge of the underlying details. Indeed, most, if not all, of the formulation presented here will be supplied by the vendor, perhaps even in the hardware in some implementations.

REFERENCES

Belnap, N. D., Jr. [1975]: personal communication.
Bernays, P. and Fraenkel, A. A. [1958]: "Axiomatic Set Theory", North-Holland Publishing Company (Amsterdam 1958).
Boolos, G. and Jeffrey, P. [1974]: "Computability and Logic", Cambridge Univesity Press (London 1974).
Brouwer, L. E. J. [1908]: "De onbetrouwbaarheid der logische principes", Tijdschrift voor wijsbegeerte, 2, pp. 152-158.
Bull, R. A. [1968]: "An algebraic study of tense logic with linear time", JSL, 33:1 (1968), pp. 27-38.
CODASYL [1975]: "Data Base Facility", CODASYL Journal of Deveopment, April 1975.
Corcoran, J., Frank, W. and Maloney, M. [1974]: "String Theory", JSL, 39:4, pp. 625-637.
Godel, K. [1931]:fur Untersuchungen von formalizierten Sprachen", Forschungen zur Logik und zur Grundlage der exakten Wissenshaften, n.s. 5 (Leipzig 1938).
Hilbert, D. [1903]: "Uber die Grundlagen der Logik und der Arithmetik", Verhandlungen des Dritten Internationalen Mathematiker-Kongresses in Heidelberg, Leipzig 1905, pp. 174-185.
Kleene, S. C. [1952]: "Introduction to Metamathematics", D. van Nostrand Company (Princeton, NJ, 1952).
Landau, E. [1930]: "Grundlagen der Analysis", Akademische

Verlagsgesellschaft (Leipzig 1930).

Petri, C. A. [1975]: personal communication.

...[1975a]: "Interpretations of Net Theory", Gesellschaft fur Mathematik und Datenverarbeltung MBH Bonn, Internal Report 75-07.

Prior, A. N. [1955]: "Formal Logic", Oxford University Press (London 1955).

...[1966]: "Postulates for tense-logic", American Philosophical Quarterly, 3:2 (1966), pp. 1-9.

Quine, W. v. O. [1961]: "Mathematical Logic", rev. ed., Harvard University Press (Cambridge, MA 1961).

Russell, B. [1903]: "The Principles of Mathematics", Cambridge University Press (London 1903).

SPARC [1975]: "Interim Report: ANSI/X3/SPARC/DBMS", CBEMA (Washington, D.C., February 1975).

Steel, T. B., Jr. [1975]: "Data Base Standardization: a Status Report", in Dougue, B.C.M. and Nijssen, G. M., "Data Base Description", North-Holland Publishing Company (Amsterdam 1975).

Tarski, A. [1936]: "Der Wahrheitsbegriff in den formalisierten Sprachen", Studia Philosophica, 1 (1936), pp. 261-405. (Reprinted in English in Tarski [1956].

... [1956]: "Logic, Semantics, Matamathematics", Oxford University Press (London 1956).

von Neumann, J. [1927]: "Zur Hilbertschen Beweistheorie", Math. Zeitschr., 26 (1927), pp. 1-46.

Whitehead, A. N. and Russell, B. [1950]: "Principia Mathematica", 2ed., 3v., Cambridge University Press (London 1950).

Wiener, N. [1912]: "A Simplification of the Logic of Relations", Proc. Camb. Phil. Soc., 17 (1912-1914), pp. 387-390.

Zermelo, E. [1908]: "Untersuchungen uber die Grundlagen der Mengenlehre I", Math. Ann. 59, pp. 261-281.

DISCUSSION

COMBA: As a mathematician by background, I'm not terrified by all these symbols and all these axioms, etc., but as a computer scientist I would like to see this reduced to a minimal necessary set, and I think that you have opened up so many possible controversies that should really not belong to us. For example, on the question of ontology, Quine believes that there is only one thing - that there is no distinction between sets and individuals, that individuals are just special kinds of sets. Now, I don't think we have to agree on that. I don't think we should bring up the question, except to bury it. On the question of descriptions, as you know, there are some troubles there. For example, if I say I believe that Napoleon died at St. Helena, but I don't believe that the loser of Waterloo died at St. Helena am I showing my ignorance, or lack of logical power?

STEEL: Let me comment on that one. There are ways of protecting this kind of system against that kind of difficulty. That's a much worse paradox, but the troubles with descriptions can be kept out of this kind of a formal system, I'm pretty sure.

COMBA: Yes, but it would be useful for somebody to work that out but you do open it, and now I have to worry. Is the system you propose open to such possible antimonies? Now other questions, for example, whether order is primitive or not   ou show a way in which order can be defined in terms of sets, but psychologically, it's the other way around. Try to teach a youngster that ABC is the same as CAB and it's the same as CAAAB. The set concept involves a very high level of abstraction, because the way in which most of our perceptions are ordered, and the repetition which is very difficult to understand.

STEEL: I will disagree with that.

COMBA: Another way of introducing integers is with Peano's axioms.

STEEL: That's how I do it.

COMBA: So you don't have to reduce integers to sets. So why don't we try and start with the minimal set of assumption that are generally agreed on. On the integers, I don' think we have to define the integers in this room here. Finally one more point on the level of formalism that is needed by the theory.
 It is likely that we need some formalism and yet there are some theories that we call scientific that have a rather small amount of formalism like evolution.

STEEL: Try teaching evolution to a computer. When you can do that, then I'll agree with you.

COMBA: Yes, but we are talking about a description of a firm. You cannot describe a firm precisely so perhaps we are misplacing the precision. We have to bridge the gap between people and computers. If we want a schema that people can understand, perhaps as much as possible, it should be in English. You can't have theories expressed in English. I'm raising these questions, but I'd like to stress that my main point is that we should try to avoid going to the foundations beyond where it is necessary, but at the point where it is necessary, we should try to explain clearly; to explain and state what our concepts are. For example, the integers will always have the same ordering. We know what it means and we can state the axioms. We do not have to define it further in terms of further theories. Take a starting point and build on top of that.

STEEL: That's what I did. I took a starting point and built on top of it. You just disagreed with the starting point.

COMBA: Yes, I think it could be closer to our experience as non-mathematicians.

STEEL: What I've shown here is the underlying underpinnings. I would expect that the typical conceptual schema designer would indeed be working with and using the ordinary way, numbers, and things of that sort. As far as the psychological problems are concerend, I'm going to make a remark that I tried to put in the introduction to the interim report and the Study Group wouldn't let me. It was an observation that enterprise administrators are presumably going to be fairly senior people, are going to be quite well compensated, and it wouldn't hurt to have them learn a little. I'm not sure that's a direct quote, but that's the thrust of the observation.

TAYLOR: The artificial intelligence community, what I know of it, has worked for a couple of decades with various approaches to modelling complex systems, and there is a significant school in that community that feels that approaches based on a theorem proving methodology are ultimately bound to fail, because human systems are full of self contradictions, full of exceptions. A more operational procedure has to be sort of a framework in which the more formal theorem based approach is embedded and theorems by themselves will not work. Marvin Minsky will expound at great length on that. Would you comment on why you think that human organizations like enterprises are so consistent that a theorem approach will work.

STEEL: I think a great deal of what we want to model is precise enough to do with the approach that I've taken so far. Second, I believe that the recent work on fuzzy subsets is going to go a long way toward dealing with that problem. Are you familiar with that work?

TAYLOR: Up to a point. I guess my response is, it seems to me the burden of proof is, at present, on the people who take a more formal approach, in the sense that there are demonstrable systems using frames and operational procedural definitions of semantics right now which do a great deal more than the corresponding systems based on theorem proving.

STEEL: I fully agree. This approach is going to have to be worked out, thrown against concrete examples and seen to work. If it doesn't work, chuck it. In some sense it's got to be an experimental approach to the thing. I think these difficult situations have to be somehow dealt with, if they can't be in a reasonably straightforward way, then the approach is wrong.

COLLINS: The purpose of my comment is to get some clarification for myself and also clarify it for people who think like I do. It seems to me that we have two proposals here. One I would restate in the form that formal mathematics is an extremely suitable and perhaps the only language in which to express conceptual schemas. Is that correct?

STEEL: That's correct, yes.

COLLINS: The second thing you've done is given a specimen of a conceptual schema, and, in fact, the one, as far as you developed it, would necessarily, it seems to me, be part of every enterprise's conceptual schema. People could disagree with you on two levels. Is formal mathematics appropriate, especially since there is a hint here that this is where we should put our main emphasis? There was also a little hint of discouraging the development of new ideas. I'd like to take a little exception to that, because even if formal mathematical language is the proper language for a conceptual schema, and I feel that it ultimately must be, I would still like to see new ideas. I'd like to simultaneously encourage new concepts, not discourage them. On the level of the choice, you've made a number of choices for us...

STEEL: Let me interrupt and comment to that last point first. There's no way you're going to stop Jardine's students from generating new ideas, no way in the world!

COLLINS: What I'm proposing, therefore, is that they not be considered competitors and we resurrect the great new debate, but that they be considered as test cases to see whether a particular schema is a good one. If there is something I feel I can properly say using some bright new idea, and you can't show me how your logical theory can handle it, then maybe you need to change your logical theory. On the choice of theorems we use, the basis of which we discussed a few minutes ago, I'm not anywhere near competent, nor would I ever spend the energy even if I were competent, to get into that to see where you're going. So let me address that just from the point of some very elemental user concerns. I noticed in the beginning that you made a statement that you should choose the entities very carefully. I don't want to choose my entities carefully. I want to have a great deal of freedom, and you're telling me that if we go down that route, there'll end up being some things that I just can't discuss with my data base management system, which I might have discussed had I forced the conceptual schema to go another route. I'm a little unhappy there, and I'm not sure where I stand.

STEEL: I didn't say choose the entities very carefully, I said choose the fundamental entities very carefully.

COLLINS: And the field will free up as we proceed?

STEEL: Then you build on top of that.

COLLINS: When I get to employee, would I....

STEEL: Well, should you think of 'employee' as fundamental, or should you pick 'person' as fundamental? That's the kind of care that I'm talking about.

COLLINS: I'd have to agree with that. I'd like to point out though, that when you make a definition, it's not as harmless as you may have represented. Mathematically it's harmless enough, but on a human scale what it represents is a value distinction. You've chosen to segregate something out so you can express it compactly, and being human beings we tend to focus our attention on things we can easily express. So, in a sense, there is a value judgement behind.....

STEEL: O.K. Now you have just reinforced my point about choosing entities carefully and removed the 'fundamental' from it. You're saying be careful what definitions you write down.

COLLINS: I'm also saying that when I go to talk about it, I'm going to have to talk in Homeric myths, because I'm not going to be able to speak about what I want to speak about using the carefully chosen things I've chosen!!

KIRSHENBAUM: The reason you went back to your starting point is the reaction to what can loosely be called 'it is intuitively obvious to the casual user' that we have been seeing in this business for the past couple of years - perhaps an overreaction - but nonetheless a reaction to the rather loose use off terminology in this business, and you did an 'I'll show you guys'. What do you feel the level of mathematical sophistication for education of a practitioner?

STEEL: I would expect if the Equitable were to get into this business, and we had such a system, I would expect that somebody like you or people who have reported directly to you with a one semester course in the appropriate topics would be doing this kind of work. Does that answer your question?

KIRSHENBAUM: Name the subjects that you think would be involved. Just personal curiosity.

STEEL: Mainly logic.

KENT: I have the feeling that what you're talking about on the whole is a purely descriptive mechanism which is really non specific with respect to model concepts and it's essnetially a descriptive thing which side-steps some of the model discussion and arguments that we're having. If I could use the same basic form of logic notation to describe a model that I want to think of as entities and relationships, or if I want to·have a model where I think of events and processes, or if I want to have a model where I think of records and data items as my basic model, the formal logical system that you're talking about is equally applicable. So what you're proposing doesn't really address the various issues that go on between the components of the various models. You're just offering a way describing whichever one wins, or all of them. Is that accurate?

STEEL: That's about accurate. I don't believe any one of them will win. I think there are too many proponents on each side. From the point of view of the work the Study Group has been doing, the desire is to accommodate any and all models. I think what I've done, and that you accurately perceive, does, in a sense, side-step the issue, and permit arbitrary choice of form. That was deliberate.

KENT: In effect what you're saying is if anybody comes out with a database product which has a formalism for dealing with the conceptual model, don't choose the Senko model, don't choose the Abrial model, don't choose the Tsichriitzis model, but instead sidestep that question in your product. Come out with this kind of language, which doesn't even force a choice of these models. That's your specific, in effect, it's your alternative, counter argument to the whole interim model.

STEEL: That's right. Then the user of the product, when he develops his particular conceptual schema for his enterprise, chooses the model for his instance, and another fellow over here, may choose another model.

COLLINS: It's possible to state the thing this way, but what we were saying is take a language which clearly has the capability to describe many of these models and probably most of the ones we've been discussing locally. Don't take a preconceived pattern, like a network or a tree. The pattern you are to have in your mind while you're using this language is an enterprise itself, and we're not saying model the enterprise, express that model in this language and you'll be happy, we're saying express the enterprise in this languae and you'll end up with a model of the enterprise, which is what we want.

STEEL: Yes, that's fair.

KENT: I don't argue that position, I don't challenge that position, but then there's a corollary problem. If somebody comes out with one of these products, it's going to have certain fixed things in it, certain fixed procedures and languages, and what not, and even though you can be as flexible as this in the descriptive aspect of the conceptual model, other things that you want to be able to do is have mappings from the other levels, external and internal. If you're this loose about what goes on at the conceptual model, we don't even have any canonical concept of the kinds of objects that are there. It becomes a little fuzzy for me to understand how one can talk about the mapping constructs from the external level to these formless objects at the conceptual level and corresponding mapping down to the internal level, and I need to see a new kind of thinking to address that problem.

STEEL: Well, I don't have any good words to answer that question. I have some sort of intuitive feelings about how it can be implemented, but nothing that I can prove. I guess all I can say is that I have faith.

KENT: There was a comment in one of these early discussions, by Bob [Taylor]. It said something about theorem proving mechanisms, and I'm a little puzzled or confused as to what the relevance of that is, because I think of using the form of logic primarily as a language and a description that is a static description at the conceptual level.

STEEL: That is my intention, and I thought I had said somewhere in the talk that I was not talking about automatic theorem proving, and I don't quite think that was the thrust of Bob's [Taylor] remark anyway.

KENT: So you're agreeing withmy observations that theorem proving mechanisms and techniques are not relevant to what we're talking about.

STEEL: That's right. It might someday be useful if it ever got good enough, but it's not an essential.

CHINLUND: I've had some experience with the theorem proving versus heuristics issue, and I do think Bob Taylor does have a point, although I'm in favour of the more formal approach. It can be true in practical situations that less formal methods are more immediately effective. However, as I understand it, your whole purpose of introducing this mechanism is to establish consistency, and that's very important, and sort of underlines it. I think there's been a lot of confusion about whether this is a pattern for the conceptual schema, which I don't think it is. It's more of an underpinning, to guarantee the correctness of the whole thing in an efficient way. I ask if that's correct.

STEEL: It is intended as the underpinnings of the language or set of macros that are added in to define the conceptual schema. It is not itself, a conceptual schema.

CHINLUND: Exactly, but I think there's been some confusion about that.

STEEL: When I was disagreeing with Bill [Kent], or agreeing with Bill, or whatever I was doing with Bill, about the automatic theorem proving point, I was agreeing with the point he was making but disagreeing that he was correctly interpreting the point that Bob Taylor was making. And I agree that it may well be the possibility that some of the less formal methods turn out to be necessary. As I say, I have faith, but who knows??

CHINLUND: Let me suggest that the description of the ANSI/SPARC study group position as given in the summary paper seems to make the description of an Aristotelian horse with a white attribute and a leg attribute, quantity 4, and so on, look like the kind of thing that's being done. I refer particularly to the notion that there would be attributes, conceptual attributes, conceptual groups and records and so on. This might belong in some model based on the system for certain types of users, but it's certainly not fundamental. That's kind of in support of your position, and along that line, I wanted to say I'm glad to see the removel of normalization questions at this level. For example, in trying to describe a university environment, we have students, they have names and addresses, and take courses. They don't take course numbers. The courses are complex entities. In turn, courses, which can be treated as relations again, not normalized, not that theology, but as relations in the logical sense, also have complex constituents like instructors, not instructor numbers.

STEEL: I think that if one chooses an internal model that is relational, there is where the concept of normalization becomes significant because its related to the efficiency of processing. I fully agree with you that at the conceptual level it is inappropriate.

KIRSHENBAUM: I think that amongst other things what the formalism that you've introduced does, is allow things like relations, and relations in the sense we've been using it here up until now, and the DDLC 'sets' to be described. It achieves two things. First, it's a common framework, so you can say this is different from that in the following ways and is the same in these ways, and that's useful. Second, if any of these data models have, in fact, inconsistencies, I would presume that this kind of formal notation would immediately pull out that kind of inconsistency if you attempted to do it in this notation.

STEEL: On that latter point, I'm not sure they would automatically fall out, but you'd have a better chance of finding them.

KIRSHENBAUM: Than ordinary English.

STEEL: Yes.

KIRSHENBAUM: You say there is a mechanism for handling data objects, there's a mechanism for handling processes. Is there a mechanism for handling time?

STEEL: Yes.

COLLINS: Bill Kent brought up a point a minute ago, asking you whether this approach to conceptual schemas is going to have the power to cope with the necessary mappings that the external schemas and internal schemas will require in everything, and while, probably in practice the answer will have to be yes, I'd like to suggest that this may be missing part of the point here. We're presently asking the man at the terminal to look at the model and think in terms of the data model, while he uses the terminal to get the information he wants, and I think what we all want is we want him to look at the reality. Consequently, the ultimate inside schema must be aware of that reality, and maybe we can get away from this need for, to some extent, probably not entirely, of simple crutches, like various data models. Now this bears on the point Larry Cohn brought our attention this morning on the importance of query. I don't think we'll ever free up on the query issue until the user can sit there and not be thinking about how the data base is arranged but how the reality is arranged. He may get frequently disappointed when the data base doesn't support what he wants to know about the reality, but that's in the nature of it.

STEEL: Yes, I think that's a fair comment. I would anticipate, although this is pure speculation, that if something like this were put into place as a mechanism for defining conceptual schemas, you would fairly rapidly

find that the external schemas took on - cut down to some extent of course
- something of this same flavour, so that even they would be more talking
about the reality rather than about the data processing system. The tough
mapping is going to be to the internal schema, because there it does have
to talk about the data base.

SWENSON: Are you predicates going to range over predicates as well? Is it
first order?

STEEL: Yes and no.

SWENSON: If it is first order, you'd need normalization, the regularity
axiom will force it, but you need normalization.

STEEL: You need the ability to normalize. Let me clarify 'yes and no' a
little bit. The answer is technically 'yes', but if you have the predicate
of membership you have the equivalent of an omega order, which is why the
unnormalized situation can go on consistently.

GRABER: There are two well known models for a computing machine. One is a
Turing machine and the other is a finite state automaton. It seems to me
that the model which is more correct for a real world computer, especially
for a real world business computer, is a finite state automaton. What
we're seeing here is more of a Turing machine model. The proper model for
a data base, at least a business data base, is a regular set rather than a
recursively enumerable set, as something related to a finite theory, a
completable theory, and not to something that is so open ended as the
theory of the Turing machines or the mathematical theory you have
presented.

STEEL: I know more about this approach than about your approach. There are
a number of constructs that one needs, or appears to need, in order to talk
about enterprises that I'm not sure can really appropriately be grafted on
the finite state approach. Remember what you're trying to do with a
conceptual schema. It is to model an enterprise, not model a data model of
an enterprise. The finite state approach is probably correct if you are
going to formalize with equal kind of precision the internal schema.   Then
it might be the appropriate paradigm to use.

GRABER: I do think if is essential that when we get down to defining these
things, particularly as we move toward standardization, that we do base our
definitions with mathematical rigor. This is a similar point to the one
Mr.   Comba made. There is no need to go back to the very first principle
and derive everything from basic set theory. I think one can begin at some
place close to the top, perhaps at the assumption that everyone
understands, perhaps all of arithmetic and all of set theory, and perhaps
even all of graph theory. Begin at that point, using these as assumed
terms everyone knows, or if they don't know can go back to text books and
mathematics and learn. There's no need for us to start with the basics of
set theory, we can start at a much higher mathematical level.

STEEL: Yes, you can assume the mathematics, but the conceptual schema
designer will be generating predicates and axioms about the predicates that
talk about the things of interest to the enterprise. These things are new.
They're not part of traditional mathematics and unless you have available
the elementary mechanisms to operate with appropriate interaction among
those things and sets, you may have a problem. I would expect, as I tried

to respond in answer to Mr. Comba, that the typical enterprise administrator will indeed be using integers and he knows what they are and he doesn't worry about what's behind it. We'll be using sets in a naive set theory sense, not worrying about what's underneath it. But I think there will be times when one will have to have the underlying fundamentals exposed in some corners in order to deal with problems that come up with the newly introduced predicates and objects.

GRABER: Coming back to my view that managers have different needs, I'd like to clarify a little bit about my comments yesterday where I indicated that I didn't think Mike Senko's model would be acceptable to the members of the GUIDE committee. I don't think your model would be acceptable to the members the GUIDE committee. I want to make the point, however, that I think there is a place for your model, or Mike Senko's model, or similar models in the overall picture of the data base management system. In fact I think it is essential that this picture be there some place in the system. However, it is not what my committee thought of as what they call the entity set rather than the conceptual schema. It comes from a comment made a few days ago that if this is what the conceptual schema is, it is not something that is going to be produced by someone called the enterprise administrator. It may be produced by someone called the chief data base architect or something, but an enterprise administrator that is actually going to be controlling this in a business sense is not going to be performing this kind of activity. Someone else will be doing that, and there is a need, perhaps for this type of activity, but there is also a need for another interface which is specifically oriented toward the needs of the practicing businessman.

STEEL: Let me remind you, for anybody else who's forgotten for the 49,000th time, administrators are people in roles, and this superman, with the bald head and the pot-belly is the enterprise administrator, is a manager. Presumably, in a big enterprise he would be a manager of a staff. In a small shop, one person might perform all three of those roles, so let's not get hung up on what the enterprise administrator is. It's a person or a set of people or a part of a person in a role. It is, perhaps, comparable to the operations research kind of function, but there are some experts who know how to do this job. They are managed by a traditional manager and the communication is between the businessmen and this staff of experts, and their job is to translate the ordinary business descriptions of what goes on, into some kind of formal mechanism.

GRABER: I'll accept that as one possible approach. I think there is an alternative possible approach in which there are two interfaces. One interface is designed for the use of the person who is constructing a sophisticated mathematical model of the enterprise or its data. Another interface is used for a businessman who is attemptingg to exercise some control over the operation of the enterprise and this data.

SENKO: I happen to be something of an iconoclast with regard to men who have invented things earlier than us. I believe that if the Greeks had had pants, Aristotle would have put them on one leg at a time. I think these men have been quite brilliant but they don't know all of our traditions. For example, if we believed in some of the Greeks, we would still be working in terms of earth, air, fire and water. There is a great truth and a great tradition and we should take care to revere it where it is appropriate. But there are cases where we might have to make slight changes, and I think that we may not disagree.

STEEL: First of all, we are still working in terms of earth, air, fire and water. It´s called solid, liquid, gas and plasma. We just changed the names. With respect to historical tradition, my point was not that these were necessarily such brilliant people, that they were so much brighter than we are. It´s that what´s been done has been around a long time, has been studied, has been analyzed and many of the holes found already, and that´s my point of suggesting that we try to stick to them as long as they work.

SENKO: That´s the point - as long as it works in what we´re doing, and sometimes it does and sometimes it doesn´t. Most of logic, for example, deals with extensions rather than intensions, and our sets are intensional rather than extensional, so we have to be a little bit careful there.

SEVCIK: One lesson learned in the area of security and protection was that it is far safer to give permission explicitly rather than trying to prohibit all the cases that don´t allow it. It would be my hope that in getting to a way of describing the conceptual schema that we could go the route of stating things that are, rather than trying to think of all the things that are not, and disallowing them one at a time.

STEEL: Don [Jardine] pointed out that there´s more than one way to do it. I would like to make one comment about the problem that we had with money. That´s a problem that´s going to have to be solved, obviously, for conceptual schemas relating to business enterprises. But our problem was not with describing what money was, but understanding what money was.   It was not that we got hung up because the mechanism couldn´t describe it.   We couldn´t quite figure out what money is, and I think somebody´s going to have to worry about an appropriate model.

COHN: [as a user] If I could reverse the usual question asked of IBM, and this time addressing the.. [as a conceiver]

STEEL: No comment.

COHN: Addressing the philosophers, mathematicians, researchers, and so forth, of the world, some of whom have gathered here, talking in terms of different models, different formalisms, different this, that or the other thing, I don´t think there is any question about the importance of this conceptual schema that we've been discussing, and I would also assume that there ought to be some desire to eliminate the frustrations of waiting for things for a long period of time. When would you guess that the arguments will converge in this vast multitude of thinking process that´s going on and we might see something that represents concrete recommendations from your philosophical academic, mathematical community on the subject.

STEEL: I would estimate that it is going to take another three years to, in some sense, settle the arguments and kind of shake it out. Then I suppose I should ask you how long it´ll take to build it after the arguments are shaken out.

COHN: Can I start from where Aristotle started?

STEEL: I brought up Aristotle, not so much to give Mike [Senko] something to quip me about but rather to warm up Jardine, who brought up Locke and Liebnitz.

TURNER: The example of operations research has been used before.   I think we have to be terribly careful about the examples of that sort.   The people in management science have been concerned for many years about the inability of operations research to really influence the decision making within organizations. The people that practice it often feel somewhat on the side of the enterprise. Certainly top management is often not aware of the supposed benefits of operations research. I think it depends on what industry you're in and there have been many positive things that have been done. But in many industries, operations research is really not an intimate part of the operation of the enterprise, and so it isn't quite clear to me what the connotation will be of the analogy of data processing or the data base administrator or the construction of the conceptual schema with the results to date in operations research.

STEEL: I think there is one significant difference.   If our data base management systems are being used by the enterprise to produce data, reports, results, and various sorts of things, and if our data base management system requires a conceptual schema to function, top management better pay attention to the enterprise administrator, or the whole business will come crashing down around their ears. They can afford to ignore operations research. All they'd do is be a little bit less efficient and don't even know it. I think there is a real difference there.

KIRSHENBAUM: The way that operations research people are in fact dealt with in many ways is as technicians. There might be a class of technicians who are concerned with formalisms and a class of mmanagers that are concerned with using those formalisms to do a real job.

TURNER: This gap does exist between manageement and the technician and it would be unfortunate if such a gap continued to exist between the data processing technician and professional management. I'm sure the conceptual schema would simplify the construction of our information systems. I'm terribly concerned with the implication, though, that by creating a processing mechanism that uses a conceptual schema, we're going to change the way that management perceives the data processing function.   That's a criticism that's been levelled against people in data processing for a long time, that we require the enterprise to change, that we require the people to perform their functions differently.   It may be that there are many advantages if we could get people to change, and perform their functions differently.   It seems unfortunate that that's a requirement for our effective use within organizations.

STEEL: Data processing is a tool, and tools can be used well or badly. Once you have tools with certain properties, people's habits and the things they learn do have to change. It used to be that every politician in the country knew how to ride a horse. Now they know how to ride in the back of chauffeur-driven limousines. Times change, the tools change, and people's habits have to change. If we're going to use data processing and use it effectively, somehow, the part of the world that interfaces with it in any respect, is going to have to change some of their habits. Now one would like to minimize the number of what are perceived to be good habits that it's necessary to change.   We do a bad job of it now because we produce piles of paper very high and all sorts of awkwardnesses.

TURNER: I suspect it was a lot less costly when the politicians rode horses.

STEEL: You're right! But there was a pile of something on every street when that happened.

TURNER: The thing implicit in what you're saying is that change has certain characteristics. It takes a bit of time and it requires a bit of force, but there are processes which expedite change and make it easier. We must very consciously understand some of the implications of what we're saying. There's a great danger, and this is what I want to prevent, that we begin to talk about building a fairly accurate and detailed model of the enterprise, when I submit that it is enormously difficult to define the enterprise in any model: I don't even care about the semantics of what we use to define it. We can even use English, which, although lacking the precision of a formal language does have a richness of ambiguity and interpretation, and I submit that it would be enormously difficult to take a relatively simple enterprise and describe it in sufficient detail to replicate the conceptual schema. That, to me, means the conceptual schema has to be an abstraction of the enterprise in some way. The key, then, is to make that abstraction in a manner that still allows you to do many of the integrity checks and the internal derivations that are necessary for our systems to function. There is a need to describe this process and to somehow bound our objectives, maybe not our desires, but what's likely to be accomplished.

STEEL: I know it's possible within the schema technique I'm talking about, and it probably is in a lot of others, to have controlled ambiguity. I think that's really what you want. Mike Senko is shaking his head 'no'. Why don't you two argue.

SENKO: I would agree with you, though, in the sense that I feel that the conceptual schema idea which has been put forth here will, in fact, give us greater flexibility to move with the organization and conceptual schema should not be interpreted as meaning that we are going to do a lot of inessential work describing the thing. We're only going to describe it as much as we have to to do the data processing. It will be an abstraction and should be simpler than the abstraction than we have now in terms of files, records, and so forth.

STEEL: There is a point that I suppose really ought to be put into the report and emphasized. It's there, but it isn't really emphasized. The enterprise, from the point of view of what we are talking about, is that portion of the organization that is pertinent to what is going to be in the data base. Enterprise does not equal corporation. I think that point ought to be emphasized, and I think that's consistent to what you've just said.

SENKO: With regard to your estimate, I would tend to agree with you. I think that there is a fair amount of hope with regard to coming to a reasonable definition of the conceptual schema within three to five years, or something like that. There is, much more, I think now, in the last year or so, particularly witnessed by the Freudenstadt meeting and some of the discussions here, of real attention to the facts of the matter, rather than to just banging things up against each other, and I think that we've got a really good chance to do something. The work that we've heard here such as the comments of whether we want to deal with employees or employee numbers, are now getting us down to a level of discussion where we can decide things.

STEEL: I agree with that. I think what we're beginning to see evolving are some criteria for what the properties of the conceptual schema really ought to be, and once we agree on that, then the various proposals can be looked at in that light, and hopefully that will lead to real convergence.

COLLINS: I'd like to change the subject very slightly, but with the thought of shedding some light on this conceptual schema language proposal I want to paint a little picture of the enterprise administrator. We all recognize that one of the things the conceptual schema is going to do for us is somehow marry the internal and external. It also is going to do something for the enterprise administrator. TThe ultimate power in our society is the power to change the way we think about things and the way other people think about things. If I can change the way you perceive me or perceive the objects with which you have to deal, I'm exercising the ultimate in power or control or authority over the situation.

STEEL: Called 'Fascism'.

COLLINS: It is what happens with human beings. This is what we try to do and it is called 'communication', also. Let's suppose that we are somewhere in the middle of the situation, and there is a data base and there are data elements to find, and everything is running along smoothly, but a particular data elements called 'return on investment' has not yet been invented at this point. Some financial vice president goes to his terminal one day with a brilliant idea on a way of viewing the corporation that will be useful to his purposes. He invents one of the variations of return on investment by sitting down and asking for an elaborate query against the data base where he pulls off all these little figures that have to go into ROI, assuming that they're not aggregated already, for the moment. He instructs the machine how to aggregate them and he comes up with this one number. He then goes off happy with that and uses it in various ways. He begins to talk to his fellow executives about this, and before you know it there is a demand withint the corporation to the effect that I don't want to go through all that nonsense to get ROI, but I want to ask ffor the data 'what's the ROI today, 'what's the plan call for it to be three years from now'. So they go to the enterprise administrator, who has to be involved at this point if we're going to interject a new data element to the thing. So the enterprise administrator looks at that financial V.P.'s original query, which was, What is the ROI, and he looks at it and he matches it against the other things in there. At this point he consults the accounting people because he's got to get this right. As he gets into the logic he can't have inconsistencies there, the system won't support that, so he's got to get it. He's got to develop it as a logical concept. I'm also supposing that it's going to go into the annual report. It's one of the thing we report on. He's going to end up to finding it in a way which could be used in a legal way. The whole corporation has to recognize that at some point a government agency will come along and say, 'Exactly how do you compute this ROI. We claim you're fooling investors'. That's going to be in there so that they're really doing an official corporate act. This enterprise administrator is going to be the coordinator of that whole company's attempt to define what ROI is, in a way consistent with all their aims and problems and everything else. Being very conversant with this language and with other elements, and being mainly concerned with this sort of activity, he's going to be rather good at suggesting that if you do that, this is going to connect to that, and we're not trying to call attention to that, and so on. The result is, people are going to look to him for leadership in defining ROI which is one of the things that corporation is then going to use to think about itself. As an example, I picked that one deliberately, because it´s a famous one that has caused various problems that sounded like a good idea. We held it up and said that was the goal. The next thing you know other things began to go wrong; it had that sort of history. But, this is one of the roles I think the enterprise administrator will play, and I think by that scenario, it shows the rather enormous amount of power he´s going to have, a sort of combination of the power of the accounting controllership people and the corporate lawyers. He´s going to have a say in these issues, because he´s going to be able to show the rest of the corporation what the implications of doing something like this are. Of course, in that particular instance, ultimately, the president´s liable to say ´forget all the lies, you´re going to have to do the query every time, you´re not going to peel that out as something somebody can ask for, go to your terminal and erase the log tapes when you´re done´.

COMBA: Can we expect now that the study group will actively start to look at a notation like the one that was put forth and others like it, and next time around propose a standard for this notation? Is that the plan?

STEEL: We have no plan yet. Our meeting this weekend is to determine what the next steps and objectives are, so whether that´s the plan or not is something I can´t concretely answer. I suspect the answer to it will turn out to be ´no´.
 There are things that will seem more significant and more pressing at the moment, given the still somewhat preliminary state of some of the ideas that have been thrown around for conceptual schemas. I suspect the study group will feel that more research and development work has to be done before it´s appropriate for the committee to dive into it.

JARDINE: One of the things that concerns me about possible candidate languages or formal descriptions for the conceptual schema, depending on how formal you want to make formal, is what are the criteria by which we judge the adequacy of the language for the conceptual schema. There´s all sorts of candidates around, and one gets very intuitive feelings about this having to do with richness of expression, convenience of views, understandability and usability by the people that are going to have to use it, and all the usual things that one can say about programming languages. One of the ways, clearly, of doing this is to try to express a number of fairly complex situations. This is a nontrivial amount of work, mostly because we don´t understand the situation. I wonder if the ANSI/SPARC group might not consider the possibility of constructing one or two cases, a framework, if you like, for evaluating possible approaches. I´m not looking to them to spend all of the time of sitting down and writing down the conceptual schemata in five different formalisms, but what would be possibly useful is a couple of cases that show the kind of complexity and the kinds of things that we think ought to be dealt with in the conceptual schema. Make them not so big that they require seven man-years to express in any of the possible formalisms, and then say, here are some test cases. There would be people all over the place who will start writing them down in the various approaches. I tihink that might be a very useful exercise to collect those and to have a discussion about how well did those particular languages or formalisms fit those two or three specific cases.

STEEL: What you´re suggesting is a prose description of many enterprises. Don, that is the most preposterous suggestion I have ever heard. It´ll be 365 days a year 24 hours a day. I applaud your suggestion, but I think it´s impractical unless we all go away to Bermuda and stay there.

PEEBLES: The feeling that I've gotten throughout this few days of discussion is that in talking of conceptual models a lot of people seem to be going back to the early 1960's when everyone had the bright idea of building management information systems whereby we could make neat strategic decisions about how to run a business by having information available to managers and they could build models of the enterprise. People just ran into brick walls and brick walls and brick walls. When people are trying to decide what should we put into conceptual schemas and how should we approach the language, and what should this language be able to do, it seems to me that the place to start is to look at operation support. Try to set up a conceptual schema that enables us to describe just the day to day operations type of work that goes on in a business, and see where things go from there.

COLLINS: The enterprise administrator taken in one sense is very reminiscent of the MIS activity of a number of years ago, and I certainly hope that we don't do that again. I think, though, part of that was a question of being oversold. We certainly have put in things which gave management information. I guess I would just have to agree that there is that analogy, and if we oversell it again, we can expect the same result, maybe worse.

STEEL: I think there are a couple of significant differences, though. First, it is fifteen years later, and we've learned something about how to do things. More significantly, the objective of a conceptual schema is different than the objective of the MIS effort. Theconceptual schema is basically communicating information down to the data processing system, not trying to communicate information up from the data processing system to top management. That's a significant difference as we understand somewhat better what our intended target is.

MOEHRKE: I do get somewhat of a warm cuddly feeling when we have a formal mathematics underlying the tools, and I don't think we ought to accept any formal tools which aren't provable somehow. I don't necessarily say they've got to show up that way when they're done. I don't think you do either, but when we start from the top down, and work with operational systems and so forth in order to communicate and try to validate these things with top management and everything, one has a terribly difficult time getting precise. We say we'll start off in this direction which is very pragmatic and very loosely defined, and I would argue very useful, but on the other hand, if we're also starting at the bottom with a formalism, how do we assure that there is any kind of meeting of the paths.

STEEL: I think probably there are some ways. If the in-between tools can be built correctly, you know, what sits on top, it may be possible then to match the informal communication that is essentially verbal, between people, which is the top management kind of interface, bound to some fairly high level tools in terms of the kind of thing I was talking about, which then sort of mechanically work their way down into whatever is the appropriate level at the bottom. Somebody, during coffee break pointed out that the kind of formalism that I was showing here would ultimately be on a chip in the machine. It's buried and essentially hidden from the day to day practitioner, but it's there to validate what's going on.

PEEBLES: I disagree with your first response and sort of agree with your second one. I don't think that we have learned a great deal in fifteen years, certainly not about what I was talking about, how to model the "intelligent" behavior, intelligent in quotation marks, of top management, and with regard to the second thing, yes, I understand your motivation of having the conceptual schema provide a method of stepwise refinement going down and developing operational operations models. All I'm asking is that they be restricted initially to that kind of effort and not trying to do exotic ccorporate modelling but rather the simplistic sort of thing.

STEEL: Let me try again. Corporation does not equal enterprise. The enterprise refers to that portion of the organization that is appropriate to model for what's to be in the data base management system. Now the content of most data bases today, only consist of data that is essentially operational, so, per force, enterprise is just what you're asking for.

PEEBLES: That's good, then. I'm happy. But it's my sense that there is some confusion among the community as to just what level these things are going to go on.

STEEL: Some of the discussion today has clearly implied a broader based thing than we really intended to have.

COLLINS: The purpose is not to build a model. The enterprise administrator doesn't take it upon himself to decide to model the thing, and even if he did he's not building a dynamic model. I used an over-sexy example of a data element that would have a profound implication simply because we could all relate to it and see clearly that it could matter. But I'm referring to the thing that most analysts do regularly, which is that they, in answering user needs and requirements and helping the user to find what it is he needs to do his job, occasionally help him develop new data elements that are not simple source data collection items and are not historically accounting specified items, but new things, things that go into exception reporting. This is the thing that happens all the time anyway, and in the process of doing that, the analyst is helping that manager look at his job. Once that is implemented and wound up, and the reports come flooding through, and things happen, that will change the way that manager thinks about his job. That's the nature of our tool. If I operate a steam shovel day after day, I'll begin to think of myself as a steam shovel operator. We keep talking about information systems. I'd like to mention that most of the cost effective applications going in today are more the nature of operational systems, and some of them even neglect the informational aspect in the sense of telling somebody what's going on or keeping some file up to date. So, as that becomes more true, the effect of these data elements and the things specified in the conceptual schema, will have even a more dramatic effect on the conduct of the business of the corporation than it did when it was merely carrying information from one spot to another.

STEEL: That's certainly true, but I can quibble with you a little bit in that, for example, one of the things that an operational system does which really makes it an information system, is tell the customer how much he has to pay, when it produces the bill, so it's conveying information. In some sense you can look at the whole thing as an information system. It's just that some is more routine than others.

COLLINS: But when, it prints a check for a vendor, what it's doing is not telling the vendor that it acknowledges that they owe that much, it's paying the vendor.

STEEL: No, it's telling the bank how much to pay the vendor.

DISCUSSION OF FUTURE DIRECTIONS OF ANSI SPARC DBMS STUDY GROUP

STEEL: The object of the session is two fold. It is clear from comments that at least some parts of the ANSI/SPARC Report are being misinterpreted or misunderstood. I would like to get some discussion on where the report needs improvement. Remember, it is called an Interim Report and, at least in principle, the committee is supposed to polish it and issue a more final report. Unfortunately there are several thousand copies of the report circulating around the world, so I'm not sure that a final version is going to really do the trick. In any event, it's important to try to identify the weaknesses in the report. The second item is future directions for the Study Group.

JEFFERSON: The idea of peeling the onion applies equally well to reading the report as to constructing a description of a data base. The report should be presented in layers to appropriate people so that those who needed to look at only the first layer, would be aware of only the first layer.

STEEL: In one sense we tried todo that, on the grounds that Chapter 1 of the report, was supposed to be an overview of what was going on. Maybe the introduction should've had more content.

JEFFERSON: It is not so much the content, or whether there's an overview. You need a deliberate restriction on what items are covered at certain points. Some people need to be aware of only certain things, in which case don't tell them about other things, because that only adds to the length of presentation. All the user really needs to be aware of is the interface he must deal with. For an administrator, of course, a great deal more is necessary.

STEEL: I think I understand what you mean. You're suggesting that, for example, we break out a discussion of external schemas as a separate piece that could be thenhanded to the appropriate place, that a discussion of the DML interface be pulled out separately.

MOERKE: My biggest concern is that you were unable to communicate well the concept of the conceptual schema. It's clear there are a number of opinions, on what the conceptual schema is, or could be. They are quite divergent, and something has to be done about that.

STEEL: Similar comments have come from lots of places. It's quite clear that the purpose of the conceptual schema has not been adequately explained, and we must do something about that.

SWENSON: Perhaps my criticism of the CODASYL effort could be applied to the SPARC effort also. Small tutorial examples of internal schemas, external schemas, conceptual schemas and the roles of various administrators, would reduce confusion. This would lengthen the document somewhat, but it's already 261 pages, and so another 25 or 30 are not going to make it any less readable.

MANOLA: It would be extremely helpful to try to separate as much as possible discussions of what the conceptual schema is, or what it's intended to be used for, from what language approach you use to define it. We in DDLC have had problems trying to understand what the architecture is all about. There's a large overlap between you [Steel] and Charlie Bachman as far as the purpose of the conceptual schema is concerned. The problems are the linguistic approaches that ought to be adopted to specifying it. There's a vast disagreement there.

I can understand your feeling that something like the CODASYL DDL is not suitable for the conceptual schema.

STEEL: My approach is data model independent. I do not in any sense talk about the syntax of the language, only its semantics. That's key to understanding what concepts ought to be included.

KENT: I guess I'm going along the same line as everybody else. I want to reinforce the fact that I think an awful lot more talking needs to be done about the conceptual model. I'm hoping that there'll be enough time for discussion tomorrow...I personally have the feeling that I could get cranked up, and a number of people could get cranked up after your presentation tomorrow, that it may be worth considering more than one session on it, or continuing it off line because I could rattle off half a dozen situations that just aren't accommodated in the kind of record oriented structure that is currently defined in the study group document and also in the DDLC CODASYL document. I would like to discuss tomorrow the implications of these various situations that aren't covered by the record oriented model; whether they're important, who cares about them, and whether we should all go back and rethink what the purpose of the conceptual model is. Is it significant that there are a half dozen or a dozen efforts going on in the area of data semantics that just don't in any way look like record structured models? Tsichritzis put a picture up as his starting point for the semantics of what he was talking about. Abrial has done a lot of work in that direction. Senko's work looks a lot more general graph structured and network structured; it's very hard to find a record in that work. Langefors in Sweden is working along those lines, and it seems that everybody that's doing the formal standardization directed work seems to be moving along as though none of that work exists. In addition to a critique of the content of the document, I would also say that these remarks are addressed as future directions to the study group. Spend a little time looking at the alternative approaches to data semantics and why they're being modeled this way, and whether that might give some better direction for structuring the conceptual model.

KIRSHENBAUM: The whole argument about record structures is an interesting one, because the same set of arguments went on in the study group. There were those in the study group who felt that you didn't need a lot of what are essentially named constructs. That is, prestored constructs like records where you set up a series of relationships and a series of types of relationships up and you call them a record. That implies certain things about the structure. The reason it appeared that way is that some people in the study group would like to see them used as examples of the types of structures, rather than an exhaustive list. There were some on the committee who said all there were were data items and relationships between them, period. Since you can build anybody else's world from that base, it is a necessary and sufficient set. But there were people who felt more comfortable by naming explicitly some of the possible combinations, and to keep them happy, they were left in the report.

KENT: Based on the thinking I've done, I find it hard to understand or believe the statement that anybody's model can be built up from the record oriented base.

STEEL: No, that's not what Frank is saying. He's saying that there are some people on the committee who believe the world consists of individuals, sets of individuals, sets, and the universe. That is all you really need. The constructs of fields records, groups and plexes and all those other terms are simply artificial constructs that some people feel are at an appropriate level and that's why they are in the report.

KENT: But, that's the only thing that's in the report. The report, as I read it didn't say this is an exemplary set of structures you might think about. I understood it to say those are the structures that are proposed.

COHN: One of the constructive things that took place in the IFIP Freudenstadt Meeting was the attempt on the part of some of those people whom you named, not to state that their things were different, but to work on how they actually did fit into the constructs of the conceptual schema model. This is not to say that they had to find something in what they were doing that matched every one of the constructs. We accept the criticism that most of those constructs were unnecessary for most of the models. However, there would be at least one model in somebody's mind that required some one of those constructs which maybe somebody else's model didn't need. The attempt that we made was to find constructs that would allow everybody to find a home. This was not to say that everybody had to find a home for those terms in his model.
 Most of those people that you named had representatives in the meeting. I was satisfied that those models found a home in the SPARC conceptual schema.

STEEL: Let me add one further comment. I think we did make a very serious error in the report in using terms like 'field', 'record', 'group', because they put things in people's minds. You assume what a record is when you use that word, but the alternative was to invent new terms, and that's even worse in some ways.

COMBA: I want to register mild complaint about the way the term fact is used.....

MANOLA: I think the preceding discussion about record oriented approach prejudices consideration of a model by using a data processing term. It seems to me that when I said development, for example, of the CODASYL DDL, I meant precisely that. That is to say, the essence being that you have a language which can describe things, properties of things, and relationships between things. Now if there is something wrong with that fundamental model, for example, you only want to define properties of things and relationships between those properties, or facts and relationships between facts, that's a basic thing, that's important. If you want to reject the CODASYL DDL on the grounds that it uses a term 'record' or it uses a term 'data item', which you've associated with data processing, I think that's a very superficial kind of a thing. I think those kinds of things ought to be very carefully distinguished in these kinds of discussions.

STEEL: I quite agree with you. My only reason for making the comment I did earlier, is that I think it's unfortunate that these terms do have connotations and then people do misinterpret what's being said as a result.

JARDINE: Frank Kirshenbaum said that a number of these terms were put in so that people could feel comfortable and could relate. In a definitional document, one should not be much concerned whether or not terms make people feel comfortable. I think that this document is confusing two things. It says it's an architecture. I don't believe it's an architecture in the sense that the word 'architecture' is normally used. I think it's a framework for thinking about the problem. In such a case, I do not like the idea of introducing terms that are vague, or which have associations with other designs or architectures. I admit that this document isn't the only one that's done that, but I think it could have avoided doing it.

STEEL: When we were preparing this document initially, it was not anticipated that it would go out in 40 million copies. It was not intended for that purpose. I understand why that's happened. In some sense I'm glad it happened, but that was not in the back of our minds when we were preparing it, and people ought to understand that. It was not intended for anything like the kind of distribution that it has gotten.

KIRSHENBAUM: I for one, would have liked to have seen it done in the following way. It should probably have been done with a set of the low level constructs, and then built up one or two of the more common descriptions of a record. Then say, 'see, here's how it can be done'.

KENT: I find it hard to find the exact sense in which many of the words are being used. I have to go back to an example situation. We can then use the example to say 'yes, that's the way I meant the word', or 'no, that's not the way I meant the word'. My concern is deeper than whether you just accidently used the word 'record' when you meant to say 'entity' and they're really interchangeable. There are certain concepts that automatically go along when you say the word record. The situation may be worse. If I went back and read the study group report and read the CODASYL DBTG Report, I may find words that explicitly reinforce this notion. But there are certain things that go with the record concept that aren't generally true about the real world. I want to talk about one example situation. Generally a record instance is an instance of exactly one record type. That's generally not true about an entity. The same thing that in the conceptual model is sometimes an employee and belongs to a set of things, all of which are employees, and by implication they're all human beings so there's a certain kind of set of attributes that naturally go with it. The same entity sometimes is also a customer, and belongs to a set of things which are all customers some of which are human beings, and some of which are government agencies and some of which are other companies. By virtue of that fact, the whole collection of them and this entity as an instance has a different set of properties. That's the kind of thing that ought to be reflectable in a conceptual model. This concept normally isn't conveyed to me when you start using the word 'record'. That's the kind of difference on which to continue to focus.

STEEL: I personally agree with that position. I'd like, however, to make the following comment. Something has gotten lost. There is no such thing as a materialization of conceptual data. The conceptual schema is a description, as opposed to data. It's a description of the real world. We've said that before, we'll say it again, and probably ought to say it a little harder in the report.

SHEEHAN: When talking about the conceptual schema and the enterprise administrator, we agreed the other day that we really weren't talking about

the president of the company. I do think, however, there has to be more of
a line drawn as to how much we're seeing this person as being a data
processing kind of person or a business function kind of person.

STEEL: Answering for the study group, we have floating around the study
group a picture of an enterprise administrator, a fat, balding man in a
Superman costume.

COLLINS: I'd like to ask a question about the use of the report which could
have implications for the further work of the group. I fully understand
that the genesis of the report was to identify those interfaces about which
we might want to have standards discussions. However, I'm also thinking
that in the process of doing this you've drawn some distinctions.   I
remember, historically, that for, perhaps, ten years now, many of us here
in this room have wanted the distinction we now talk about as the internal
and external side of the issue. We wanted this distinction implemented in
software. We wanted to be able to drive a wedge between those two and
address them separately. My question, therefore, is to what extent could
the vendors, whom you've invited to respond on the subject, take the SPARC
report and the interfaces they've identified, and treat these as a request,
requirement or even a user demand of some sort, that whatever the product
of the next generation at least makes these distinctions.

STEEL: That sounds more like a policy statement than a question.

COLLINS: Would it be fair to criticize the report in terms of its
suitability for drawing those distinctions that we want? And the other
side of the question, obviously - it's sort of a trap question now that I
think about it - what else would be the purpose of standardization than to
unbundle certain parts of the database management edifice?

STEEL: Of course it's fair to criticize the report, on that basis, but
obviously those of us who have prepared the report believe we have made
that distinction, and made it adequately. If someone thinks not, then we'd
like to hear about it.

COLLINS: And that therefore, any products should make those distinctions.

STEEL: Yes.

COHN: There were vendors on the study group, and I know Charlie [Bachman]
isn't here, and neither is Manny [Lavin], but I think the vendors on that
committee are perfectly comfortable in understanding what the motivation
and meaning of the separation of the schemas was when the SHARE/GUIDE
Report separated it in this report. I think the message was loud and clear
and understood.   I think the write-ups in Chapter 4 [of the study group
Report] describing the role of the administrators is certainly clear in its
intent, although perhaps not in every last detail.

JEFFERSON: I'd like to go back to a point that Jardine made which I think
has been completely forgotten, and that was that the study group report is
a framework for thinking about the problem, not an architecture, and I
think all of the comments that have come since that remark have been
addressing the report as an architecture. Kirshenbaum said we should have
some examples about how to build up a record which is certainly what one
expects not from a framework of thinking but from an architecture.   Now I
would suggest that a the present stage of the study group's work, it's must

more appropriate to think of it as a way of thinking about the problem, a way of structuring an attack on database management but it really should not be confused as an architecture. I'd like to hear some response from the study group on that point.

STEEL: I can give you my response. I agree with what you say, in fact. I agreed with you before you said it because Jardine made that same remark to me in the hall last night and I agreed with him then. You're right, the choice of the word 'architecture' is unfortunate.

KIRSHENBAUM: Did we ever use the word architecture?

SWENSON: It is on the title of the paper.

STEEL: "The paper" does not mean the ANSI/SPARC Report, it means Bea Yormark's paper at this conference.

COHN: Oh, it's her [Yormark's] architecture!

YORMARK: It's my framework! I got a letter and a phone call from Tom Steel saying we would like you to discuss the ANSI/SPARC Study Group on database management system architecture.

STEEL: So, it's my fault!

KIRSHENBAUM: Just to clear it up, on page 9 of the report where the master diagram appears, the title is "Database System Prototypical Architecture".

STEEL: Then it's Charlie Bachman's architecture! Charlie drew the diagram. The original was a blueprint.

SENKO: On of the problems with the document at the present time is that the levels have not been filled in. Thus we're tending to discuss very vague concepts and everybody has their own opinion as to what those might be. I'm going to show you just a little bit about DIAM as an example. It's not necessarily the best thing that exists, but it will at least give you some feeling for what various levels might be and how you build records out of these concepts. I think the ANSI/SPARC separation into three levels is an excellent idea. It provides exactly the kinds of functions we want at three levels. The internal level separates out the computer efficiency problem. The conceptual level should be canonical, that is, there should be only place for a fact in the structure rather than multiple places as we have in files at the present time.
The external level hopefully gives us some way of single individuals interfacing with the system. The point is the following: If you have a user who's interested in departments and employees and asks separate questions about these two items. The best thing for him to have is two separate files. Another user asks questions about employees in departments. It's the same information, but there are different efficiency considerations. You'd like to provide him a hierarchical structure, because that's a very nice way to ask questions. If he becomes a predominate user, what you'd like to do is give him a storage structure which is almost an image of that. Sometimes you might even want to have two copies of the fact. What you want is a place where you can control all this. If we can define the conceptual schema to have one location per fact, we can get control over the integrity of the information. For instance, records have a number of problems. Schmitt and Swenson noticed that they're not really

SYSTEM OVERVIEW

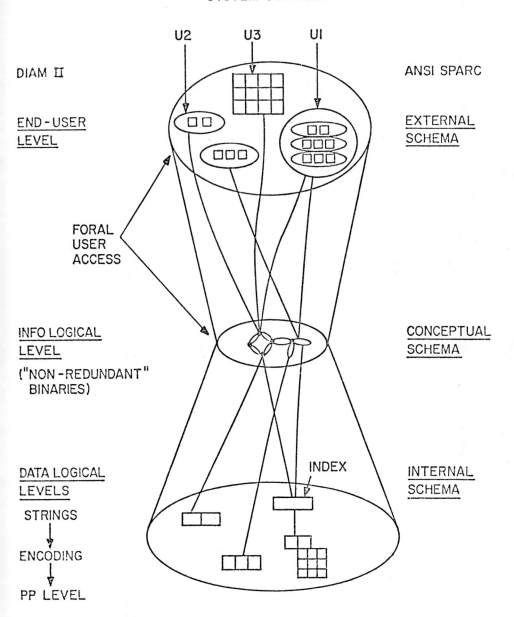

DIAM II

ANSI SPARC

END-USER
LEVEL

EXTERNAL
SCHEMA

U2   U3   UI

FORAL
USER
ACCESS

INFO LOGICAL
LEVEL

("NON-REDUNDANT"
 BINARIES)

CONCEPTUAL
SCHEMA

DATA LOGICAL
LEVELS

STRINGS

ENCODING

PP LEVEL

INDEX

INTERNAL
SCHEMA

WHY LEVELS ?

DIAM II - ANSI SPARC

. STAGED, SIMPLIFIED PROBLEM SOLVING

STRUCTURED PROGRAMMING

. INTERNAL LEVELS

SEPARATE OUT COMPUTER EFFICIENCY PROBLEM

. CONCEPTUAL LEVEL

CANONICAL STRUCTURE
DATA BASE CONTROL
SEMANTIC INTEGRITY

. EXTERNAL LEVEL

HUMAN EFFICIENCY
COMPATIBILITY WITH EXISTING SYSTEMS

NEW DIAM INFOLOGICAL LEVEL
BINARY ASSOCIATIONS
SEMANTIC INTEGRITY

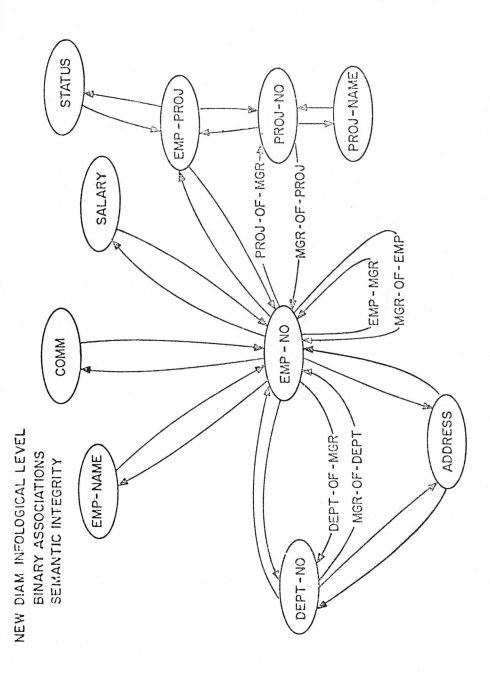

semantic in the sense that you have spurious operations. Another aspect of record structures is that they're noncanonical. You can have several record structures containing similar facts. Another problem is you have to have a different representation for a 1:M relationship than for a M:1 relationship. If you have a M:1 relationship such as employee to department, then you can store the department number in the employee record. If you want to ask questions about employees in departments, then you have to go to a different file, and use a completely different kind of language. A number of people have come up with different proposals, and there's a lot in common among them and there are a few minor differences. Those at the conference in Freudenstadt [IFIP TC-2 conference Jan. 1976] tended to believe that what they wanted as a basic unit of description was something very small, probably binary, in the sense that you have names for two things and the way you describe one thing is by associating its name with another thing. Part of the problem, I believe, is that the ANSI/SPARC paragraph is somewhat inconsistent. The problem happens to be a question of whether there is a difference between a description and a name for a thing. When you knock down the ashtray, you're really giving a name for a thing. If you talk about the colour of the ashtray, then you're giving a description of it. That's a very fundamental problem in logic and the distinction is an important one to make. You can build up all you want to describe about a system in this fashion. In such a case, I use names of individual items rather than of records. If you have just employee numbers and department numbers, etc., you can describe anything you like and you don't run into stored representation dependence. It also forces you to be very careful. For example, if you put manager in an employee record, which is quite an easy thing to do, you find out that you really don't know what kind of manager he is. In the diagram, there are three types of managers. This kind of diagram forces you to be much more explicit. Department managers must be associated with departments, project managers must be associated with projects, and managers of employees must be associated with employees, so there is much more semantic content. There is no such thing as perfect semantics, in a sense, because that involves a complete knowledge of the world.

However, some models have more semantics than others. How do you get records out of this? We looked at the questions of categorization, that is, what things do you put in various categories. We had essentially four levels in the internal model. We developed a language for following access paths, and its very much like a simple version of DML. We defined two kinds of strings, one string whichis called an I-string, which connects those items which bear a 1:1 relation to each other. A T string connects those things which are related 1:M. The T-string starts to look something like a record, and the T string looks something like a file, and in fact it has many aspects of a set.

JARDINE: It isn't clear whether this is an example of what the ANSI/SPARC document talks about as a conceptual schema. I'm going to suggest that it isn't. I don't see anything in your diagram that talks about the things in the real world. I see employee numbers, but I don't see any employees; I see addresses, but I don't see any houses; I see department numbers but no departments. Possibly something in the ANSI/SPARC document could be clarified. The conceptual schema is a description of the real world in some symbolic notation; there's another level where one describes the things you do, but still with generalized relations. This is not an internal view, it clearly is not an external view. I'd like some clarification of where your diagram, which is clearly necessary in our analysis, sits in the Study Group framework.

SENKO: There's considerable discussion recorded in the Freudenstadt documents on just this point. In fact, I could put the employees in circles, departments in circles, and so forth. There are certain trade-offs which I've tried to discuss my in my Freudenstadt paper. These are names for entities rather than the entities themselves, and there are some nice aspects of having entities in the circles. On the other hand you get more nodes that way, so there's a trade-off.

KENT: It doesn't bother me to see all those things in one model, because they're all facts about the real world, that employees exist, and that they have employee numbers, and that there are houses and there are addresses. That's all a description of the real world, so it doesn't bother me to have the two kinds of things described in the conceptual model. Secondly, I want to go back to Dennis's [Tsicritzis] way of grabbing psuedo-records out of that picture by clustering things together. I can either agree or disagree with that depending on whether he lets me draw overlapping circles from one bunch of attributes that'll group together. When I want to think of this entity as an employee, I will gather together one bunch of nodes into a record. When I want to think of this person as a customer, and it happens to be the same person, on my model I want to represent it as the same entity, but with respect to records about that entity I'm going to draw my circle which represents a record around a different cluster of ovals in that diagram. So that whether or not you can collapse this thing into little clusters and say that's what you meant by records, is to me, correct or incorrect, depending on whether you allow overlapping mappings when you draw these records. I suggest that's one of the things that has to be clarified when you start talking about records.

SENKO: Well, I would come back to the first point that Don [Jardine] made and you made also, that the circles and arrows there could be entities rather than otherwise. In fact, it is possible to do it either way.

COHN: There's something that should be obvious about our methodology from the discussion that's gone on, and that is wheuther people were unaries or n-aries the methodology that we employed was to ask whether we could find a home for their model in our architecture, and not whether we agreed or disagreed with any particular person's modelling technique. We were not judges of whether they were good or bad, we merely tried to find a home for them. If any person has a data model and thinks it doesn't fit in what we did, we'd be very interested in having direct interface with that person because we have not yet found anyone whose model did not fit. There is a second point I'd like to make relative to the word record. It was not put in there just to make people happy. There's part of the conceptual schema's role that is not being covered by those people who talk about structure and that is that it has a role in control. Dealing in the control vehicle, which is one of the very important requirements that has been passed to the study group, one does think of a quasi-materialization of a record, not a real materialization of a record, at the conceptual level. A quasi-materialization because the external levelis in part derived from the conceptual level and you do materialize at the external level. This quasi-materialization at the conceptual level is often helpful in considering validities, security, integrity, etc., that might be occurring at any particular materialization. So 'record' becomes useful to any of those people who are designing and implementing at the conceptual level.

SENKO: I disagree. You can do the control at the basic fact level, and it's easier to do it, as you saw this morning in the security paper. There are problems with controlling relations because you have several facts stored in the same record. Control may, in fact, be easier this way, but it's another question which we would have to go through and actually look at the arguments, and I can't say that I have a proof one way or the other.

GRABER: As former chairman of the GUIDE Data Dictionary Committee, I have several points to make, and I'd like to start by asking a question. When Mike [Senko] got up, he said he was going to show what his view of a conceptual schema looked like. I'd like to ask Tom [Steel] if he thinks this is essentially in agreement with the view off the SPARC study committee.

STEEL: There are number of things left out, from the point of view of the study group's view of what a conceptual schema is.

GRABER: I'm glad to hear you say that because one of the points I was going to make is that my committee would also find this view at least partly unacceptable. That doesn't mean I don't think this is a very good view. I think this is an essential view, this idea of actually analyzing things down to the simplest components which may be simple binary relations. I think this is a very essential part of any good future database management system, where things are, in fact, analyzed to their most simple mathematical concept. However, there is a need for another level, and perhaps I'm echoing Jardine's suggestion that we need four levels instead of three, although I hate to do that. There is a need for a level which represents the model of an enterprise administrator. Someone who does represent, at least in spirit, the views of the chairman of the board. Someone who is looking at the entire picture from a business point of view and is also actually exercising control over the various applications. The use of the conceptual schema to exercise control over the various application schemas is one of the key factors that was emphasized most heavily in the GUIDE committee I worked with. This requires the ability to build a model, a model that would be natural to someone who thinks like a high level business man. This model is something quite different than this mathematical type model we're seeing here. I think yet there's a need for both these models to be represented in a good and useful database product. The one, because unless the manager has something he can use, he won't use the product; the other one, because unless the mathematician has something he can get hold of, the internals just won't work or will be very inefficient. There's a need for both of these things. Part of the confusion is that both the managers and the mathematicians are trying to latch onto the conceptual schema and it won't serve both of them, you have to have something for each of them.

SENKO: First of all, I would agree with you that this is not complete. I think a lot of people would put in consistency constraints, and so forth, which I believe are appropriate. But, you must have some sort of formal model and I fought with mathematicians for a long time myself. I don't consider this to be a mathematical model in the strongest sense of mathematics. What would you propose that would be less? I don't believe that managers can afford to talk to other people in terms of just prose. You have to have some picture to tell the relation between things, and that's essentially what we tried to do here.

GRABER: I think that is one of the reasons why there is this great theological debate, because different people do have different views of the world, and in many cases the manager wishes to choose his view and impose it on his subordinates. If he happens to be a network man, and his subordinates are relational men, they're going to have to do the translating, or vice versa.

SENKO: I submit that those are efficiency considerations, first of all, and second of all they can be given to the people at the external level and at the internal model. If you do put those in, you find out that what you're doing is putting in a lot of spurious associations that do not occur in the real world.

GRABER: Perhaps the ideal model would be something like prose, something very close to the English language.

SENKO: Then you've got problems communicating.

GRABER: But, failing the ability to do that, and I think we all must admit that the state of the art has not come that far, you are going to have to allow the manager to choose a model that he feels comfortable with, which I submit, will be something that does not have the desirable properties of this binary model. It will be something that perhaps is cluttered with inessentials and extra structures, and so on, because that is, in fact, the way that manager's mind works; it includes that extra structure. It may be the technique which he learned when he was starting in the world of business or data processing. He will stick with the model and the method of expressing himself that he is familiar with.

STEEL: You're not going to like my presentation tomorrow at all. Let's hold that argument, we're kind of running out of time.

KENT: I really want to respond to something Larry [Cohn] said, but we can pick it up tomorrow.

STEEL: No, go ahead. What I didn't want was more discussion about whether managers ought to be mathematicians or not.

KENT: Larry [Cohn] several times has said that it's his belief and the committee's belief that you have provided a broad enough foundation in the conceptual model that everybody else's model can find a home there. For the situation I've been talking about, where the guy is both an employee and a customer, I now have to write two separate conceptual records. I define an employee type conceptual record and a customer type conceptual record. I don't know of anything in a conceptual model that allows me to say that some instances of those two record types, overlap. That there are some entities that are really the same entity, and that's one of the kinds of model properties that I'm looking for in a conceptual model that I don't see has a home in the present description of the conceptual model.

COHN: I know of nothing in the report that precludes that.

SENKO: If you go to the entity level that Don [Jardine] suggested earlier, there are trade-offs because the model becomes more complex and you may not want to do that. I think a lot of these things are issues on which there is some very nice discussion at Freudenstadt, and people who are interested in the area should look there. At the conceptual level there is a case for getting the best properties at that level. Some of the properties that I mentioned earlier, one location for a fact and so forth, are not possible in the co-existence model or the anarchy that Larry [Cohn] talks about where you can have many many data models. I think that I would agree that you can provide those things at the external schema, but it's really a question of tearing down the thing rather than just accepting all possibilities.

COHN: You use the word 'location', which doesn't make any sense to me when I'm talking about the conceptual schema. As a comment to what you said and what Bill [Kent] said, there are explicit statements in the interim report which state that a conceptual field can be a member of any number of conceptual records, and that is in open disagreement with DIAM. I'm not here to discuss DIAM, I'm primarily here to discuss the interim report, but if you want to construct a model that has a conceptual field in only one conceptual record, then DIAM can be modelled. However, for those people who choose to model with conceptual fields in more than one conceptual thing - call it a record if you will, or not, I don't care - then they can model as well, including Bill Kent's employee thing and customer thing.

SENKO: I would agree with you on that. The question is can you gain something when you add those possibilities. In a number of cases you get properties that you might not wish to have. People can then argue as to whether those properties are more valuable or less valuable than the other ones.

Mr. Edward Altman
IBM Research
Monterey & Cottle Rds.
San Jose, CA. 95193

Mr. Robert Bellman
Computer Corp. of America
575 Technology Sq.
Cambridge, MASS. 02139

Mr. James Black
Sperry Research Center
100 North Road
Sudbury, MA 01776

Mr. Charles Blose
United Banks Service
5700 S. Ulster Parkway
Englewwood, COLO. 80110

Ms. Lorraine Borman
Northwestern University
2129 Sheradan
Evanston, IL. 60201

Mr. Joseph Brawly
Canadian Natl. Coord. Trans.
935 La Gauchetiere ST., W.
Montreal, Quebec H3C 3N4
CANADA

Mr. Gerald L. Brody
Standard Oil of Calif.
P. O. Box 3495
San Francisco, CA. 941196

Mr. Kenneth Bush
European-American Bank
865 Merrick Ave.
Westbury, NY 11590

Mr. Matt Camarota
Coopers and Lybrand
1251 Ave of the Americas
New York, NY 10020

Mr. L. R. Case
CDP Support A-B
Aetna Life ´ Casualty
151 Framington Ave.
Hartford, CONN. 06156

Dr. Thomas Chinlund
Columbia Univ. Computer Center
612 West 115th Street
New York, N.Y. 10025

Mr. Neal Clarke
CINCOM Systems Inc.
2300 Montana Ave.
Cincinnati, OH 45211

Mr. Larry Cohn
IBM Corporation
Dept. R40/123
Monterey & Cottle Rds.
San Jose, CA. 95112

Mr. W. Kenneth Collins
Consultant
23 Rocky Point Rd.
Old Greenwich, CT. 06870

Dr. Paul Comba
IBM
545 Technology Square
Cambridge, MA. 02139

Mr. Terry Curtis
319-3 Place Ville Marie
Montreal, Quebec
CANADA

Dr. Alfred G. Dale
Computer Science Dept.
Univ. of Texas at Austin
Austin, TX. 78712

Mr. L. Delport
Mgr. Administrative Data Proc.
Univ. of Leuven (K.V. Leuven)
de Croylaan 58
B3030 Heverlee, BELGIUM

Mr. William Ferone
CINCOM Systems Inc.
2300 Montana Ave.
Cincinnati, Ohio 45211

Mr. William Hosken
Penn State University
3107 Whitemore Lab
University Park, PA. 16802

Ms. Joanne M. Gallitano
Hunter College
695 Park Ave.
Box 608
New York, N.Y. 10021

Mr. Bernard Jeannin
STO XGSK
c/o Harrison
SAS 138-02 Queens Blvd.
Jamaica, NY 11435

Mr. James S. Graver
Library of Congress
Washington, D.C. 20540

Dr. Donald Jardine
Dept. of Computing & Info. Sci.
Goodwin Hall
Queen's University
Kingston, Ontario, CANADA

Mr. John Green
United Services Automobile Assn
USAA Building
San Antonio, TX 78288

Dr. David K. Jefferson
Code 188
David Taylor Naval Ship R&D Ctr
Bethesda, MD 20084

Ms. Estelle Grinoch
Mgr. DB Administration
RCA
30 Rockefeller Plaza
New York, NY 10021

Ms. June Jodeit
Software AG
4825 Fremont Ave. S..
Minneapolis, MN. 55409

Mr. Timothy L. Grimes
SPERRY UNIVAC M.S. 4823
P. O. Box 3942
St. Paul, MN. 55165

Ms. Linda Jones
Con Edison Company
4 Irving Pl.
New York, NY 10003

Mr. Alden Guillory
Mgr. DB Administration
American National Ins. Co.
One Moody Plaza
Galveston, TX. 77550

Mr. Roger Jones
Cibar, Inc.
Suite 1204
2850 W. Serendipity Circle
Colorado Springs, CO 80917

Mr. Lloyd Harper
IBM Corporation, G.P.D.
1501 California Ave.
Palo Alto, CA. 95304

Mr. William Kent
IBM Corporation
1512 Page Mill Rd.
Palo Alto, CA. 94304

Ms. Suellen K. Harris
Sperry Univac M.S. 4823
2276 Highcrest Drive
Roseville, MN 55113

Mr. Frank Kirshenbaum
Equitable Life Assur. Soc.
1285 Ave. of the Americas
New York, NY 10019

Mr. Walter Klaus
U.S. Army
88-22 Burbank Rd.
Annandale VA. 22003

Prof. Eugene Kozik
Penn State University
Graduate Center
King of Prussia, PA. 19406

Mr. Harold Kunecke
Boeing Computer Services
M. S. 8M-64
P. O. Box 24346
Seattle, Wash. 98124

Mr. Eugene I. Lowenthal
MRI Systems Corporation
12575 Research Blvd.
Austin, TX 78766

Mr. Charles E. Mairet
Deere & Company
Moline, Illinois 61265

Mr. Frank Manola
Code 5403
Naval Research Laboratory
Washington, DC 20375

Prof. E. J. McCauley
University of Illinois
Center for Adv. Comp.
Urbana, IL 61801

Mr. W. F. McClelland
IBM Corporation
Armonk, NY 10504

Mr. Harry Melzer (J3)
Fedral Reserve Bank
33 Liberty St.
New York, NY 10045

Mr. Don P. Moehrke
A. O. Smith Corporation
P. O. Box 584
Department 9240
Milwaukee, Wis. 53201

Dr. Howard L. Morgan
Univ. of Pennsylvania
Office of Computing Activities
3609 Locust Walk
Philadelphia, PA. 19104

Mr. David Nelson
127 Forrest Rd.
Moorestown, NJ 08057

Mrs. Patricia L. Nichols
Data Crown Ltd.
650 McNeill Avenue
Willowdale, Ontario M2H 2E1
CANADA

Mr. Michael O'Reilly
Quasar Systems Ltd.
1129 Carling Ave.
Ottawa, Ontario
CANADA K1Y 4G6

Ms. Sherrill Overfield
TRW Def. & Space Sys. Group
One Space Park, E1/3016
Redondo Beach, CA. 90278

Prof. Richard Peebles
Dept. of Computer Science
University of Waterloo
Waterloo, Ontario
CANADA N2L 3G1

Mr. Russell Pratt
Johns-Manville Co.
1PC - Greenwood Plaza
Denver, COLO. 80217

Mr. Bruce W. Puerling
Bell Telephone Laboratories
Holmdel, N. J. 07733

Mr. Gary J. Rasmussen
LDS Church, Room 2033
50 East North Temple St.
Salt Lake City, UT. 84150

Mr. Richard Rinderknecht
General Mills, Inc.
P. O. Box 1113
Minneapolis, MN. 55440

Mr. Gary Robertson
Control Data
215 Moffet Park Drive
Sunnyvale, CA. 94086

Mr. Michael Roberts
Deputy Dir. Ctr f. Info. Proc.
Encina Hall 224
Stanford University
Stanford, CA. 94305

Mr. Randall Rustin
Chase Manhattan Bank
1 Chase Manhattan Plaza
New York, N.Y. 10015

Ms. Jane N. Ryland
Virginia Dept. of Comm. Col.
911 East Broad Street
Richmond, VA. 23212

Mr. R. M. Sage
Systems & Programming
Dominion Textile Ltd.
1950 Sherbrooke St., W.
Montreal, Que., CANADA

Mr. Ralph E. Salamone
Mgr. DB Systems
European-American Bank
865 Merrick Ave.
Westbury, NY 11590

Dr. Harold Schwenk
BGS Systems
Box 128
Lincoln, MA. 01773

Mr. Marvin Schaefer
System Development Corp.
2500 Colorado Ave.
Santa Monica, CA. 90406

Prof. Stewart A. Schuster
Dept. of Computer Science
University of Toronto
Toronto, Ontario
CANADA M5S 1A7

Mr. Richard D. Secrest
Amoco Production Company
P. O. Box 591
Tulsa, OKLA. 74102

Mr. M.E. Senko
IBM
P. O. Box 218
Yorktown Heights, NY 10598

Prof. K. C. Sevcik
U. of Toronto,Comp.Sys.Res.Grp.
Sandford Fleming 216
10 King's College Rd.
Toronto, Ont., CANADA M5S 1A7

Mr. Stanley J. Sewall
CINCOM Systems, Inc.
2300 Montana Ave.
Cincinnati, OH 45211

Miss Diane Sheehan
Chase Manhattan Bank
1 New York Plaza 5J04 18 Flr
New York, NY 10013

Mr. A. P. Smith
IBM Corporation
1133 Westchester Ave.
White Plains, NY

Mrs. Jean G. Smith
SPERRY UNIVAC
P. O. Box 500
Blue Bell, PA. 19422

Mr. Leon Smith
Bankers Trust Company
Computer Services Dept.
Bankers Trust Plaza, 36th Floor
New York, NY 10015

Prof. Frank Tompa
Dept. of Computer Science
University of Waterloo
Waterloo, Ontario
CANADA N2L 3G1

Mr. G. G. Specker
General Mills, Inc.
9200 Wayzata Blvd.
Minneapolis, MN 55440

Mr. Frank M. Toth
Sperry Univac M.S. 1C2-SE13
P. O. Box 500
Blue Bell, PA. 19422

Mr. Michael Spillum
Employers Insurance of Wausau
2000 Westwood Drive
Wausau, WI 55401

Prof. Dennis Tsichritzis
Computer Science Dept.
Univ. of Toronto
Toronto 181, Ontario
CANADA M5S 1A7

Mr. Thomas B. Steel, Jr.
Equitable Life Assur. Society
1285 Ave. of the Americas
New York, NY 10019

Mr. Jon A. Turner
Center for Computing Activities
Columbia University
612 West 115th St.
New York, N.Y. 10025

Mr. Chester Suski
Employers Insurance of Wausau
2000 Westwood Drive
Wausau, WI 55401

Mr. Marc Van Den Berge
IBM Belgium
Avenue Galilee, 5
B1030 Brussels
BELGIUM

Mr. J. R. Swenson
Dept. of Computer Science
University of Toronto
Toronto, Ont.
CANADA M5S 1A7

Dr. C. P. Wang
DB Systems and Design
IBM Mohansic Lab
2651 Strang Blvd.
Mohansic, NY 10598

Mr. Bruce S. Swist
Data Base Project Manager
Gilbert Associates, Inc.
P. O. Box 1498
Reading, PA. 19603

Mr. Richard Winter
Computer Corp. of America
575 Technology Square
Cambridge, MA. 02139

Mr. Robert W. Taylor
IBM Research
Dept. K55/282
5600 Cottle Rd.
San Jose, CA. 95123

Ms. Beatrice Yormark
The Rand Corporation
1700 Main Street
Santa Monica, CA.

Mr. Terry Tessian
Cincom Systems, Inc.
220 Forbes Rd. - 4th floor
Braintree, MA. 02184